Reform of the International Monetary System and Internationalization of the Renminbi

Reform of the International Monetary System and Internationalization of the Renminbi

Li Ruogu

The Export-Import Bank of China, China

World Scientific

EW JERSEY · LONDON · SINGAPORE · BEIJING · SHANGHAI · HONG KONG · TAIPEI · CHENNAI · TOKYO

Published by

World Scientific Publishing Co. Pte. Ltd.

5 Toh Tuck Link, Singapore 596224

USA office: 27 Warren Street, Suite 401-402, Hackensack, NJ 07601

UK office: 57 Shelton Street, Covent Garden, London WC2H 9HE

Library of Congress Cataloging-in-Publication Data

Li, Ruogu.

Reform of the international monetary system and internationalization of the renminbi / Ruogu Li, The Export-Import Bank of China, China.

pages cm

Includes bibliographical references and index.

ISBN 978-9814699044 (alk. paper)

1. International finance. 2. Banks and banking, International. 3. Currency substitution. 4. International liquidity. I. Title.

HF5548.32.L5195 2015

332.4'5--dc23

2015031940

British Library Cataloguing-in-Publication Data

A catalogue record for this book is available from the British Library.

国际货币体系改革与人民币国际化

Originally published in Chinese by China Financial Publishing House

Copyright © China Financial Publishing House, 2012

In-house Editors: Chandrima Maitra/Qi Xiao

Typeset by Stallion Press

Email: enquiries@stallionpress.com

Printed in Singapore

Preface

What happened during 2007–2009 has caught economists, scholars, bankers, and even the general public in the world by surprise. In March 2008, Bear Stearns went bankrupt and half a year later in September, Fannie Mae, Freddie Mac, and AIG were taken over by the U.S. government one after another. At almost the same time, Lehman Brothers declared bankruptcy, Merrill Lynch was acquired by Bank of America, and Goldman Sachs and Morgan Stanley became bank holding companies. In just six months, the top five U.S. investment banks all disappeared. New York is the cradle of international financiers and Wall Street is the symbol of global fortune. Why were they so fragile? Just a wave of subprime lending turned what for a century had been the center of global financial services into the center of financial storm. The whole world was shaken, and a global stock market crash ensued. From March 2008 to March 2009, the Dow Jones Indices and the S&P 500 Index dropped by more than 40% respectively. The U.S. economy was hit by the most severe recession since the 1930s, and U.S. unemployment skyrocketed.

Confused and disoriented, people attributed the crisis to the financial derivative — subprime debt — and then pointed finger at the financial regulatory authorities. They believed that the blind development of financial derivatives was the cause of the financial storm. The reason behind this situation was the failure of financial regulatory authorities to fulfill their due responsibility. This charge sounded reasonable: if the regulatory authorities had done their job, subprime debt would not have emerged; or, even if it had occurred, it would not have developed to such an extent. While this may sound convincing, it is actually misleading. The people who hold this view ignore, knowingly or unknowingly, the heart of the matter: How did financial derivatives come into being in the first place? And why did the regulatory authorities fail to live up to their responsibilities? Financial derivatives are a natural product of the free market economy. Participants in the market economy invariably seek to maximize their personal (or corporate) gains. They are therefore bound to use all means to pursue this goal. According to free market theory, the market is capable of automatically adjusting itself and there is no need for external adjustment. It is believed that market mechanism is capable of correcting any disequilibrium. In my opinion, however, it is the blind belief in free market theory that has led to the failure to exercise diligent regulation.

I believe that in order to prevent such a crisis from occurring again, it is necessary to reconsider the theory of the free market economy. In other words, it is necessary to seek right balance between the internal market mechanism and the external adjustment of governments. Such balance is dynamic and constantly moving. As there are different ways for different countries to reach such balance at different stages, attempts to find an unchanging and "optimal" method can only be futile. Trying to judge the performance of financial markets on whether supervision is strong or weak is, in a way, misleading. Philosophically speaking, imbalance is constant, while balance is relative; crisis is bound to occur, while the absence of crisis is relative. It is through addressing imbalance and overcoming crisis that progress is made. The world would stop developing if there were no imbalance and crisis. Therefore, what is important is not avoiding imbalance and crisis, but preventing them from getting out of control and causing destructive impact on economic development.

What kind of market forces give rise to such a large number of financial derivatives? I believe they are the "American dream" and the notion of "housing for all". Over the past few centuries, it was the combination of this dream and idea that drove Americans and those who yearned for America to try every means to take advantage of the market to get rich. There has long been imbalance between saving and consumption in the

United States as well as imbalance between the service sector and the manufacturing sector. Within the service sector, there has been imbalance between financial service industry and other service industries. The dollar, as an international currency, and the dollar-based international monetary system have made it possible for such imbalance to persist in the United States. Taking advantage of this system, the United States has been thus able to use the savings of other people to satisfy its own consumption and maintain growth.

Why is the international monetary system responsible for the global financial and economic crisis? As it will be explained in greater detail in this book, I will only address the issue briefly here.

There was a post-World War II consensus that to avoid a repeat of the great calamities that occurred during World War I and World War II, it was necessary to set up a more equitable international political and economic system. In August 1941, U.S. President Franklin Delano Roosevelt and British Prime Minister Winston Churchill discussed the reshaping of the political and economic system aboard the U.S.S. Augusta in the Atlantic Ocean, thus starting the process of the post-war rebuilding of the international political and economic system. The idea of building an international political–economic system with the United Nations as the mainstay was later adopted at the Yalta meeting and the Cairo meeting. In response, 44 countries convened an international financial and monetary conference in Bretton Woods, New Hampshire, during which decisions were made to establish the International Bank for Reconstruction and Development (World Bank) and the International Monetary Fund (IMF) as well as the fixed exchange rates system. Under this system, the dollar was to be linked with gold, while all other major currencies were linked to the dollar. In October 1946, U.S. Secretary of Finance John Snyder sent a letter to the President of IMF, stating that the United States accepted and would abide by this arrangement. The dollar thus became the only international currency after World War II.

As an institutional arrangement based on international law, the system of fixed exchange rates played an important role in economic reconstruction and development after World War II. If this arrangement had been maintained, the Unites States would have been able to tackle imbalance that emerged in its economy. Admittedly, it would cause other problems for U.S. economic development. The United States would have difficulty in maintaining normal growth and face the "Triffin Dilemma". However, when this arrangement became unsustainable owing to U.S. domestic policy needs, the right approach should have been for the whole world to negotiate a way to replace the dollar as the international currency, rather than allowing the United States to unilaterally declare that the fixed price between the dollar and gold would not be maintained. The United States' decision to abandon its solemn pledge to the international society without the IMF's consent was unlawful under international law.

In order to maintain the dollar's position as an international currency, the United States opposed any new international monetary arrangement — including giving a new role to the Special Drawing Rights (SDR). But it was either unwilling or unable to fulfill its responsibility and obligations as the issuer of international currency. Instead, the United States advocated the gimmick of "floating exchange rates". As the issue of the floating exchange rates will be discussed in this book, I will just touch upon the essence of "floating exchange rates" here: only the United States may have an independent monetary policy, while the monetary policies of other countries have to be subordinated to the needs of the United States. This explains why the United States did not demand the devaluation of the renminbi when the value of the dollar was rising, but now demands a sharp appreciation of the renminbi, when the dollar is devaluating. No international conferences or treaties forbid a country from linking its currency with another currency. Why would the United States help other countries or economies design the currency board system, which fixed their exchange rates with the dollar, but not allow a stable exchange rate between the renminbi and the dollar? The floating exchange rates system is a system in which the dollar can float freely, while other currencies must float according to the needs of the dollar. This is typical logic of robbers. Using this method, the United States hit the Japanese economy hard, and it now wants to do the same thing to weaken China's development. But I do not think it will succeed.

The models and theories preached by the West to China are hardly persuasive. Now, even the West itself has abandoned the theories and practices they long advocated. This shows that there are no standard and unchanging development models and theories in the world, but only development models and theories that meet the need of particular countries. Blindly following the theories and models advocated by the West can only lead to failure. We must develop in an innovative way new models and theories to meet our own development needs. This is how China has succeeded in its revolution. This is also what we need to do to make China's development a success.

Now I wish to address the exchange rate of the renminbi. In an article published in the *Financial Times* on December 4, 2002, then Japanese Deputy Minister of Finance, Haruhiko Kuroda, claimed that the undervalued renminbi was the cause of international imbalance, and demanded that the renminbi be revaluated and float freely in the foreign exchange market. At the time, many people made the same charge against the renminbi and accused China's exchange rate policy of being the culprit of global economic imbalance. In order to clarify this issue, I published some newspaper articles and gave speeches at various international conferences. I pointed out that, rather than being the cause of global economic imbalance, China was actually a victim of the current unjust international economic and monetary system. I was invited to attend a number of G7 meetings of deputy finance ministers and deputy central bank governors and similar meetings held by the Group of Twenty (G20). In the 2 years before I left my post at the People's Bank of China, I had extensive and in-depth discussions with foreign banking officials on the renminbi exchange rate. I repeatedly asked the following questions: If the fixed exchange rate was the source of all evils, why were the two decades before 1971, when the fixed exchange rate was the norm, a period of the most stable global economic development? What exactly are floating exchange rates? What does floating mean if there is no parameter? If there is a parameter, what is it? While the fixed exchange rate after World War II did not lead to global economic imbalance, how is it that the issue of renminbi valuation has now become the source of imbalance?

No one could answer these questions. Why? It was simply because the so-called renminbi exchange rate issue is a false proposition invented by those pseudo-scholars, or those who have a hidden agenda. This false proposition is fundamentally flawed. If there had been no financial tsunami, some naïve people would still believe that the renminbi exchange rate was the key problem. A greater number of people would still believe in the myth that floating exchange rates are superior to fixed exchange rates. However, this unprecedented financial crisis revealed the true color of those pseudo-scholars. Their so-called "theory" is designed to maintain a favourable environment for their own development at the expense of others. This situation is aptly described by an old Chinese saying: "Magistrates are free to burn down houses, but ordinary folks are not even allowed to light lamps." I simply cannot understand how a decent scholar could fail to see that as the issuer of the dollar — the major international currency — the United States should fulfill its due responsibilities. According to those so-called scholars, only the United States, not other countries, has the right to adopt its own monetary policy and determine the value of its own currency to suit its needs. Such a position is so absurd that there is no way it can be satisfied.

Again, there are Chinese sayings that describe such a situation: "A thief cries 'thief!'", and "the more one tries to cover something up, the more attention one will attract". "A thief cries 'thief!'" refers to the fact that Western countries are fully aware that their own policies and the dollar-based international monetary system have caused the current global economic imbalance. But they shift the blame to China's exchange rate policy and seek to, through forcing appreciation of the renminbi, weaken the competitiveness of China's economy and derail China's economic development, or at least, make China take longer time to catch up with the developed world. "The more one tries to cover something, the more attention one will attract" refers to the fact that Western countries try to deny that the mismatch between responsibilities, obligations, and benefits of the dollar's position as an international currency is the very reason behind the global economic imbalance. But the harder they try to shift the blame to the renminbi exchange rate, the more obvious the absurdity of the existing international monetary system becomes. The outbreak of the financial crisis has laid bare this cover-up attempt.

How can the dollar-based international monetary system be reformed? To achieve this goal, we should promote the internationalization of the renminbi and diversify the international monetary system. Breaking the monopoly of the dollar is crucial for reforming the international economic and financial system. An old building needs to be demolished before a new one can be erected in its place. There is no construction without destruction. The commencement of destruction is also the beginning of construction. Disorder is an essential prerequisite for reaching a new global order. "Disorder" here means the process of forming a diversified international monetary system, a process that will eventually lead to the emergence of a unified international monetary system. Many people, both in China and overseas, do not believe that the renminbi will become an international currency. Some think it will take a long time for this to happen. Although I have studied this subject for years, I would not make prediction. I just want to point out that, at the founding of New China, few people believed that the Communist Party of China could run the country successfully. After the political turmoil in 1989, some people in the United States predicted that the Chinese government would collapse within two weeks. When China began reform and opening-up, no one believed that, within three decades, China could reach the level of development today. During the Asian financial crisis, no one believed that the renminbi could resist the pressure of devaluation. However, with six decades of development behind them, the Chinese people have accomplished these missions impossible. History will surely tell whether China can succeed in its development endeavor and whether the renminbi will become an international currency.

This book is dedicated to the 60th anniversary of the founding of the People's Republic of China.

August 27, 2009

Contents

About the Author

 Mr. Li Ruogu received Master of Laws degree at Peking University in 1981 and a Master of Public Administration degree at Princeton University in 1983. He is now Chairman and President of the Export-Import Bank of China. His previous positions include the following: Deputy Governor of the People's Bank of China (PBC), China's Executive Director of the Asian Development Bank, China's Alternate Governor of the International Monetary Fund, the Caribbean Development Bank, and the Eastern and Southern African Trade and Development Bank. From April 2003 to September 2005, he served as a member of the Monetary Policy Committee of the PBC.

Mr. Li Ruogu is also Master Candidate Supervisor and Member of the Degree Evaluation Commission of the Graduate School of the PBC and Member of the Academic Committee of the Post-doctoral Station of the PBC Research Department.

Mr. Li Ruogu has written Institutional Suitability and Economic Development, China's Financial Development in the Face of Globalization, and China's Financial Development in the Age of Globalization. He was editor-in-chief of Comparison of Global Economic Development Patterns, Economic Globalization and China's Financial Reform, International Economic Integration and Financial Regulation, and Thesis on International Finance. He has translated *The Order of Economic Liberalization: Financial Control in the Transition to a Market Economy* by Ronald I. McKinnon.

Part One

Evolution of the International Monetary System

The international monetary system has gone through four stages in its evolution: (1) the gold standard (1880–1914); (2) the gold-exchange standard (1925–1933); (3) the Bretton Woods system (1944–1971); and (4) the Jamaica system, also known as the floating exchange rate system (1976–present).

Each international monetary system has its own political and economic background. The history of the international monetary systems is also a history of the rise and fall of economic powers and a history of modern international economic relations. By studying the evolution of international monetary systems and their political and economic background, we can gain insight into changes in and development of the current international monetary system and work to improve it.

Chapter 1

The Gold Standard

The gold standard has been long abandoned. However, as the initial form of international monetary system, it had an extremely important position in the evolution of the international monetary system. And many conflicts and problems in today's international monetary system have their roots in the era of the gold standard.

1.1 Origin of the Gold Standard

Gold is a basic element in Nature. It was the first metal discovered and used by mankind, much earlier than copper and iron. The use of gold by mankind dates back to the Neolithic Age, 4,000 to 5,000 years ago. As a Chinese saying goes, that which is scarce is precious. Gold is extremely scarce and the cost of its mining and smelting is very high. More importantly, gold is valued as it can be preserved for a long period of time because of its high degree of stability. With the emergence of the commodity economy, gold acquired a unique social role when it began to circulate as currency and became an important means for people to keep their wealth. As Karl Marx wrote in *Das Kapital*, "Although gold and silver are not by nature money, money is by nature gold and silver".

From 16th through 18th centuries before the introduction of the gold standard, the new capitalist countries, including the United States and

European countries, had adopted a bimetallic system in which gold and silver acted as equivalents. But it was an unstable currency system. In the Elizabethan Age during the 16th century, Thomas Gresham, a financial agent of the Crown, discovered what is now known as Gresham's Law, which stated that "bad money drives out good" if exchange rate is set by law. At that time, the exchange rates between gold and silver coins in different countries were legally fixed by governments and remained unchanged over a long period of time. But prices of gold and silver fluctuated in response to market supply and demand. As it was more difficult to mine gold than silver and the deposit of gold is much smaller than silver, the relative value of gold inevitably went up against silver, and often surpassed the statutory exchange rate. Therefore, people preferred to smelt gold coins into gold bullions and convert them into silver coins on the market. This way, gold coins could be exchanged for silver at a better rate than official exchange rates. Over time, the number of gold coins (the "good money") on the market gradually dropped, whereas silver coins (the "bad money") flooded the market. This created chaos in commodity prices and trading in those countries using the bimetallic standard between 16th and 18th centuries.

The bimetallic standard caused great losses to Britain, and casting silver coins in the 1790s began to phase out. After the Napoleonic Wars, Britain began to issue gold coins. According to the Bank Charter Act of 1844, only the Bank of England was authorized to issue bank notes with the support of an adequate gold reserve. This Act formally established the gold standard in Britain. However, as it was not yet introduced in other countries, the gold standard had not yet become international.

Britain was the first country in the world to industrialize. The Industrial Revolution began in Britain in the 1760s. Driven by the development of modern industry, Britain became the "world's factory" by the mid-19th century. There was huge global demand for Britain's industrial products, particularly textiles. After Britain introduced the gold standard, other countries which had close trade relations with it had to follow suit. In 1871, after extracting a huge sum of war indemnity from France, Germany adopted the gold standard by issuing the gold mark as its standard currency. Russia and Japan also adopted the gold standard in 1897.

In the late 19th century, a unified international monetary system — the gold standard, began to emerge among Western countries. During the process, because of Britain's dominant position in international trade, the British pound sterling became the principal means of payment and the main reserve currency in the international monetary system. The British pound sterling gained recognition in the world and became an international currency equivalent to gold. Gold flowed into Britain in large quantities due to the appeal of Britain's economic might.

With huge capital, British banking industry registered robust growth and conducted active lending overseas. By the mid-19th century, London had become the financial center of the world.[1] Therefore, the gold standard — which was used before the World War I — was referred to as the "British Pound Standard" by some economists. According to renowned American political economist Robert Gilpin, the international monetary and financial system under the conventional gold standard was organized and managed by Britain. The monetary system under the gold standard was dominated by Britain, next to which were the new financial centers in Western Europe.[2] It should be noted that the formation of the gold standard was not the result of negotiations among countries. Rather, it was the product of market selection in response to changes in the global economic environment and the economic relations between countries. This stands in sharp contrast with the establishment of the Bretton Woods system after World War II.

1.2 Characteristics of the Gold Standard

The gold standard lasted 35 years, from 1880 to 1914. Under the gold standard, different countries issued small change and bank notes, which could be converted freely to gold coins or gold according to certain proportion. Exchange rates between bank notes of different countries were determined by the ratio of their respective values in gold, and were fixed. For instance, the value of one British pound sterling (GBP) was fixed at

---

[1] Xia Yande (1991), p. 408.
[2] Robert Gilpin (1989), p. 139.

113.00 grains[3] of pure gold, while the value of one U.S. dollar (US$) was 23.22 grains of pure gold. Thus, exchange rate between the two currencies was US$ 4.86 to GBP 1.

Under the gold standard, governments of different countries allowed some fluctuation in managing their respective exchange rates, which was kept within limits between the gold-export point (the exchange parity plus the shipping cost) and the gold-import point (the exchange parity minus the shipping cost). If the exchange rate of a particular country surpassed the gold-export point, gold within its territory would be shipped out in exchange for foreign currencies. Once gold was shipped out, demand for its currency would shrink, pressing down its exchange rate. If the exchange rate of that country fell below the gold-import point, gold would flow in pushing up its exchange rate. To keep their monetary systems and international trade running, governments kept their respective exchange rates within limits. Therefore, gold standard was strictly a fixed exchange rate system.

Under such a strict fixed exchange rate system, balance of payments of countries was self-adjusted. Scottish economist David Hume first referred to this system of self-adjustment, known as the price-specie-flow mechanism, in *Political Discourses* published in 1752. Hume found that, under the gold standard, if a country maintained a surplus in foreign trade, its domestic gold reserve would continuously increase and this would trigger domestic inflation. Rising domestic prices would lead consumers of that country to buy more imported goods, while foreign nationals' demands for that country's goods would also decline. This would lead to a drop in trade surplus, a gradual decrease in its gold reserve, and a continuous price decline. Thus the country's balance of payments would return to equilibrium. The price-specie-flow mechanism worked before World War I mainly because all industrial economies strictly followed the"rules of the game"for the gold standard: the monetary authorities of the trading countries denominated the value of their currencies in terms of gold, and the money supply was restricted by a country's gold reserve. Free exchange between gold and currencies was permitted and gold could be shipped freely across borders.

---

[3] 1 grain = 64.799 mg.

1.3 Breakdown of the Gold Standard

The gold standard was dominant from 1880 through 1914. During this period, the capitalist economy further developed, and important progress was achieved in science. This led to the Second Industrial Revolution featuring the use of electricity. The United States and Germany greatly benefited from this industrial revolution, and they saw a boost in their industrial production. But Britain failed to promptly upgrade its industrial capacity and adopt the latest technologies. Thus, Britain's economic status in terms of industrial output dropped sharply. From 1870 through 1913, Britain's share of global industrial output dropped from 32% to 14%. Once the number one industrial country in the world, Britain now slipped to number three. The United States' share of global industrial output rose from 23% to 36% and became number one. Germany gained the second place, surpassing Britain.[4]

The causes for the decline of British economic status were many and complicated, on which in-depth studies have been conducted. English scholar Martin Wiener is well known for his interpretation of England's decline from a cultural perspective. Wiener believed that the English culture was anti-capitalist, which considered free market economy unfair as it only benefited factory owners, and that the working classes were its victims. Despite the completion of industrialization in Britain after 1870, the British society very much remained what it had been in the pre-industrial age and was not prepared to meet the challenges of modern society. This viewpoint was widely recognized in Britain, but it also caused much controversy.[5]

---

[4]Liu Zongxu (2005).

[5]For a detailed discussion, refer to Chen Xiaolv (2002). According to Martin Wiener, English culture is essentially in opposition to entrepreneurial spirit. Such opposition is best represented in the British education system, especially the free public schools and universities. Since the early period of the Victorian era, these institutions have been the main places for British merchants to receive education. The main objective of these schools was to cultivate gentlemen, while industrial and commercial activities were not considered irrelevant. Besides, English culture at that time had a strong tendency of anti-urbanization; it considered the pastoral life in England before industrialization as the most ideal social state and that life of landholding nobles was far higher than urban life.

Cultural factor might have, to a certain extent, hindered Britain's industrial development after 1870. But I think there were at least three other factors behind Britain's decline.

First, while other countries had not yet begun to industrialize themselves or lagged behind in industrialization, Britain, the first industrialized economy was naturally the champion leader. However, when capitalist countries, such as the United States and Germany which have bigger territories, entered the stage of industrialization, it was difficult for Britain, an island country with limited land, to maintain its position as the leader of the industrialized countries. In this sense, Britain's decline was, in fact, a normal result in historical development.

Second, Britain's decline was due more to the rapid economic development in the United States and Germany. Between 1859 and 1909, U.S. industrial output grew 6 times; between 1870 and 1913, German industrial output grew 4.7 times, while Britain's growth was only 0.9 times.[6] Similarly, there are many causes for the rapid growth of the United States and Germany, a main one of which was research and innovation. Take the United States for example: from 1870 to 1913 — in less than half a century — a surprising number of inventions and patents emerged, including many new manufacturing methods and production procedures. Light bulb was invented by Thomas Edison in 1879, the alternating current (AC) was invented by Nikola Tesla in 1894, and the Model T automobile was invented by Henry Ford in 1908. During this period, the U.S. government made major investments in both basic research and applied research. In fact, many of today's leading American research universities were established with the support of the federal government and state governments during the second half of the 19th century. They include Massachusetts Institute of Technology (founded in 1865), University of California, Berkeley (founded in 1868), Stanford University (founded in 1885), and California Institute of Technology (founded in 1891).

Third, Britain, as the biggest colonial power at the time, controlled a vast market and supplies of raw materials. So even without a very high level of technology, British businesses could still reap huge profits. Therefore, Britain did not have adequate incentive to carry out innovation

---

[6] Liu Zongxu (2005).

and responded slowly to technical innovation created in the Second Industrial Revolution.

Factors undermining the stability of the international monetary system were also increasing due to the unbalanced economic and political development of capitalist countries and the increasing conflicts among them, and factors undermining the stability of the international monetary system also increased. Using their economic strength and military force, Britain, the United States, Germany, France, and Russia amassed two-thirds of the global gold reserve by 1913.[7] The distribution of gold reserves in the world was severely unbalanced, and the basis of many countries' currencies was seriously weakened. This undermined a key rule of the gold standard, namely, that all countries issued their currencies according to the amount of their respective gold reserves. At the same time, to prepare for war, some countries sharply increased government spending and could only cover the budget deficit by issuing a large number of bank notes. Therefore, rule free exchange between currencies and gold was undermined. After the outbreak of World War I, all the participating countries stopped free exchange between bank notes and gold. Gold export was also prohibited. Thus, all the rules that underpinned the gold standard were violated. The stability of the international monetary system was no longer ensured, and the gold standard collapsed all together.

There was a deeper cause for the disintegration of the gold standard. Currency serves as a lubricant of economic operation, and money supply of an appropriate amount is essential for an economy to grow. Neither excessive nor inadequate money supply is good for the smooth functioning of an economy. The two industrial revolutions accelerated the growth of the world economy, but the supply of gold could not catch up with it. The gold standard thus gradually lost its justification. In this sense, even without World War I, the gold standard would still come to an end anyway.

1.4 Evaluation of the Gold Standard

The advantages of the gold standard, as the first international monetary system, were obvious. First, as the value of different currencies was based

---

[7] Chen Biaoru (1996), p. 11.

on their value in gold, exchange rates between different currencies were relatively stable. Stable exchange rates played an important role in promoting international trade and investment and thus optimized the international allocation of resources. Second, as the issuance of currencies was limited by the amount of the gold reserve, inflation was effectively controlled. A country's gold reserve came mainly from two sources — gold mining and the balance of payments surplus. Due to limitation in gold mining technology, growth of the money supply was not only slow, but even negative from time to time. Therefore, during the period of the gold standard, price levels were relatively stable.

However, the automatic balance of payments adjustment mechanism under the gold standard was imperfect. First, the intervention by different countries' monetary authorities prevented this mechanism from operating normally. When the inflow or outflow of gold led to changes in a country's domestic money supply, the monetary authorities in that country would control the money supply in a way similar to open market operations. This intervention, through the price-specie-flow mechanism, would hamper the inflow (or outflow) of gold and increase (or decrease) of the price. This means the automatic balance of payments adjustment mechanism could not achieve its normal, desired effect. Second, international lending limited the use of gold for international settlement. This, to a certain extent, also hindered the operation of the mechanism. If a country experiences a current account deficit, it could make up for it by getting international loan. Conversely, if a country experiences a surplus, it could reduce this surplus by investing overseas. The frequent use of international loans also shows that a country's money supply would not increase or decrease due to trade surplus or deficit, as indicated by the price-specie-flow mechanism. During the 35-year period of the use of the gold standard, the flow of gold among countries was, in fact, infrequent. This was not only because trading countries abided by the rules of the game, but also because international lending weakened the effect of the price-specie-flow mechanism and reduced its function of regulating the international balance of payments.

Chapter 2

The Gold-exchange Standard

The gold-exchange standard was an alternative to the gold standard adopted after a failed post-World War I attempt to return to the pre-war gold standard. It lasted less than a decade, from the 1920s through 1933.

2.1 Origin of the Gold-exchange Standard

During World War I, exchange rates were extremely volatile, making it almost impossible to conduct international trade and foreign payments. After the war, rebuilding of the international monetary system became urgent. However, as gold supply was insufficient to meet increasing demand that resulted from economic expansion, it was impossible to return to the pre-war gold standard. On April 10, 1922, 29 countries[1] — including Britain, France, Italy, Belgium, Japan, and the Soviet Union — held an international monetary and financial conference in Genoa, Italy on the rebuilding of the international monetary system. The Genoa Conference was also the world's first international economic conference. To narrow the gap between gold supply and economic growth, the conference proposed the adoption of an international monetary system that would not use gold directly, i.e., the gold-exchange standard.

---

[1] The United States sent officials as observers to the conference.

2.2 Characteristics of the Gold-exchange Standard

Gold-exchange standard is also called "virtual gold standard". It was obviously a virtualized copy of the post-World War I gold standard, by actually encompassing two types of monetary systems — the gold-bullion standard and the gold-exchange standard. Because a bigger number of countries adopted gold-exchange standard after the Genoa Conference, the international monetary system during the period was named accordingly. Germany was the first country to use the gold-exchange standard in 1924. Around 30 countries, including Austria, Italy, and Denmark, also introduced the standard later. Britain and France adopted the gold-bullion standard in 1925 and 1928, respectively, while the United States continued to use the gold specie standard. The gold-exchange standard thus came into being in the 1920s.

The gold-exchange standard was essentially a form of the gold standard with conditions attached. This standard had four main characteristics: first, gold still served as the foundation for the international monetary system. Countries were still required to set a certain proportion of gold to back up its paper currencies, which acted as means of payment and settlement that had been previously handled by gold. Second, bank notes were pegged to gold in two ways: either directly linking a country's currency with gold, or indirectly, linking its currency to a gold-linked currency. In both ways, the national currencies directly or indirectly achieved a fixed-parity rate with gold. Third, when indirectly linked, a country could only obtain gold by purchasing a directly-linked currency (foreign exchange). To maintain the exchange rate, it needed to deposit a certain amount of foreign exchange and gold as the stabilization fund in the country whose currency was directly linked to gold. Finally, gold or gold coins were not in circulation domestically, and gold could only be used as an instrument of international payment as the last resort in the case of disequilibrium to maintain exchange rate stability.

Although it still used gold as the basis for issuing currency, the gold-exchange standard was different from the gold standard in several ways. First, although gold's position as the basis for issuing bank notes did not change, its functions were weakened and bank notes were no longer redeemable for gold freely. For example, to purchase gold from the Bank of England, a single transaction had to be four hundred ounces of gold or above. In countries using the gold-exchange standard, domestic currency could not be exchanged for gold and could only be exchanged for the currencies of countries using the gold-bullion standard. These conditions limited purchase of gold from central banks. Second, the number of currencies functioning as international currencies increased. Under the gold standard, only gold and the British pound sterling were international currencies. Under the gold-exchange standard, countries with currencies directly linked to gold included not only Britain but also the United States and France. The dollar and franc, thus, also functioned as international currencies. Third, the position of British pound sterling in the international monetary system declined. After World War I, the inflation rate of Britain was much higher than that of the United States. However, to maintain the pound's status, the British government kept the exchange rate fixed at the pre-war rate of US\$ 4.86 to GBP 1. This evaluation of pound sterling was obviously too high which made people unwilling to hold it. The position of pound sterling in the international monetary system was thus weakened.

2.3 Breakdown of the Gold-exchange Standard

The gold-exchange standard established after World War I was, in fact, a variant of the pre-war gold standard and did not break new ground. Moreover, compared with its role in the pre-war gold standard, the role of gold as the basis for issuing currency was weakened under either the gold-bullion standard or the gold-exchange standard. Consequently, the gold-exchange standard was unstable.

After functioning only for a short period of operation time, the fragile gold-exchange standard eventually collapsed under the impact of the Great Depression from 1929 to 1933. The outbreak of the depression in the 1930s initially manifested itself in an increase in "bank runs". Banks around the world faced great pressure, when people rushed to banks to convert their bank notes into gold. On September 21, 1931, Britain was forced to announce that it would abolish the gold-bullion standard in order to stave off the rush to convert currency into gold. Then, other countries using the British pound sterling also abandoned the gold-exchange standard. In 1933, when the dollar was also in crisis, the United States, too, abandoned the gold-bullion standard. The gold-exchange standard collapsed.

In June of 1933, delegates from 66 countries held an international conference in London to discuss ways to resolve the problem of stagnation in global trade and save the world economy. However, in a bid to establish a new global economic order, the United States, with its financial power, hoped that Britain's leading position would go with the old economic order. U.S. President Franklin Delano Roosevelt did not attend the conference and he announced that the United States would not negotiate any agreements pertaining to monetary stabilization. The conference thus ended in failure.

After failing to agree on a common policy for stimulating international trade and the world economy, Britain, France, and the United States began a fierce monetary war, which gave rise to a British pound group, a French franc group, and a U.S. dollar group. These three competitive currency groups imposed foreign exchange control internally and vied to depreciate their currencies. Britain further depreciated the pound sterling and established a foreign exchange stabilization fund to intervene in the foreign exchange market and keep the British pound's exchange rate from rising. The United States chose to allow the dollar to depreciate to maintain its competitiveness in international trade and purchased large quantities of gold. France converted all of its foreign exchange reserves into gold. This beggar-thy-neighbor policy caused persistent fluctuation of exchange rates, a sharp decline in international trade, severe damage to the world economy, and undermined the credibility of currencies in the capitalist world. To some extent, the self-centered policies pursued by the three major currency groups caused Japan, Italy, and Germany to remedy their economic woes by militarizing their economies, thereby planting the seeds for World War II.

2.4 Evaluation of the Gold-exchange Standard

The gold-exchange standard was essentially an international monetary system still based on gold, so it had the same advantages of the gold standard in terms of checking inflation, stabilizing exchange rates, and regulating balance of payments. Additionally, an important objective of adopting the gold-exchange standard was to limit the use of gold. So such a system was justified to some extent. However, it failed to overcome the inherited defect of the gold standard — the gap between limited gold supply and continuous economic expansion. At most, it only temporarily eased this problem.

Although the gold-exchange standard only existed for less than 10 years, it was still important in the historical development of the international monetary system for the following four reasons. First, the gold-exchange standard was the product of the first international economic conference and can be viewed as the start of economic consultation and cooperation at an international level. Second, the gold-exchange standard was used by Britain — whose economic influence declined and who lost its position as the global economic leader — to restore the British pound sterling to its original international standing. But the result was not what it expected. Not only did the British pound sterling lose to the U.S. dollar in the international competition, but the gold-exchange standard rapidly collapsed as well. This illustrates that the position of a country's currency in the international monetary system is determined by that country's economic strength. An international monetary system incompatible with countries' economic power is unstable. Third, the gold-exchange standard weakened the link between currencies and gold. It was an important breakthrough in monetary history, as it was the first step away from a gold-based monetary system and towards a credit-based system of the modern economy. Finally, the Bretton Woods system established after World War II was a monetary system under which currencies were pegged to the U.S. dollar and the dollar was in turn pegged to gold. It, too, was a kind of gold-exchange standard. The introduction of the gold-exchange standard, therefore, laid the foundation for the establishment of the Bretton Woods system after World War II.

Chapter 3

The Bretton Woods System

After World War II, dollar-based international monetary system was built under the sponsorship of the United States. This system established the dominance of the United States and the dollar within the international monetary system. This period lasted from 1944 through 1971.

3.1 Origin of the Bretton Woods System

After World War II, tremendous changes took place in the power equation in the Western world. The British economy was heavily damaged during the war, and the United States became the biggest creditor in the capitalist world and the most powerful country. This made it possible for the dollar to secure dominance. Before the end of World War II, the United States had begun to build a dollar-based international monetary system.

Both the United States and Britain wanted to establish a new international monetary order that met its own interests. On April 7, 1943, the two countries presented their proposals, namely, the American "White Plan"[1] and the British "Keynes Plan".[2] The two plans reflected change in the

---

[1]Proposed by U.S. Assistant Secretary of Finance, Harry D White, also known as "Stabilization Fund for United and Associated Nations".

[2]Drafted by British Financial Advisor, Lord Keynes, also known as "International Clearing Union".

relative economic strength of the two countries and their struggle for global financial leadership.

Under the Keynes Plan, Britain proposed to build an International Clearing Union (ICU) and create an international currency called the Bancor, which would have a fixed gold value. Member countries would treat it as gold and use it for international clearing. The Keynes Plan proposed the following: (1) The ICU would issue the Bancor for clearing between central banks or ministries of finance. A fixed parity rate would be established between the Bancor and gold. (2) Various currencies would have fixed exchange rates with the Bancor, which could be adjusted. But countries would not be allowed to unilaterally carry out any competitive devaluation, and due procedures should be followed before any change could be made in the exchange rate. (3) Central banks would open accounts in the ICU and Bancor would be used in account clearing. When a country experienced a balance of payments (BOP) surplus, it would deposit the surplus into its own account. When there was deficit, it could apply either to overdraw or to withdraw funds from its account, according to specified quota. The total sum of overdraw would be US$ 30 billion.

The international monetary system envisaged in the Keynes Plan was designed to address the flaws of the previous systems. Regulation of currency, exchange rates, and BOP imbalance was proposed. The amount of Bancor issued would be determined by the needs of the world economy and without being restricted by gold. The exchange rate with Bancor would be fixed but could be adjusted, and countries were prohibited from engaging in competitive currency devaluation. Regarding regulation of the BOP, the Keynes Plan expanded the payments between two countries to an international multilateral clearing system. Upon clearing, if a country's loan balance were to exceed a certain proportion, countries with surpluses and deficits would have to take action to address the disequilibrium and both would share responsibility for carrying out such regulation.

In the White Plan, the United States introduced the concept of "Stabilization Fund for the United and Associated Nations" and proposed to set up an international stabilization fund, with the following provisions: (1) Member countries would contribute capital to set up a stabilization fund of US$ 5 billion. Member countries would decide upon their quota subscriptions according to their gold reserves and national incomes, which would determine the foreign exchange position a country could borrow to adjust its BOP deficit. (2) An international monetary unit named "Unita" with specified value in gold would be established. The Unita was only a unit of account, not a real currency, but could be transferred among member countries or exchanged for gold. All currencies should maintain a fixed exchange rate with the Unita. (3) Foreign exchange control and direct bilateral clearing would be prohibited. (4) The fund management authority would have the right to supervise and intervene in the domestic economic policies of member countries and would have the right to trade gold. Member countries' currencies could be borrowed or lent out subjected to the consent of member countries. (5) The fund's management office would be set up in the country which held the largest share.

The major differences between the Keynes Plan and the White Plan show that the United States and Britain were competing for domination of international finance. After World War II, the United States far surpassed Britain in terms of both economic strength and gold reserve. From 1937 to 1945, the United States' gold reserve increased from US$ 12.79 billion to US$ 20.08 billion, while that of Britain dropped from US$ 4.147 billion to US$ 1.918 billion.[3] If the gold standard were to be restored after the war, leadership of international finance would have certainly fallen into the hands of the United States. Therefore, the White Plan, which represented U.S. interests, emphasized the stabilizing effect of gold and called for the use of gold as the basis of the monetary system. The Keynes Plan, which represented British interests, however, criticized the flaws of the gold standard. It claimed that limited gold deposits would hinder the development of the world economy, and advocated substituting gold with an international credit currency for international clearing. In addition, the Keynes Plan called for the establishment of an international clearing union and proposed that a deficit country should be able to make up for its deficit by applying for permission to overdraw. By overdrawing, Britain could relieve the pressure on its inadequate gold reserve. The White Plan, however, prohibited overdrawing, maintaining that overdrawing could not fundamentally resolve the BOP disequilibrium. The real

---

[3] Meng Xianyang (1989).

reason was that such overdrawing would cause a large amount of gold to flow out from the United States and into deficit countries.

In September 1943, a delegation of British financial officials visited the United States and, along with delegates from 39 other countries, held heated discussions. But such discussion actually became a bilateral negotiation between Britain and the United States on international monetary arrangements. John Maynard Keynes and Harry Dexter White proposed the aforementioned plans on behalf of Britain and the United States respectively. Under strong U.S. influence, nearly all countries present at the meeting accepted the White Plan.

In July 1944, 45 countries convened the United Nations Monetary and Financial Conference in Bretton Woods, New Hampshire, and adopted the Articles of Agreement of the International Monetary Fund (IMF) and the Articles of Agreement of the International Bank for Reconstruction and Development (IBRD) — collectively called the Bretton Woods agreements — based on the White Plan. The Bretton Woods system was thus officially established. The Bretton Woods Agreements aimed to: (1) establish a permanent international monetary institution to promote international cooperation on monetary issues, for which the IMF was established; (2) stabilize exchange rates, establish a multilateral payment system, and prevent competitive currency devaluation, for which adjustable peg system was established; and (3) offer member countries financial aids when needed to regulate BOP imbalance.

The international monetary system created by the Bretton Woods system was a double-linkage arrangement. First, the dollar was still a gold standard currency with a fixed relationship to gold of US$ 35 per ounce. Secondly, other member countries maintained an adjustable pegged exchange rate by tying its currency to the dollar, with a fluctuation of plus and minus 1% of the parity. The monetary authorities of other member countries would intervene in foreign exchange markets to maintain the dollar's official gold price. Except in the case of a BOP "fundamental disequilibrium" which was subject to the IMF's approval, member countries were not permitted to change their par values. The arrangements under the Bretton Woods system actually set up a relative price system among different currencies with gold as a benchmark. Because the dollar was the sole currency backed by gold, it became the reserve currency.

What the Bretton Woods system introduced was essentially a "dollar standard", with the dollar being superior to all other currencies. This actually gave the United States a leading position in the international monetary system.

3.2 Characteristics of the Bretton Woods System

Some called the Bretton Woods system the gold-exchange standard or "gold-dollar standard", viewing it as the same with the gold-pound standard used in the mid 1920s in nature. Strictly speaking, the Bretton Woods system was not entirely new, but it was distinctively different, in certain aspects, from the gold-exchange standard. First, the most notable difference is that during the period of the gold-exchange standard, there were three international currencies — the British pound sterling, the U.S. dollar, and the French franc — with each having its own respective spheres of influence. But after World War II, the U.S. dollar became the only international currency. Therefore, compared to the pre-war gold-exchange standard, the Bretton Woods system was a real international monetary system. Furthermore, under the gold-exchange standard, people could exchange their U.S. dollars, British pounds, and French francs for gold from the monetary authorities. Currencies were also much more closely linked to gold. Under the Bretton Woods system, however, the United States only allowed foreign monetary authorities to exchange U.S. dollars for gold from the Federal Reserve Bank under specified conditions, and private gold exchange was prohibited. Therefore, the Bretton Woods system was a type of gold exchange standard in which free gold exchange was extremely weakened. Finally, fixed exchange rates were practiced under the gold-exchange standard, while under the Bretton Woods system, adjustable pegged exchange rates were adopted, which increased the flexibility of exchange rate regulation.

As a whole, the Bretton Woods system consisted of the gold-exchange standard, fixed exchange rates, and foreign exchange control.

First, the Bretton Woods system was similar to the gold-exchange standard in some ways: member countries must set a parity of their currencies in terms of U.S. dollar; they needed to maintain the exchange rate within plus or minus 1% of the parity; they were not permitted to take quantitative restriction and differential measures for the purpose of balancing their current accounts; they were required to have U.S. dollar and British pound sterling as part of their international reserve.

Second, there were similarities between the Bretton Woods system and the fixed exchange rate system: banks or foreign exchange balancing funds of member countries controlled the market exchange rates within a specified range by means of foreign exchange trading. If a fluctuation in foreign exchange supply and demand was only temporary, no adjustment of a country's exchange rates would be allowed. Only when BOP was in a fundamental disequilibrium could member countries change the par value upon approval of the IMF. Third, one similarity between the Bretton Woods system and foreign exchange control was that, when deemed necessary, IMF member countries could control capital transactions.

The Bretton Woods system also had some new features, the most prominent of which was that the establishment of the IMF created a supranational player for the first time in the international economic system. This means that the world economic order began to evolve into a system with multiple participants. In fact, the founding of the IMF shows that countries were becoming increasingly interdependent and it heralded the emergence of global economic governance.

3.3 Development of the Bretton Woods System

Three dollar crises exerted an important impact on the evolution and disintegration of the Bretton Woods system. For two decades after the establishment of the Bretton Woods system, the international monetary system was stable, and adjustment of exchange rate between member countries was rare. In 1947, U.S. Secretary of State George Marshall announced the European Recovery Program (ERP), a large-scale aid program known as the Marshall Plan. The program started in July 1947 and lasted for 4 years. During this period, West European countries received US$ 13 billion in financial, technical, and equipment assistance.[4] The large amount of U.S. aid greatly relieved Europe's post-war fund shortage and enabled it to carry out economic reconstruction and development. Because the dollar

---

[4]Michael J Hogan (1987).

was the *de facto* international currency, other countries needed to increase their dollar reserves, which was only possible when the United States had a deficit in its own international BOP. In the mid- and late-1950s, the United States shifted from having a BOP surplus to having an annual BOP deficit of US$ 1 billion,[5] while Europe and Japan began to have surpluses. Because such deficit was not large, it was not a source of much concern. As long as the United States' gold reserve was larger than its U.S. dollar debts, the Bretton Woods system could maintain normal operation. However, things began to change in the 1960s. The United States had pursued an active fiscal policy and monetary policy over a long period of time, and Europe and Japan, which were undergoing economic recovery and whose economic positions were continually rising, accumulated a huge amount of dollar. The United States had to recover all the surplus dollars at a price of US$ 35 per ounce of gold under the fixed exchange rates. As the United States' debt exceeded its gold reserve, it was difficult to maintain the fixed parity between the dollar and gold, and this triggered the dollar crises.

3.3.1 *The first dollar crisis*

The first dollar crisis took place in 1960, caused by the worsening U.S. BOP since 1958. In 1960, U.S. foreign debt for the first time exceeded its gold reserve, leading to an overflow of the dollar.[6] As many countries began to exchange dollars for gold from the U.S. government, the U.S. gold reserve sharply decreased. Due to the pessimistic market expectation on the dollar, many people sold dollars in panic and purchased gold from the United States and hard currencies of other surplus countries. Within just one month, the value of German mark and the Netherlands guilder rose by 5%.

Rapid loss of its gold reserve caused concern of the U.S. government. In order to maintain the stability of the foreign exchange market and the price of gold and retain convertibility of the dollar and the fixed exchange rates, the United States asked European countries for cooperation within the IMF

---

[5] Barry Eichengreen (2004).
[6] *International Financial Statistics*, additional edition, 1972.

framework. It signed the Reciprocal Agreement with Europe and Japan to set up the General Agreements to Borrow and a "gold pool" within the IMF. The Reciprocal Agreement was signed by the United States and 14 other countries to intervene in the foreign exchange market and stabilize exchange rates with currencies of the counterparties within a specified period and amount. For instance, when U.S. dollar relative to German mark faced pressure for devaluation, the United States could borrow German marks from the Federal Republic of Germany in the amount specified in the agreement, and then sell the marks to purchase dollars. By doing so, the United States could ease the speculative shock on the dollar and stabilize the exchange rate against the mark, and thus indirectly stabilize the parity rate of the U.S. dollar against gold. Subsequently, within the specified period, the United State would repay the borrowed German marks in lump sum or installments. When the agreement was signed in March 1962, its total amount was US$ 11.73 billion, which then increased to US$ 19.78 billion by March 1973.

The General Agreement to Borrow was signed by the IMF and 10 industrial countries[7] in November 1961 and went into effect in October 1962. Its main purpose was to borrow funds from nine countries other than the United States to support the dollar and ease the dollar crisis, so as to keep the international monetary system functioning. The United States was the main borrower under the General Agreements to Borrow.

The gold pool was set up in October 1961 under an agreement reached by the central banks of eight countries, namely, the United States, Britain, France, the Federal Republic of Germany, Italy, the Netherlands, Belgium, and Switzerland, to stabilize gold price and maintain the normal functioning of the Bretton Woods system. Under this agreement, the eight countries jointly contributed gold worth US$ 270 million to set up the gold pool, of which the United States contributed 50%, Germany, Britain, France, and Italy each 9.3%; and Sweden, the Netherlands, and Belgium each contributed 3.7%.[8] The gold was then managed by the Bank of

---

[7]The 10 industrial countries include United States, Britain, France, Canada, Federal Republic of Germany, Japan, Italy, Holland, Belgium, and Sweden, being the member countries of the subsequent G10 (Group of Ten).
[8]Jiang Boke (2008).

England, the British central bank. When gold price rose, the gold pool was to sell gold in the London market; when gold price dropped, it was to buy in gold. The gold pool was thus to regulate the supply and demand and stabilize market price. Initially, it was successful in stabilizing the public confidence. But as the trade volume of gold in the international market was excessively large, the US$ 270 million worth of gold was soon sold out. After the United States introduced the two-tier gold system in 1968, the gold pool came to an end.

3.3.2 The second dollar crisis

After the Vietnam War began in 1961, the United States became deeply involved in it and its spending on the war rose sharply. With the burden on its budget increasing and inflation becoming more serious, the dollar again came under great pressure of devaluation. International confidence in the dollar sank, and people rushed to buy gold. Many countries converted their dollar holdings into gold. Within two weeks, the U.S. gold reserve decreased by US$ 1.4 billion. If this trend were to continue, the U.S. gold reserve could hardly maintain the fixed parity between the dollar and gold. In response, the United States announced the introduction of a "two-tier gold system"[9] in March 1968.

The second dollar crisis made people see that inadequate natural reserve of gold would inevitably limit the development of the global economy. To resolve this problem, the IMF created Special Drawing Rights (SDR), known as "paper gold", in 1969. SDR is a virtual currency that substitutes gold for dollar. It could function like gold as an international reserve asset, and IMF member countries could also use SDR instead of the dollar to clear their BOP. The parity rate of SDR to gold was the same as that of the dollar: one ounce of gold equaled SDR 35. By supplementing the dollar, the SDR caused the international monetary system

---

[9] The "two-tier gold system" implies that gold has two markets. One is the official market in which one ounce of gold exchanges for US$ 35; the other is the private market in which the parity rate of gold to US$ is determined completely according to the gold supply and demand in the market. With the flourishing gold demand, the gold price in the private gold market boosts up, showing an increasingly big gap with the official parity price.

to transition from the gold-dollar standard to a gold-dollar/SDR standard. The creation of SDR shows that the international society became aware that an international monetary system based on the currency of one country was inherently unstable and wanted to create an international credit currency to resolve this problem.

The SDR was designed to replace the dollar, but its allocation failed due to U.S. opposition. The share of SDR in the foreign exchange reserves of countries was insignificant. The first allocation of SDR in 1969 amounted to merely US$ 3.1 billion. In 1971, SDR occupied just 4.5% of the total reserves of international currencies. In 1976, its share dropped to 2.8%.[10] As SDR was too small in size to function as an international currency, the dollar remained the key international currency.

3.3.3 *The third dollar crisis*

In 1971, the United States' short-term foreign debts rose sharply, but its gold reserve continued to drop. From 1961 to 1970, the U.S. gold reserve dropped from US$ 16.95 billion to US$ 11.07 billion, a decline of 38%, while its short-term foreign debts increased sharply from US$ 22.94 billion to US$ 46.96 billion, a growth of 148%.[11] The American gold reserve could no longer bear the growing burden of debts. Faced with the excessive issuance of the dollar and inadequate gold reserve, U.S. President Richard Nixon announced the New Economic Policy (NEP), ceasing convertibility between the dollar and gold. This action, known as "the close of gold window", marked the collapse of the Bretton Woods system.

The severance of exchange between the dollar and gold caused chaos in the international financial market. Fearing that their currencies would become targets of speculation, West European countries with strong currencies immediately closed their foreign exchange markets, and international trade and investment came to a standstill. On December 18, 1971, after four months of negotiation, G10 reached the Smithsonian Agreement in Washington. It introduced dollar depreciation, with a new parity of US$

---

[10] Ma Yaobang (Ben Mah) (2009).
[11] *International Financial Statistics*, additional edition, 1972.

38 per ounce of gold, and appreciation of currencies of countries with surpluses, such as Japan and West Germany. The fluctuation margin for exchange rates was increased from 1% to 2.25%, and the United States dropped the 10% import surcharge. This agreement showed the decline of the dollar's international position and the rise in the international influence of the currencies of countries with surplus. It marked the arrival of an era of diversified international reserve currencies and a turning point that saw the international monetary system move away from the Bretton Woods system towards the Jamaica system.

3.4 Evaluation of the Bretton Woods System

Although the Bretton Woods system was an American initiative, its establishment also involves the participation of many other countries based on the practices of the gold standard and the gold-exchange standard. The Bretton Woods system played an active role in global economic development between the two world wars.

First, the establishment of the Bretton Woods system created a unified standard for governing relationship among international currencies, and thus played its role in promoting the post-war growth of international trade and the world economy. The dollar became the major international reserve currency and, to a certain extent, eased the shortage of international reserve due to inadequate gold supply. The linkage of different currencies to the dollar restricted fluctuation in exchange rates, and the value of currency was kept at a relatively stable level. This promoted the international flow of goods and capital. From 1948 to 1971, global exports saw an average annual growth of 8.4%,[12] up from only 0.7% between 1913 and 1938.[13]

Furthermore, during the initial period of the Bretton Woods system, the United States exported a huge amount of dollar to the world through aid, credit, and the purchase of foreign goods and labor services. It thus facilitated the expansion of world purchasing power and made positive contribution to the post-war recovery and redevelopment of the global economy.

---

[12]WTO Database.
[13]Li Ruogu, "Financial Crisis and Reconstruction of International Monetary System", a presentation at Conference on Reconstruction of Bretton Woods System in 2008.

Finally, the establishment of the Bretton Woods system gave the dollar a central position in the international monetary system, which created significant advantages for the United States: (1) a considerable amount of seigniorage;[14] (2) increased flexibility in pursuing economic policy, which enabled the United States to tolerate a higher balance of payments deficit without the need to make immediate adjustment; and (3) promotion of export of American goods and capital and expansion of U.S. political, economic, military influence, and technical standards overseas. The significance of such promotion and expansion could not be measured in monetary terms.

While the Bretton Woods system played an important role in promoting post-war economic recovery and bringing about significant benefits for the United States, the system had many inherent flaws that could not be overcome.

First, the Bretton Woods System had one fatal flaw: the use of one national currency (the dollar) as the main international settlement and reserve asset was unstable by nature. As the global economy and trade grew, demand for the settlement and reserve currency grew accordingly. Under the Bretton Woods system, this could only be met by sustaining U.S. trade deficit. The prerequisite for the dollar being the core international currency was the stability of its value. This required the United States to keep surplus, or at least equilibrium, in its BOP. These two requirements were contradictory, which is known as the Triffin Dilemma.[15]

Furthermore, the Bretton Woods system could not adapt to changing trends in economic development among different countries. When the Bretton Woods Agreements Act was signed, the United States was the center of global finance, led the world in industrial production and international trade, and held most of the world's gold reserves. However, two decades later, the international economic landscape changed. The economic strength of Japan and the European industrial countries grew rapidly. They accumulated large international trade surplus and their

---

[14]The income resulting from the difference between the currency's production cost and its face value owned exclusively by a government or a body which is authorized to issue a currency is defined as seigniorage.

[15]For the detailed analysis, refer to Robert Triffin (1960).

currencies became stronger. By contrast, the United States' relative economic position declined and the conditions underpinning the dollar's dominant position changed as well. But the unchanging Bretton Woods system could not adapt to these changes, which eventually led to its collapse.

Finally, the Bretton Woods system was unable to resolve the issue of addressing BOP imbalance while maintaining exchange rate stability. In the case of a fundamental disequilibrium of BOP, the Bretton Woods system allowed its member countries to apply to the IMF for exchange rate adjustment. But in reality, no country was willing to do so. As a key country, the United States would not devaluate the dollar, as this could trigger a crisis of confidence. If the United States wanted to control the deficit, the only thing it could do was to adopt a tight monetary policy at home and keep the deficit at a controllable level. However, this was not what the United States did. None of its administrations was willing to see domestic economic shrink, and almost every president wanted to adopt an easy monetary policy to carry out domestic social reforms and promote economic growth. Thus, U.S. BOP deficit inevitably persisted. Similarly, governments of other countries with deficits were not willing to devaluate their currencies either, as this would be viewed as incompetent. Most governments were ready to promise to achieve higher employment, but few of them were willing to use a tight policy to control the deficit. The majority surplus countries were unwilling to appreciate their currencies too. For instance, in the case of Germany and Japan, currency appreciation would weaken the competitiveness of their export. Export was a major factor behind their rapid economic development, and they naturally had no incentive to have their currencies appreciated.

Chapter 4

Patterns in the Evolution of the International Monetary System

The evolution of the international monetary system from the birth of the gold standard to the disintegration of the Bretton Woods system lasted for about a 100 years. By analyzing its course, we can gain valuable insight and important lessons for reforming and improving the current international monetary system or even for building a new one.

4.1 A Dynamic Analysis of the Evolution of the International Monetary System

The international monetary system is the total sum of monetary relations among countries and is an extremely important aspect of the economic relations among countries. Economic relations among countries consist of relations of real economy, which include trade and investment, and monetary relations, which facilitate trade and investment. The international monetary system is created in response to the needs of international trade and investment. Therefore, the international monetary relations are subordinate to relations of the real economy. Their evolution hinges on changes in relations of the real international economy, and the international monetary system must be in keeping with these relations.

The evolution of the international monetary system from the gold standard to the Bretton Woods system was the result of the evolution of the international economy. Under the gold standard, Britain had greatest influence, because it was the strongest among industrial countries and leader in the export of manufactured goods and the top overseas investor. As Britain had dominant position in international trade and investment, the British pound sterling became the dominant currency of the gold standard. After World War I, the United States surpassed Britain to become the world's leading industrial country. But the gold-exchange standard established under Britain failed to adapt to this change in the international economy. Such a system thus had no staying power and lasted for less than 10 years, manifesting its transitional nature. After World War II, the United States became the dominant global economic power. By setting up a dollar-based international monetary system, the Bretton Woods system institutionalized this change in international economic relations. The Bretton Woods system was stable in the first 20 years of its establishment. It lost strength and finally collapsed due to the decline of relative economic power of the United States.

4.2 An Analysis of Development Trends in the International Monetary System

In the course of over 100 years, the world went through profound economic transformation and experienced two world wars. Trends of evolution of the two core elements in the international monetary system — international currencies and balance of payments (BOP) adjustment mechanism — reflect such profound underlying changes.

4.2.1 *Trend towards credit-based currencies*

The evolution from the gold standard to the collapse of the Bretton Woods system was actually a process of demonetizing gold. At the beginning when gold standard prevailed, only gold coins or bank notes that were convertible to gold could directly circulate in the economy. During this period, gold and bank notes basically meant the same thing. During the period of the gold-exchange standard, there were certain restrictions on the exchange between bank notes and gold. In countries using the gold-bullion standard, there were limits on converting bank notes into gold, which were fixed at a relatively high level in most cases. In a country using the gold-exchange standard, one could acquire gold only by first converting the country's currency into the currency of a country using the gold standard (or the gold-bullion standard) in an amount as stipulated by that country. In addition, under the gold-exchange standard, with the exception of the United States, gold could no longer be used as a circulating currency. Just as its alternative name, the "virtual gold standard", suggests that the relationship between currency and gold existed only in name under the gold-exchange standard. Under the Bretton Woods system, the linkage between currency and gold was further weakened because only governments from other countries, but no individuals, could exchange dollars they held for gold with the U.S. government.

The demonetarization of gold was actually a process moving towards credit-based currency. Any monetary system based on precious metals or any other real good was not likely to bridge the gap between money supply and economic expansion. At present, only credit-based currency can meet the demand for money created by economic growth. It is unlikely to return to an international monetary system based in precious metals or any other real good.

4.2.2 *Trend in evolution of BOP adjustment mechanism*

The mechanism for international BOP adjustment is also a key part of the international monetary system. Under the gold standard, the BOP was regulated mainly by self-adjusting mechanisms such as the price-specie-flow mechanism. However, in this process of self-adjustment, countries with a BOP deficit would undergo a painful process of economic contraction and had to pay the cost of economic recession and increased unemployment. Consequently, under the gold-exchange standard, governments set aside a certain amount of British pound sterling as an international reserve to adjust the BOP imbalance outside the price-specie-flow mechanism. Under the Bretton Woods system, member countries fixed their exchange rates at a predetermined level. Temporary BOP imbalances were corrected by market forces with the assistance of the International

Monetary Fund (IMF). However, in case of fundamental imbalances, countries would address such imbalances by adjusting exchange rates and setting up trade barriers. In such cases, the role of government intervention would be far greater.

The tendency was towards more government intervention, while the role of market adjustment decreased. However, government intervention and market adjustment are the two basic means of regulating the economy. History of the evolution of modern economy proved that neither one of them alone is desirable. A combination of government intervention and market adjustment is the best way to ensure healthy economic growth. Therefore, one can reasonably expect that, in the future international monetary system, the BOP will still be managed by a combination of government intervention and market adjustment. The only question is how to maintain a proper balance between the two.

4.3 Lessons Derived From the Evolution of the International Monetary System

The current international monetary system is completely credit-based, which is fundamentally different from all the previous international monetary systems. Yet, there are valuable lessons one can draw from the evolution of earlier monetary systems from the gold standard to the Bretton Woods system.

First, any international monetary system dominated by a single currency will face the Triffin Dilemma and will be unstable. The creation and the operation of an international monetary system cannot depend excessively on one single currency, as was shown by the collapse of the Bretton Woods system.

Second, international monetary relations are a product of the constantly developing real economy. Therefore, an international monetary system should contain institutional means for dynamic adjustment, so that the relationship between various currencies can adapt to changes in the real economy. Otherwise, the international monetary system will become unstable if there is a mismatch between a country's economic strength and the position of its currency. The collapse of both gold-exchange standard and Bretton Woods system resulted from an imbalance between the relative economic strength and the monetary position of the key country in the international monetary system concerned.

Finally, the creation of Special Drawing Rights (SDR) by the IMF offers a new approach and model for resolving core issues confronting the international monetary system. To some extent, SDR can function like gold as an international reserve asset and act as a substitute for the dollar in correcting a BOP imbalance. The creation of this mechanism shows that the international society has begun to try to create a universal fiat currency and transform the international monetary system based on one currency. SDR therefore is significant as a historical milestone.

Part Two

The Current International Monetary System

After experiencing many dollar crises between 1960s and 1970s, the Bretton woods system finally collapsed. In 1971, the United States abandoned the convertibility of the dollar into gold, thereby starting an era of floating exchange rates. Even though the United States was no longer obliged to convert the dollar to gold when required, its core status in the international monetary system remained unchanged. This caused many unfair and unequal practices in international economy. This part begins with an analysis of the characteristics and the functioning of the current international monetary system. It then makes an appraisal of the system, pointing out both its positive functions and the inherent conflicts in it. It ends with a conclusion on the unsustainability of the current international monetery system.

Chapter 5

Characteristics of the Current International Monetary System

Following the collapse of the Bretton Woods system, the international monetary system again sank into chaos. The international community made many attempts to rebuild the international monetary system. Some proposed the restoration of the gold standard, while others proposed to set up a system based on a basket of hard currencies, but no progress was made. It was only after experiencing five chaotic years in the financial market that the international community finally concluded the Jamaica Agreement. The international monetary system thus entered the "age of floating exchange rates".

5.1 Establishment of the Jamaica System

In January 1976, the International Monetary Fund's (IMF's) Interim Committee of the Board of Governors on the International Monetary System met in Kingston, capital of Jamaica. After fierce debate, the Jamaica Agreement was concluded and signed. In April of the same year, the IMF Council adopted the "Second Amendment to the Articles of Agreement of the International Monetary Fund". The amendment recognized significant changes in international finance since 1971 and adopted new rules for the international monetary system, thus ushering in the era of the Jamaica System.

The Jamaica System inherited some of the merits of the Bretton Woods system and rectified many defects that had caused chaos in the financial sector. The Jamaica Agreement had the following provisions: (1) The parity between two currencies was allowed to float freely, thus formally legalizing the regime of floating exchange rates, which would co-exist with fixed exchange rates, and member countries were allowed to freely select their own exchange rate arrangement.
(2) Exchange rates between currencies were to be based on respective economic status and political–economic strength of individual countries. Such an arrangement would prevent possible collapse of the system due to decline in power of dominant countries. The monetary system as a whole would therefore be dynamic and respond to changes in the international economic system.
(3) Demonetization of gold was introduced. The agreement abrogated the role of gold in the international monetary system, deleted the article on gold in the Articles of Agreement of the IMF, and abolished the official price of gold. Member countries could now freely trade gold according to its market price. Gold would stop serving as a clearing currency for international trade, and would only be an investment asset as a precious metal.
(4) The role of Special Drawing Rights (SDR) was strengthened. The IMF expanded the use of SDR in general transactions. The share of SDR also increased from SDR 29.2 billion to SDR 39 billion, a rise of 33.6%. The status of SDR as an international reserve vehicle was enhanced as a result.
(5) Financial support to developing countries increased. With proceeds made from selling gold, the IMF established a trust fund to improve credit and loan conditions of developing countries, Limit on credit loan was increased from 100% to 145% of the member countries' shares. Additionally, limit on the Compensatory Financing Facility (CFF) on export price fluctuation was increased from 50% to 75% of the member countries' shares.

5.2 Characteristics of the Jamaica System

As one of the three major pillars of the international monetary system, the Jamaica system did not specify any standard currency, nor had any unified exchange rate system or unified coordination mechanism for balance of payments. The international monetary order was in chaos. Therefore, the

Jamaica System is also known as the "International Monetary Non-system" (Dooley *et al.*, 2003). The following are the major characteristics of the Jamaica System in its 30-year evolution.

5.2.1 *A dollar-dominated multi-currency structure*

The Jamaica system brought about demonetization of gold. The international currency standard was completely decoupled from any physical or material value. The status of gold in the international reserve fell significantly, dropping from a high level of over 50% to the present level of 10%. Credit-based currencies of leading economies became major world currencies, accounting for 80–90% of the international reserve (Table 5-1). SDR also began to function as a new international reserve. From 1977 to 1990, its use as international reserve increased from SDR 9.315 billion to SDR 21.479 billion.[1] Nevertheless, SDR failed to play its expected role. Since the mid to late 1980s, the share of SDR in the international reserve began to fall and today stands at less than 0.5% of the total international reserve. It is thus jokingly referred to as the "scorned lady".[2] Generally, the international reserve under the Jamaica system consisted of foreign exchange reserves, gold reserves, and SDR, with foreign exchange reserve acting as the mainstay of the international reserve, gold coming next, and SDR last (Table 5-1).

Table 5-1 International Reserves (1977–2008)

(Percent)

	1977	1978	1979	1980	1981	1982	1983	1984	1985	1986	1987
Forex Reserve	54.88	52.29	38.80	38.36	44.52	39.43	43.58	49.48	50.57	50.35	54.91
SDRs	2.53	2.19	2.09	2.28	3.27	2.97	3.03	3.04	3.12	2.97	2.58
Gold	38.00	42.31	57.42	57.89	49.73	54.58	48.87	42.30	41.16	42.07	38.87
Others	4.59	3.20	1.69	1.48	2.49	3.01	4.53	5.19	5.16	4.62	3.64
Total	100	100	100	100	100	100	100	100	100	100	100

(Continued)

---

[1] IMF, International Financial Statistics Database.

[2] Mengdaier (2003), p. 115.

Table 5-1   (*Continued*)

	1988	1989	1990	1991	1992	1993	1994	1995	1996	1997	1998
Forex Reserve	59.47	62.09	67.22	69.91	71.27	70.82	73.78	76.11	78.97	82.19	80.71
SDRs	2.58	2.44	2.36	2.32	2.27	2.02	1.95	1.75	1.56	1.48	1.49
Gold	34.70	32.68	27.93	25.08	23.79	24.72	21.91	19.29	16.93	13.17	13.68
Others	3.24	2.79	2.49	2.70	2.67	2.44	2.36	2.85	2.54	3.16	4.11
Total	100	100	100	100	100	100	100	100	100	100	100

	1999	2000	2001	2002	2003	2004	2005	2006	2007	2008
Forex Reserve	82.37	84.79	85.16	84.66	85.57	87.99	88.91	89.26	89.35	89.24
SDRs	1.37	1.23	1.12	1.03	0.90	0.78	0.65	0.57	0.47	0.43
Gold	12.99	11.45	10.85	11.23	10.79	9.23	9.60	9.78	9.93	9.81
Others	3.28	2.53	2.87	3.08	2.74	2.00	0.83	0.39	0.24	0.51
Total	100	100	100	100	100	100	100	100	100	100

Source: IMF, International Financial Statistics Database.

There are striking changes in the composition of international foreign exchange reserve. Global economy moved towards multi-polarity owing to the rise of the relative economic strength of Western Europe and Japan. A new multi-currency reserve system emerged, replacing the dollar which used to be the sole reserve currency. Between 1977 and 1990, shares in world reserves of the then German mark and Japanese yen rose from 8.2% and 1.2% to 19.7% and 9.1% respectively, while that of the dollar dropped from 79.4% to 56.4%.[3] The creation of the euro posed a stronger challenge to the central role of the dollar.[4]

Despite the weakening of its relative position, the dollar continued to play a major role in international trade, foreign exchange reserves, and foreign exchange trading. Especially in the 1990s when the U.S. economy entered a period of steady growth, the position of the dollar recovered as a result. At the end of 2008, share of the dollar in the currency composition of known foreign exchange reserves stood at 64% (Figure 5-1). In 2007,

---

[3]Chen Yulu (2000), p. 57.
[4]Gabriele Galati and Philip Wooldridge (2006); Freddy van den Spiegel (2005).

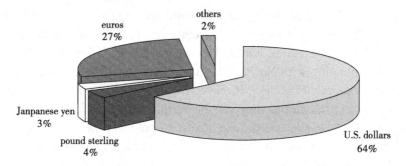

Figure 5-1   Currency Composition of Global Foreign Exchange Reserve by the End of 2008

Source: Currency Composition of Official Foreign Exchange Reserves (COFER), IMF (2009).

dollar related trading accounted for more than 40% of the global daily average foreign exchange transactions.[5] The United States accounted for only 11.5% of global trading in goods and services that year, but over 50% of the total global trading was settled with the dollar.[6] Furthermore, most countries have continued to take the dollar as the benchmark currency in their exchange rate regimes.[7] Thus, to a great extent, the current international currency system remains a "dollar standard" (McKinnon, 2001).

5.2.2 Emergence of diversified exchange rate regimes featuring a core vs. periphery framework

The Jamaica Agreement did not restrict the exchange rate arrangements of its member countries, which could formulate exchange rate regimes in light of their respective national conditions and choose between strict fixed exchange rates and complete floating exchange rates.

Having undergone over 30 years of evolution, the international exchange rate regimes have become increasingly diversified. According to IMF classifications based on the degree of regulation and the width of fluctuating band, the current exchange rate regimes fall into seven

---

[5]BIS (2007), p. 11.
[6]Calculated as per relevant data of International Trade Statistics 2008.
[7]Li Ruogu, *China Today* (2008).

categories: Exchange Arrangements with no Separate Legal Tender,[8] Currency Board Arrangements,[9] Conventional Fixed Peg Arrangements,[10] Pegged Exchange Rates within Horizontal Bands,[11] Crawling Pegs,[12] Managed Floating with No Predetermined Path for the Exchange Rate,[13] and Independently Floating.[14] If related monetary policy arrangements are taken into consideration, they can be further classified into more than 20 types of exchange rate arrangements. In practice, the following four exchange rate regimes are most widely used: Independently Floating (13%), Managed Floating (27%), Conventional Fixed Peg (28%), and With No Separate Legal Tender (22%) (Table 5-2).

Global exchange rate arrangements exhibit the characteristics of a core vs. periphery framework. The few developed countries that issue international currencies are at the core and use floating exchange rates, and these currencies float independently or jointly according to the respective countries' interests. On the periphery are the numerous developing countries, which, because of historical reasons, economic strength, and economic structure, use fixed exchange rate regimes that are pegged to major currencies (currency basket). The exchange rate arrangements of IMF member countries can thus be classified into three rough

---

[8]The currency of another country circulates as the sole legal tender, or the member belongs to a monetary or currency union in which the same legal tender is shared by the members of the union, such as countries in the Euro Area.

[9]A monetary regime based on an explicit legislative commitment to exchange domestic currency for a specified foreign currency at a fixed exchange rate, combined with restrictions on the issuing authority to ensure fulfillment of its legal obligation; for example, as Hong Kong.

[10]The country pegs its currency at a fixed rate to another currency or a basket of currencies. The exchange rate may fluctuate within narrow margins of less than ±1% and the Central Bank stands ready to maintain the fixed parity through direct intervention.

[11]Similar to the conventional fixed peg arrangements, but with the fluctuation margins of more than ±1%.

[12]The currency is adjusted periodically in small amounts at a fixed rate or in response to changes in selected quantitative indicators.

[13]The monetary authority attempts to influence the exchange rate without having a specific exchange rate path or target.

[14]The exchange rate is market-determined, with any official foreign exchange market intervention aimed at moderating the rate of change and preventing undue fluctuations in the exchange rate, rather than establishing a level for it.

Table 5-2   *De Facto* **Exchange Rate Arrangements of IMF Member Countries**

	Exchange rate anchor				Monetary aggregate target	Inflation targeting frame-work	IMF-supported or other monetary program	Other
Exchange arrangements with no separate legal tender (41)	Another currency as legal tender (9)	ECCU (6)	CFA franc zone (14)		—	—	—	Euro area (12)
			WAEMU (7)	CAEMC (7)				
Currency board arrangements (7)	7				—	—	—	—
Other conventional fixed peg arrangements (52)	Against a single currency (47)				5	—	—	1
	Against a composite (5)				—	—	—	—
Pegged exchange rates within horizontal bands (6)	Within a cooperative arrangement (4)		Other band arrangements (2)		—	3	—	—
Crawling pegs (5)	5				1	—	—	—
Managed floating (51)	—				20	7	7	19
Independently floating (25)	—				5	16	1	4

Note: The figures in the above table represent the number of relevant classified countries and regions. Additionally, during the investigation, some countries or regions adopted more than one exchange rate regime, so the item figures may differ from the summary figure.

Source: IMF staff reports, IMF recent economic developments, and IMF Staff estimates, July 31, 2006.

categories: (1) floating exchange rate arrangements of the core countries, including managed floating and independent floating; (2) pegged exchange rate arrangements, including exchange arrangements with no separate legal tender, currency board arrangements, and conventional fixed peg arrangements; and (3) intermediate exchange rate arrangements that are obliged and committed to the rates established by the former two arrangements, including pegged exchange rates within horizontal bands and crawling pegs.

5.2.3 *Co-existence of global and regional coordination mechanisms*

Another major characteristic of the current international monetary system is the diversity of coordination mechanisms. There is the global coordination mechanism which is derived from the Bretton Woods system, namely, the IMF. There are also regional multilateral coordination mechanisms such as the Eastern Caribbean Currency Union (ECCU), the Western African Economic and Monetary Union (WAEMU), the Central African Economic and Monetary Community (CAEMC), euro area, and the current East Asian monetary cooperation that has drawn much attention. In addition, against the backdrop of the U.S. financial crisis, a number of bilateral coordination mechanisms have emerged, such as the local-currency swap agreements China has respectively signed with South Korea, Belarus, Malaysia, and Hong Kong.

There are profound causes for the diversification of coordination mechanisms. First, as analyzed earlier, since the exchange rate arrangements are complex and the international financial situation is volatile, it is necessary to employ different types of international coordination mechanisms to cope with such volatility. Second, the sequence of the emergence of various coordination mechanisms shows that it was the failure of global coordination mechanisms that made countries enter into extensive regional and bilateral coordination and cooperation. For instance, it was the failure of the IMF in handling Southeast Asian financial crisis that led to the formation of the Southeast Asian monetary coordination mechanism.

5.2.4 *More diversified but still imperfect balance of payments (BOP) adjustment mechanisms*

Under the Bretton Woods system, there were limited means of regulating BOP imbalances, which was primarily conducted through IMF lending and, when necessary, by changing exchange rates. Under the Jamaica system, countries can apply to a variety of measures to regulate BOP imbalances, thereby making such regulation more timely and effective. These measures include exchange rate adjustment, interest rate adjustment, international cooperation and policy coordination, international commercial bank financing, etc.

The Marshall–Lerner condition[15] is the prerequisite for using exchange rate adjustment to achieve BOP equilibrium. Adjusting exchange rate can trigger hot money attacks, which will aggravate instead of alleviating uncertainty in regulating BOP. Commercial lending can only work temporarily in easing BOP disequilibrium but cannot address the root cause of the problem. Therefore, under the Jamaica system, enhancing international policy coordination has become the main approach for resolving BOP problems.

International financial institutions created by the Bretton Woods system, e.g., the IMF, World Bank, and other multilateral institutions were naturally principal vehicles through which international cooperation and policy coordination were to be undertaken. Unfortunately, since the IMF has no binding power to perform regulatory function, its regulatory effect was limited, especially in relation to big powers. So, in case of any BOP disequilibrium, the affected country or region could mainly depend on its own actions. As a result, BOP disequilibrium has persisted and become a global trend in recent years, severely affecting the stability of the international monetary system.

5.3 Evolution of the International Economy under the Jamaica System

In late 1978, Iran's oil export stopped after the outbreak of the Iranian Revolution. The unexpected decrease of supply in the international market triggered panic oil buying. Daily global oil shortage reached five million barrels, 1/10th of the world's total consumption. As a consequence, price

---

[15]Provided that the sum of the price elasticity of demand coefficients for exports and imports is greater than one then a fall in the exchange rate will reduce a deficit and a rise will reduce a surplus.

of oil rocketed from US$ 13 per barrel in 1978 to US$ 32 per barrel in 1980.[16] This led to the second oil crisis, which also triggered and aggravated a worldwide economic crisis. From 1980 to 1981, the Western economy was plagued by stagflation — development nearly grounded to a halt, unemployment rose, and inflation surged.

In the early 1980s, the U.S. Reagan Administration adopted supply-side economics and launched major reforms to combat inflation and improve the performance of its economy. These reforms included: (1) relaxation of economic control and a massive reduction in tax in order to invigorate the American economy; (2) a large-scale increase in defense expenditures to stimulate the domestic economy; and (3) implementation of a tight monetary policy to cut liquidity and an unprecedented increase in the Federal Funds Rate to contain inflation. As a result, sharply increased interest rate and improving economic condition attracted a huge inflow of international capital into the United States. The dollar saw persistent increase in value during these years, so much so that from January 1980 to March 1985, in what came to be called the dollar's glorious period, its nominal effective exchange rate rose by 50%.[17]

The dollar's continuous appreciation resulted in rapid growth of the U.S. current account deficit and the rise of trade protectionism, much to the apprehension of the international community. Such apprehension led to the Plaza Accord. On September 22, 1985, finance ministers from the United States, Japan, the Federal Republic of Germany, France, and Britain held a meeting at New York's Plaza Hotel. The governments of the participating countries came to realize that under the floating exchange rate regime, countries were domestically focused on formulating policies, causing lack of international coordination. In order to ensure the stability of the foreign exchange market, countries must enhance coordination in policy-making. The reaching of the Plaza Accord helped bring about the dollar's devaluation. At the same time, the United States undertook to reduce expenditures and cut its deficit, and Japan agreed to open its financial markets and to appreciate the yen to a level that would reflect Japan's economic strength.

---

[16] IMF, IFS Online (2009).
[17] *Ibid.*

The Plaza Accord caused the dollar to devaluate faster than expected. Seeing that dollar devaluation showed no signs of stopping, the Western countries had to intervene again. In February 1987, the G7 finance ministers convened a meeting at the Louvre Palace in Paris. The G7 countries realized if the dollar continued to devaluate, the United States would experience inflation, while Japan and Europe could face a decline in export and economic depression. So they decided to intervene in the foreign exchange market again to maintain the dollar's exchange rate at the level at the time. For the first time, a dollar exchange rate target zone was set up to allow the dollar to float within a certain margin. For instance, under the agreement, US$ 1 could exchange for JPY 145.83 to JPY 161.18. If the dollar fell below the reference exchange rate of JPY 145.83, the U.S. and Japanese monetary authorities would jointly intervene in the foreign exchange market by selling Japanese yen and buying the dollar. On the other hand, if the dollar rose above JPY 161.18, the monetary authorities of the two countries would sell the dollar and buy Japanese yen in the foreign exchange market.[18] This came to be known as the Louvre Accord. The exchange rate target zone established under the Louvre Accord was maintained mainly through intervention by monetary authorities, while market regulation served as a supplementary tool.

By the 1980s, the U.S. stock market had been bullish for nearly four decades, with its total valve jumping from US$ 2.4720 trillion in 1980 to US$ 5.9950 trillion in 1986. It thus attracted huge overseas capital. By 1987, the daily trading volume of the New York Stock Exchange had reached 1.806 trillion shares. With expanding liquidity on the rampage, the asset bubble was on the breaking point, and a massive upheaval in U.S. stock was unavoidable. On October 19, 1987, the U.S. stock market crashed. Dow Jones Industrial Index lost 508.32 points — a historical record, and the entire market spun out of control. Relaxed monetary policies were hastily introduced by countries after the stock market disaster, which again led to worldwide inflation. Eventually, countries had no option but to raise interest rates to fight inflation. High interest rates, however, discouraged effective investment and triggered recession in the United States and Britain in 1991.

---

[18]Kikkawa Mototada (2000).

Since the start of the 21st century, BOP disequilibrium has again caused the concern of the international society. On the one hand, relying on its political, economic, and military power and taking advantage of its position as an issuer of international currency, the United States borrowed money to maintain consumption. Through the American current account deficit, a huge amount of dollar was exported in exchange for physical resources (goods and services), while the saving rate of the United States dropped to nearly zero. According to data from the U.S. Bureau of Economic Analysis (BEA), net U.S. saving rate was 5.8% in 2000, before dropping to 1.7% in 2007 and to –0.9% in 2008. On the other hand, emerging markets led by China began to industrialize and have entered a period of sustained growth, and their national income rose. These countries reinvested the majority of their income and accumulated huge trade surpluses by manufacturing and exporting quality but low cost goods and services. Additionally, due to soaring prices of natural resources, resource-rich countries, represented by the Middle East oil-producing countries, have gained huge amount of petro-dollars in recent years. Owing to lack of substitute assets, most of these surpluses flow back to the United States

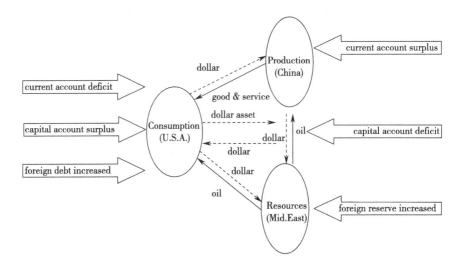

Figure 5-2　Operational Status of the Three Major International Economic Segments

Note: The solid arrows indicate the direction of flows of real resources and dashed arrows indicate the direction of flows of financial resources.

to buy dollar denominated assets (including U.S. treasury bonds and institutional bonds). Cheap capital, in turn, has stimulated consumption in the United States and boosted the real estate and financial sectors. Hence, in international finance, the consumption segment, represented by the United States, has registered persistent current account deficit, with rising foreign debts. The production segment and resource segment represented by China and the Middle East oil-producing countries, however, have maintained continuous current account surplus, with rising foreign exchange reserves (Figure 5-2). Under the dollar based international monetary system, this global BOP disequilibrium has exacerbated, making a major adjustment inevitable.

Chapter 6

Appraisal of the Current International Monetary System

The contemporary international monetary system was born out of the Bretton Woods system. Its operating mechanism was set up to correct or mitigate disequilibrium in international trade and balance of payments. Since it was an outcome of compromise among various parties, the contemporary international monetary system is bound to encounter numerous problems in its functioning.

6.1 Positive Role of the Contemporary International Monetary System

The birth of the Jamaica system was natural. Compared with the Bretton Woods system, it is more flexible and diversified, and it is no doubt more representative of the multi-polar international political–economic system than its predecessor. As has been proved, the Jamaica system has played a positive role in stabilizing the international financial market and promoting global economic growth.

6.1.1 *Mitigating the Triffin Dilemma*

Diversification in international reserve helped relieve inadequate international liquidity. Under the Bretton Woods system, in which the dollar was the only international standard currency, the Triffin Dilemma featured prominently. Under the Jamaica system, while the dollar has retained its dominant position, other currencies such as German mark, Swiss franc, and subsequently euro, Japanese yen, and British pound sterling, etc., have all become international currencies. The euro, in particular, has gained an increasingly important position in the contemporary international monetary system. Its current share of the foreign exchange reserve has exceeded one quarter of the total and is still rising. Furthermore, the Jamaica system has also strengthened the role of Special Drawing Rights (SDR), a step forward in the development of a common global currency. Under this system, by decoupling from gold and linking its value with a basket of international currencies,[1] SDR began to acquire an independent character, and its share of the international foreign exchange reserve has also gone up. To some extent, the above mentioned measures have eased the Triffin Dilemma.

---

[1] In July 1974, the International Monetary Fund (IMF) formally announced the decoupling of SDR from gold, and switched over to using a basket of 16 currencies as the standard of value. The 16 currencies included currencies of member countries that, over the 5 years preceding 1972, accounted for a greater than 1% share in world goods and labor services exports. Apart from the US$, the currencies were the DEM, JPY, GBP, FRF, CAD, ITL, NLG, BEF, SEK, AUD, NOK, DKK, ESP, ZAR, and ATS. The quoted price of SDR was announced daily based on changes in the foreign exchange market. In order to simplify the evaluation method of SDR and to enhance its appeal, on September 18, 1980, the IMF simplified the basket of currencies into the currencies of five Western currencies with a major share in world goods and labor service export, i.e., the US$, DEM, JPY, France FRF, and GBP. Their respective proportion in the SDR was 42%, 19%, 13%, 13%, and 13%. Every 5 years, their proportions underwent a readjustment. Upon its realization, the EUR replaced DEM and FRF, in the SDR "Basket of Currencies". After the IMF's latest adjustment in 2006, the SDR is composed of four currencies: the US$, EUR, GBP, and JPY, with respective shares of 44%, 34%, 11%, and 11%.

6.1.2 *Making the rigid exchange rate system flexible*

The exchange rates arrangement under the Bretton Woods system was excessively rigid and there was little flexibility in exchange rates management among countries. Therefore, in the case of balance of payments disequilibrium, the affected countries had no choice but to adjust domestic demand through domestic fiscal policy and monetary policy to correct such disequilibrium. This usually created difficulties for countries with trade deficits, which had to dampen domestic demand to restore balance of payments equilibrium. Under the arrangements of the current system, however, such countries can achieve balance of payments equilibrium by devaluating currency and expanding external demand. In this way, it is possible for them to avoid hurting their internal economy while trying to achieve external economic equilibrium. In addition, exchange rate adjustment can also play a role in resource reallocation. The famous Balassa–Samuelson effects also show that, along with increasing productivity, the value of a country's currency will appreciate.[2] Therefore, a country's exchange rate should be duly adjusted according to change in its real economy. The current system provides such flexibility.

6.1.3 *Diversified coordination mechanisms: Remedying inadequacy of bretton woods institutions*

The IMF and World Bank were created under the Bretton Woods system. But they were able to raise their profile instead of losing their influence under the Jamaica system. Still, for various reasons, the function of Bretton Woods institutions in international coordination is limited, even negative sometimes. Under such circumstances, various countries and regions have established multi-form policy coordination mechanisms. These bilateral and regional coordination mechanisms can ease the impact of crisis in a timely fashion in light of actual national and regional conditions, thus effectively remedying the inadequate coordination capacity of the Bretton Woods institutions.

---

[2] Yang Changjiang (2002).

6.1.4 *Money creation function of the dollar was good for global economic development during a particular period*

The author affirmed the role of the banking sector's money creation function in promoting China's economic development since the beginning of the reform and opening-up era (Li Ruogu, 2008). In my view, money creation by a financial system led by state-owned banks has ensured financial support for economic growth and played an irreplaceable role in China's economic takeoff.[3]

Similarly, steady increase in supply of international money is also needed to ensure global growth. Under the dollar-based international monetary system, a relatively easy U.S. monetary policy was beneficial to global economic development and played its role in expanding the world's purchasing power, and it contributed to the stable growth of the world economy during a particular period. As shown in Figure 5-2, the supplying capacity of developing countries represented by China met demands of developed countries represented by the United States over the last two decades, thus propelling rapid global economic growth. However, such supply–demand equilibrium cannot be forever maintained. Once such equilibrium ends, it will trigger a major crisis.

By analyzing the correlation between U.S. current account deficit and global economic growth, one can appreciate the role of dollar supply in boosting the global economy. Between 1982 and 2008, the correlation coefficient between the U.S. current account deficit as a share of global GDP and the global GDP growth rate was 0.64. Prior to the 1997 Asian Financial Crisis, it was even as high as 0.75[4] (Figure 6-1).

It should be noted that the dollar's stimulating effect on the global economy is conditional, namely, the volume of dollar issued must be in keeping with the need of global economic development. Otherwise, as will be discussed later, unlimited dollar supply will create excessive global liquidity and thus sow the seeds of future crisis. Eventually, it will endanger the sustainability of the dollar standard.

---

[3] Li Ruogu, *Zhidu Shiyi yu Jingji Fazhan: Jiyu Zhongguo Shijian de Fazhan Jingjixue* (2008), pp. 201–204.

[4] The relevant coefficients were calculated by the author according to Figure 6-2.

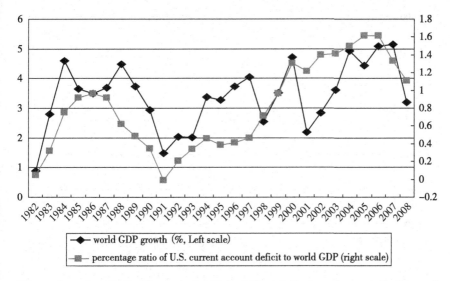

Figure 6-1　Correlation between the United States' Current Account Deficit and Global Economic Growth (1982–2008)

Source: IMF, *World Economic Outlook Database* (April 2009).

6.2 Flaws of the Contemporary International Monetary System

Despite its positive role, the Jamaica system still has many flaws.

6.2.1 *Built-in instability*

First, there is a lack of stability in its exchange rate regime. By abandoning Fixed Exchange Rates, the IMF has also given up its responsibility and obligation in policing exchange rates of its member countries. Competitive currency devaluation or appreciation occurs frequently owing to lack of discipline in international exchange rate arrangements. This has caused persistent turbulence in international finance. Countries on the periphery of the international monetary system (mainly developing countries) have been exposed to huge risks, while the exchange rates between major international currencies have fluctuated violently. For instance, in October 2000 the rate of the dollar vs. the euro was EUR 1.188 to US$ 1; by March 2008 it was EUR 0.6432 to US$ 1, a fluctuation

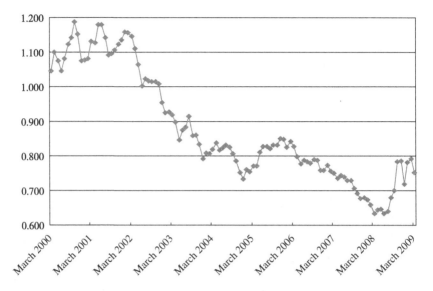

Figure 6-2   USD/EUR Exchange Rate Fluctuation (March 2000–March 2008)

Source: IMF, IFS Online (2009).

of 74% (Figure 6-2). It caused great uncertainty to other countries in terms of exchange rate policy making, trade, and finance.

Second, management of national foreign exchange reserves is made more difficult. In terms of quantitative management, instability in the international exchange rates regime and changes in balance of payments increase uncertainty for foreign exchange reserve. Under the Bretton Woods system, Robert Triffin set forth a norm — the scale of foreign exchange reserve should be able to meet the exchange demand of imports for three or four months. But now, a much higher portion of reserve is needed to handle higher international payment risks. But this leads to even higher foreign exchange risks due to instability in the international exchange rates regime. In terms of structural management, due to reasons previously mentioned, countries face higher risks in selecting currencies for foreign exchange reserve assets.

Finally, there is lack of better coordination to cope with the growing tendency of globalization in financial industries while the need for such coordination increases. Lacking comprehensive intervention mechanisms, international financial institutions such as the IMF and World Bank have done poorly when responding to a series of conflicts and crises created by the international financial turmoil. Bilateral and regional coordination do play a remedying role, but they cannot play a global role. They can play the role of self-protection for respective countries and regions, but cannot address the core problem underlying the worsening unrest in the global financial market.

6.2.2 *Unequal rights and obligations between the core and periphery countries*

Due to the dollar's position as a standard currency, the current international monetary system is a dollar dominated system. The United States enjoys the rights of an international currency, but has not undertaken its due obligations. The resultant unjust and unequal international economic relations are manifested in the following three ways:[5]

First, there is a mismatch between the benefits a country derives from the international monetary system and its obligations to the system. As the issuer of the dollar, the United States gets a large amount of seigniorage and can borrow with no limit in the world. Then, by devaluating its own currency, it can reduce the relative value of its dollar-denominated borrowing. It can thus have prolonged twin deficits and maintain excessive consumption without fearing a debt crisis.[6] While the periphery countries, especially the numerous developing countries, are in a subordinate and hopeless position in the international monetary system: they can neither influence the issuance of the dollar nor protect themselves from exchange rate fluctuations.

---

[5] Li Ruogu,"Reform of International Monetary System and Internationalization of Renminbi", presentation at the Shanghai Lujiazui International Financial Forum, May 10, 2008.

[6] If the United States undertakes its obligations as a country that tenders international currency, the supply of the dollar will naturally take into account the world economy's demand for the dollar, instead of merely the United States' demand. Accordingly, the supply of the dollar will be restrained. In so doing, the United States will partially lose the right to make its own monetary policy, while other countries will enjoy a fairer development environment. The abuse of the international currency system is therefore rooted in the United States' enjoyment of the benefits of the dollar as an international currency without undertaking any corresponding obligations.

Second, the unilateral policy pursued by the United States has deepened turmoil in the global economy. U.S. economic problems are shifted to the rest of the world under the dollar standard. For a long period of time, the United States has failed to take global demand for the dollars into consideration when adopting monetary policies, and it has issued dollars in an unrestrained manner. The Federal Reserve's expansionist monetary policy has in the past few years resulted in excessive supply of global liquidity and continued devaluation of the dollar. It has led to price hikes in oil, metals, and other commodities which are dollar priced. Pressure on global inflation has intensified as a result (Figure 6-3). Surplus liquidity has entered the real estate and financial sectors, pushing up asset prices. Seeds of bubble economy and financial crisis were then planted. To certain extent, the subprime crisis was precisely the outcome of the dollar-standard monetary system. Before the subprime crisis, the United States benefited from economic growth driven by a booming real estate market. Following the outbreak of the crisis, taking advantage of the dollar's core position, the United States has passed the risks onto other countries, which had to swallow the bitter fruit of assets devaluation and rising prices and share the costs and risks of U.S. economic growth.

Third, taking advantage of the dollar's international circulation, the United States gains dual profit. In order to protect themselves from

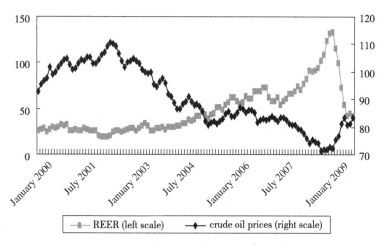

Figure 6-3 Dollar's Real Effective Exchange Rate and Crude Oil Prices (2000–2009)

Source: IMF, IFS (2009).

exchange rate fluctuations and cope with possible crisis, other countries, especially developing countries, usually hold large amounts of foreign exchange reserves, and most of these reserves eventually flow back to the United States through purchase of dollar denominated financial assets. This makes it possible for the United States to pursue a low interest rate policy which powers its economic growth. During the restructuring of global manufacturing industry, American transnational companies have invested these funds overseas (mainly developing countries) to set up factories and procurement bases to benefit from low production costs in host countries. It is earning money from developing countries by using their own capital. Developing countries only earn meager processing fees at the cost of their environment and have to bear risks caused by dollar fluctuation and the resultant reserve asset devaluation.

6.2.3 *Global economic and financial disequilibrium*[7]

The international monetary system with the dollar, a national currency, as its core, will inevitably cause worsening unbalanced global economy and global finance. In fact, the current global economic and financial disequilibrium has become increasingly acute, turning into a major factor affecting global peace, stability, and development. The global economic and financial disequilibrium under the current international monetary system manifests itself in the following four aspects:

(1) Disequilibrium in international capital flow. Since the 1970s, global capital flow has grown rapidly, but such flow is unbalanced. Generally, developed countries have a lion's share of global capital flow, while developing countries are disadvantaged. According to IMF statistics, during 1999–2007, developed economies such as the United States, Canada, Japan, Britain, and the euro zone countries absorbed 86% of total global capital flow. The capital flowing into the United States through financial accounts increased from US$ 73.7 billion in 1998 to US$ 774.4 billion in 2007, a 10-fold increase within one decade (see Figure 6-4). In 2007, international syndicated loans borrowed by developed countries accounted for 82% of the global total, and foreign direct investment

---

[7] Li Ruogu (2006).

(*Billions of dollars*)

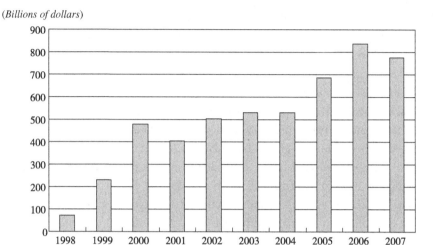

Figure 6-4   United States Capital Inflow under the Financial Account (1998–2007)
Source: IMF, IFS (2009).

absorbed by them stood at 70% of the global total. By contrast, international capital absorbed by developing countries only accounted for 22% of the global capital flow. Foreign direct investment, which is the most important external source of capital for developing countries, grew slowly, and was concentrated in a limited number of developing countries and regions.

One of the major reasons for the massive flow of international capital into the United States and other developed countries is that, to protect themselves against crisis, developing countries and emerging economies had no choice but to hold a huge amount of dollars when there were only limited international currencies for them to choose from. Consequently, capital flowed back into the United States through purchase of U.S. treasury and corporate bonds. Huge inflow of international capital caused a fall of interest rates in the United States' domestic financial market, thereby reducing the cost of its borrowing to cover budget deficit. This had actually encouraged the United States to pursue an expansionist monetary policy.[8]

---

[8]Li Ruogu, "Global Financial Crisis and Rebuilding the International Monetary System", presentation at the Conference on "Rebuilding the Bretton Woods System" in November 2008.

Under the impact of 2008 U.S. financial crisis, new imbalance has occurred in international capital flow. During previous international financial crises, investors would panic and dump currency assets of crisis stricken countries in the foreign exchange market, thereby creating tremendous pressure for devaluation of exchange rates of the currencies of the crisis countries and spreading the exchange rate fluctuation to others related currencies. But unlike the previous crises, the current global financial crisis began in the United States, the very centre of the global economy. Instead of fleeing, global capital took U.S. financial market, the epicenter of the crisis, as a safe haven. U.S. financial institutions had to write down massive amounts of bad assets. To bring their capital adequacy ratio back to normal, they needed additional capital to de-leverage their assets. Thus, large amount of capital were withdrawn from developing countries and emerging market economies back to the United States. This huge one way capital flow dealt a heavy blow to emerging market economies, in Central and Eastern Europe, Latin America, and Asia.

South Korea is a case in point. As huge amount of loans in South Korea's banking sector were borrowed from overseas, when the subprime crisis erupted, international credit suffered a sharp contraction and South Korean banks and companies encountered difficulties in capital sourcing. Anticipation of such a situation on the part of investors triggered a stock market crash and capital flight, further aggravating the balance of payment disequilibrium and causing a sharp devaluation of the South Korean won. From the beginning of 2008 to early November of the same year, the won devalued by more than 60% against the dollar. The inflow of large amount of capital into United States during the same period, however, helped maintain stability of exchange rate for the dollar. The impact of the current financial crisis fully shows that in the current international monetary system, core countries possess asymmetric rights, leaving countries on the periphery to bear additional adjustment costs and other negative consequences.

(2) Unbalanced growth of the international capital market. In 2007, the world's total global capital market was valued at about US$ 241 trillion, about 4.4 times the global GDP. The value of the capital markets in the United States, Japan, the EU, and Britain amounted to US$ 196 trillion, approximately 81% of the global capital market and roughly 5.7

times their combined GDP, higher than the average global ratio. Emerging market economies and developing countries reached US$ 47 trillion, about 19% of the global total, roughly 2.7 times their combined GDP, far below the global average ratio.[9] In terms of capital market activity, according to World Bank data for 2008, the total trading volume of stock exchanges in high income countries reached 175% of their GDP, while the figure for medium income and low income countries was 44%, about one-fourth that of high income countries.[10] This shows that the sources of funding and total amounts of funds available to developing countries were far less than those available to developed countries.

(3) Unbalanced international trade. For a long period of time, developed countries accounted for 85% of the world's total trade, and developing countries only shared about 10% of the global trade. This imbalance in international trade has been eased somewhat in recent years. By 2007, the share of developed countries in total world trade declined to 62.8%, while that of developing countries rose to 37.2%.[11] But there has been no fundamental change in the serious imbalance in international trade, which is reflected in the United States' huge current account deficit, against ever increasing surpluses held by China and other emerging economies. This persistent imbalance has resulted in emerging economies such as China accumulating huge foreign exchange reserves in the form of dollar denominated assets.

In terms of trade mix, as developed countries export mainly manufacturing products technologies as well as capital intensive goods with high added values, they enjoy advantages in terms of trading. By contrast, developing countries mainly export raw materials, primary products, and labor intensive products with low added values. As a result, they suffer from worsening terms of trading. The trading system is also distorted. Developing countries face high market access conditions, various technical barriers and high tariff rates. They are in an unfavorable position in the multilateral trade system and their legitimate rights and interests are often infringed upon. With regard to settlement currencies, developing countries

---

[9] IMF, *Global Financial Stability Report* (April 2009).
[10] World Development Indicators Database.
[11] UNCTAD, *Handbook of Statistics* (2008).

export mostly raw materials and primary products which are priced and settled in the dollar or currencies of other major developed countries. As a result, risks of exchange rate fluctuation in international trade are all borne by companies of developing countries. Due to their underdeveloped financial markets, lack of financial expertise, and a shortage of hedging instruments, developing countries often suffer huge foreign exchange losses and are disadvantaged in international transactions.

(4) Unbalanced international coordination mechanism. For decades, developed countries have dominated the IMF, World Bank, the World Trade Organization, and other international economic organizations, exercising great influence over the operation and decision-making of these organizations. Developing countries, while numerically in the majority, are in a weak position in these institutions. The IMF-led Washington Consensus and economic reforms conducted in the former Soviet Union and Eastern European countries did not achieve desired results, but negatively affected their development. By controlling the World Trade Organization (WTO) and having a major say in adopting its rules, developed countries have become the major beneficiaries of international trade, leaving little or no substantive benefits to developing countries. The Doha Round has failed to achieve any substantive progress. Developed countries have not only placed barriers on opening up agricultural and primary products markets to developing countries and refused to cancel domestic subsidies, but also resorted to trade protectionism in areas such as textiles in violation of WTO rules. This has caused many countries to be disappointed with and resist current international trade rules. To some extent, this has also triggered anti-globalization sentiments in the world.

In short, the dollar-based international monetary system has created and aggravated imbalances in the global economic and financial systems. Such imbalances have expanded to international capital flow and international trade, seriously undermining the sustainability of the current international monetary system.

Chapter 7

Sustainability of the Current International Monetary System — An Analysis

Historical experience shows that a sound international monetary system should meet the following conditions: first, it should possess a solid base for currency issuance to keep the system stable. Second, such a system should be able to adapt to changes in international economic structure and environment. Third, the growth of the international reserve should keep pace with the growth of the global economy and the expansion of international trade; and it should neither trigger worldwide inflation nor cause inadequate international solvency. Finally, it should be able to effectively regulate and remedy balance of payments disequilibrium of countries. If an international monetary system fails to meet these conditions, it will cause increasing conflicts and problems, and the pressure to reform and restructure such a system will grow, and it will eventually be replaced by a new system. The characteristics and functioning of the international monetary system show that there are deep-seated structural causes for the instability in the international financial market. This chapter will use the conditions mentioned above to analyze the sustainability of the current international monetary system.

7.1 The Dollar Cannot Shoulder the Responsibility of a Standard International Currency

Despite its declining status, the dollar has remained a standard international currency under the Jamaica system. However, such dominant position is very different from that enjoyed by the dollar standard under the Bretton Woods system, and such difference has created inherent instability in the current international monetary system.

First, no benchmark can be used to regulate the dollar exchange rates. Under the Bretton Woods system, the dollar was linked to gold at a fixed exchange rate, while other currencies were linked to the dollar. All these currencies were backed with due amount of gold reserve. In the early years of the system, countries fixed their official exchange rates at US$ 35 to one ounce of gold. As the value of the dollar was anchored to a fixed target, excessive amount of dollars put into circulation would make it difficult to maintain that fixed target. Therefore, the dollar's monetary and exchange rate policy was regulated by the agreed benchmark. The subsequent dollar crises occurred because excessive liquidity of the dollar made it impossible to keep it in line with the benchmark. In response, the benchmark was raised within the framework of the Bretton Woods system. Thus, the dollar was still regulated. Under the Jamaica system, however, since the dollar's value was not linked to gold, the United States' monetary and exchange rate policy was no longer under any check, and the Federal Reserve was no longer obliged to maintain a fixed parity between the dollar and gold. After the collapse of the Bretton Woods system, the price of gold measured in the dollar began to climb. Over the last decade it reached US$ 900 per ounce of gold, and on one occasion even topped US$ 1,000 per ounce of gold (see Figure 7-1). At the same time, the dollar's exchange rate saw frequent fluctuation. Instead of stabilizing the international monetary system, the dollar exacerbated instability in international finance and economy.

Second, the current international monetary arrangement does not reflect changes in the international economic structure. In the 1940s, the Bretton Woods system was established on the basis of the United States' dominant economic strength. In 1948, the United States accounted for 57% of the industrial output, 33% of export, and 75% of the gold reserves

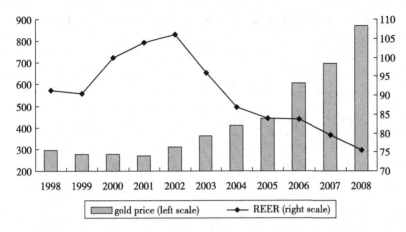

Figure 7-1 Dollar's Real Effective Exchange Rate and International Gold Price (1998–2008)

Sources: IMF, IFS (2009).

of the capitalist world.[1] But the economic rise of countries such as Japan and Germany in the following 30 years changed the international economy dominated by the United States. The weakening of the United States' preeminent economic position means that it could no longer support the dollar as an international currency. As a result, the Bretton Woods System collapsed and was replaced by a monetary non-system — the Jamaica system. During the three decades of the Jamaica system, namely, the floating exchange rates regime, even though the dollar was no longer linked to gold, it continued to serve as the world's standard currency. In the meantime, the share of the United States in the global economy continued to decline. At present, the United States accounts for only about one-fourth of the global GDP, and its share of global import and export dropped from 1/6th to 1/10th (see Table 7-1). This raises an issue: How can the United States support 60% of total global reserves deposited in dollar-denominated assets with only one-fourth of global GDP? (Li Ruogu, 2006).

Third, there is no check on the issuance of the dollar. Due to demonetization of gold under the Jamaica system, the mechanism of maintaining

---

[1] Mu Liangping (2005).

Table 7-1   The U.S. Economy and Status of the U.S. dollars (1947–2008)

(*Percent a year*)

| Year | Proportion of U.S. economy in world economy | | | Status of U.S. dollars in world currency market | |
	GDP	Export	Import	Share in forex reserves	Share in forex transactions
1947	50.0	—	—	—	—
1965	35.3	15.9	13.4	—	—
1980	25.9	12.0	12.3	—	—
1985	33.7	13.0	17.5	—	—
1990	25.8	12.6	14.2	—	45
1995	24.7	12.61	4.2	59.0	—
1998	29.4	13.8	16.3	69.3	43.5
1999	30.3	13.8	17.5	71.0	—
2000	30.6	13.7	18.4	71.1	—
2001	32.5	13.3	18.0	71.5	45.15
2002	32.2	12.4	17.6	67.1	—
2003	29.4	11.0	16.4	65.9	—
2004	27.8	10.3	15.8	65.9	44.35
2005	27.4	10.1	15.7	66.9	—
2006	26.9	9.8	15.1	65.5	—
2007	25.2	9.51	3.76	4.1	43.15
2008	24.8*	9.4*	2.5*	64.0	—

Note: *Indicates an estimated value.
Sources: World Bank, IMF, BIS.

control over the quantity of currencies issued was gone. Money supply was thus left in the hands of monetary authorities of individual countries. Without any external check, the U.S. monetary policy makers focused only on the need of U.S. domestic economy and ignored the dollar's responsibility for the world economy. The U.S. economic growth slowed down after September 11, 2001. To stimulate economic growth, the Federal Reserve pursued a policy of low interest rates and weak dollar, causing massive dollar outflow through the United States' current account deficit. In 2008, the U.S. current account deficit was as high as US$ 673.3 billion, about 4.7% of its GDP.[2] Continued increase in dollar supply has no doubt stimulated its economic growth, but its side effect, namely, excessive global liquidity and the dollar's continued devaluation, is obvious. To a certain extent, the subprime crisis and global inflation are caused by the irresponsible unilateral policy pursued by the United States.[3]

7.2 Balance of Payments (BOP) Disequilibrium — A Long-term Dilemma for the International Monetary System

In 2002, the International Monetary Fund (IMF) for the first time raised the issue of BOP disequilibrium in its *World Economic Outlook*. In 2005, Rodrigo de Rato, then acting IMF Managing Director, for the first time formally used the term "global imbalance" to refer to the phenomenon in which "one country holds a huge trade deficit, while the surplus corresponding to that deficit is concentrated in a few other countries".[4] The current global imbalance of payments manifests itself in the huge trade deficit and rapidly growing debt incurred by the United States on the one hand, and the large trade surpluses accumulated by China and other major emerging Asian economies as well as the Organization of the Petroleum Exporting Countries (OPEC) countries on the other. The United States current account balance as a share of global GDP was −0.34% in 1990; by 2007 it had reached −1.34%. During the same period, the share of the current account balance of Asia's emerging economies increased from −0.06% to 0.74%. Similarly, that of OPEC countries increased from −0.06% in 1990 to 0.63% in 2007 (see Figure 7-2).[5] In 2007, the U.S. current account deficit reached US$ 731.2, making up three-quarters of the global current account deficit.

---

[2] IMF, *World Economic Outlook* Database (2009).
[3] Li Ruogu, *China Today* (2008).
[4] Speech made by Mr. Rodrigo de Rato, Managing Director of IMF at U.S. Council on Foreign Relations on February 23, 2005.
[5] The positive sign indicates a surplus in the balance of current account, while the negative sign indicates a deficit in the balance of current account.

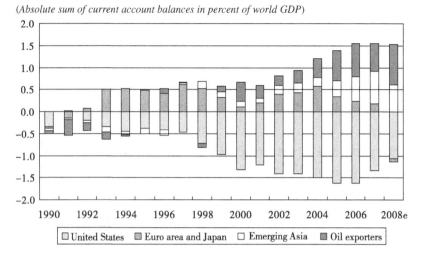

Figure 7-2　Global Imbalances (1990–2008)

Note: The oil-exporters include Middle East countries, Russia, and Canada. e indicates an estimated value.

Source: WEO Database (2008).

The global imbalance of payments is the result of a combination of factors, including a geographical shift of the global manufacturing industry and the bigger role played by comparative advantages of the world's major economies under globalization. Another key reason is the imbalance of the United States' domestic economy. According to the basic principles of economics, a country's current account balance should equal the balance of its domestic savings and investment. Although the BOP disequilibrium is an external imbalance, it reflects internal imbalance, namely, the structural imbalance of the economy itself. Therefore, the key to correcting the external imbalance lies in solving the internal imbalance. When testifying to the U.S. House Committee on Ways and Means' Subcommittee on Trade, Stephen S. Roach, Chief Economist of Morgan Stanley, pointed out that the U.S. trade imbalance is the consequence of inadequate domestic savings (Roach, 2007). Since the beginning of the 21st century, the U.S. domestic net savings have seen continuous sharp decline, which is far lower than that in the last two decades of the 20th century. The drop in personal savings is the sharpest. According to the 2007 Economic Report of the President, the U.S. personal savings ratio dropped to –1% in 2006, the lowest since World War II.[6] Meanwhile, the U.S. government has continuously increased public expenditures, including military expenditures to fund wars, thus causing persistent fiscal deficits. In most years since 1980, the U.S. government savings have been in the negative, seriously affecting the U.S. gross national savings.[7] The United States, as a result, has to attract foreign capital to fill in the domestic investment gap, thus creating a trade deficit. Figure 7-3 shows that the U.S. trade deficit as a share of GDP and its savings investment gap as a share of GDP followed similar trends over those years. This shows that U.S. trade deficit is the external manifestation of imbalance between internal savings and investment, a natural outcome of inadequate national savings. Before 2000, Europe and Japan mostly had current account surpluses. Since 2000, however, emerging Asian economies represented by China and oil-producing countries have acquired a major share of the global current account surplus. During

(Percent)

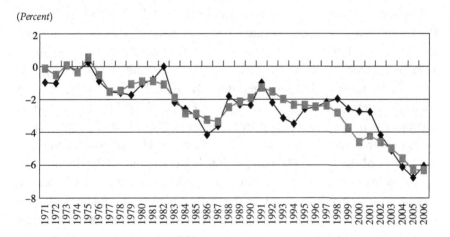

Figure 7-3 Correlation Between U.S. Trade Deficit and Saving–Investment Gap (1971–2006)

Sources: World Bank, World Development Indicators; U.S. Department of Commerce, Bureau of Economic Analysis.

---

[6] United States Government Printing Office, Economic Report of the President 2007.
[7] *Ibid.*

the same period, the United States has always had the biggest current account deficit (see Figure 7-2). This also shows that the long-term national savings/investment imbalance in the United States is a major source of its BOP disequilibrium. To bring about a fundamental solution to its trade deficit problem, the United States must bridge the gap between its domestic savings and investment (see Figure 7-3).

The fact that the United States is able to have a huge and persistent current account deficit without taking any remedial measures is because it has benefited from the dollar's position as an international currency. For the same reason, it has been able to accumulate huge foreign debt without triggering a debt crisis. By just starting the Federal Reserve's money machine, the United States can print huge amounts of dollars to purchase goods from China and other emerging Asian market countries to satisfy domestic consumption. Again, with its developed capital markets and the dollar's position as an international currency, the United States' has attracted huge investment from other trade surplus countries, thereby being able to make up much of its current account deficit. So, despite the fact that the United States has been having a trade and current account deficit since the 1970s, its BOP has always been in a state of equilibrium. If any unfavorable balance did occur, its share of GDP was quite small, being less than 1% for most of the years, and it rarely went above 1%. Only in 1998 such share reached 1.7% of GDP (see Figure 7-4). French economist Jacques Rueff (1972) noted that since the United States can do well in spite of its high trade deficit, the U.S. trade deficit could be called "deficit without tears". McKinnon (2001) also pointed out that, due to the dollar's status as an international currency, the foreign debts of the United States are similar to legal tenders issued by the central bank of a country within its own borders — they are not required to be repaid. Evidently, the unjust international monetary system is the root cause of, and an institutional factor for the perpetuation and continued expansion of the international BOP disequilibrium. Because of their confidence in the dollar and the U.S. economy, people are willing to accept the dollar as a means of payment for purchases of goods and labor services, thereby footing the bill for American consumption. The same confidence also makes them willing to hold large amount of dollar assets and thus finance United States' debt. Therefore, the sustainability of the current international monetary system,

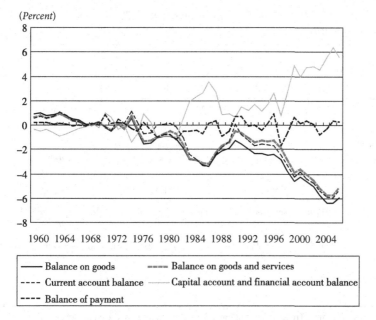

(*Percent*)

1960 1964 1968 1972 1976 1980 1984 1988 1992 1996 2000 2004

——— Balance on goods	▬▬▬ Balance on goods and services
- - - - Current account balance	——— Capital account and financial account balance
- - - - Balance of payment	

Figure 7-4   U.S. Balance of Payment Components as A Share of GDP (1960–2004)

Source: U.S. Bureau of Economic Analysis.

the sustainability of global payments imbalances and the sustainability of the United States' huge debts are all closely correlated.

The robust global economic growth spurred by U.S. consumption in the early 21st century has created the illusion that such prosperity would last forever. But an illusion is, after all, not reality. In recent years, the current account deficit of the United States has continued to grow. During the period between 1982–2008, except for 1991, the United States' current account was in deficit, and its share of GDP reached 5.9%, 6%, and 5.3% in 2005, 2006, and 2007 respectively, all exceeding the international alert point of 5%. Since the U.S. subprime crisis began, the U.S. savings have started to rise while its consumption has gradually fallen. Yet, the U.S. current account deficit as a share of GDP remained high, reaching 4.7% of GDP in 2008.[8] At the same time, U.S. foreign debt grew sharply from US$ 6.6 trillion at the end of June 2003 to US$ 13.6 trillion by the end of

---

[8]IMF, *World Economic Outlook Database* (April 2009).

Table 7-2   U.S. Government Debt (2003–2008)

(Millions of U.S. dollars)

Time	Total U.S. foreign debt	Month	Total U.S. foreign debt	Month	Total U.S. foreign debt	Month	Total U.S. foreign debt
March 2003	6570168	December 2004	8353479	June 2006	10373318	December 2007	13427103
September 2003	6712564	March 2005	8525671	September 2006	10753198	March 2008	13773135
December 2003	6946289	June 2005	8828380	December 2006	11204108	June 2008	13703567
March 2004	7391798	September 2005	9246008	March 2007	12041192	September 2008	13627459
June 2004	7744964	December 2005	9476403	June 2007	12957000	December 2008	13641807
September 2004	7957542	March 2006	9941998	September 2007	13116557	—	—

Source: U.S. Treasury: Treasury International Capital System, U.S. External Debt.

2008 (see Table 7-2), reaching an unacceptable level. Other countries have grown increasingly apprehensive about the economic imbalance in the United States, and their confidence in the dollar has dropped.

Many countries have moved away from excessive reliance on the dollar. In late 2007, Iran completely stopped using the dollar in its oil export (political considerations were also a factor). Russia also intended to use Russian ruble for pricing and settling oil and natural gas transactions. In recent years, Japan has also adjusted the size and structure of its foreign exchange reserve by gradually reducing its dollar assets. The outbreak and spread of the subprime crisis has further weakened confidence in the dollar. In July 2008, foreign investors sold U.S. institutional bonds totaling US$ 50 billion, causing foreign investment in the U.S. market to change from a net inflow to a net outflow. This fully showed that the BOP disequilibrium and the excessive U.S. borrowing for consumption are not sustainable (Wang Jianye, 2008). Many countries have begun to take a hard look at the current international monetary system. The governments of Germany and France, representative of the euro zone, both stated that between the two targets of stimulating and saving the economy and reconstructing the global economic and financial order, the latter is more important. In September, 2008, French President Sarkozy stated that it had become necessary to build a new international monetary system.[9] In March 2009, Zhou Xiaochuan, Governor of the People's Bank of China, wrote an article in which he called for creating a "super-sovereign" international reserve currency to replace the dollar.[10] This proposal has been well received by Russia, Brazil, India, and other emerging market countries as well as the United Nations and the IMF. The European Union (EU) also exerted pressure on the United States and called for reforming the existing international financial system. Furthermore, in an effort to promote the internationalization of the renminbi, China, on the basis of several bilateral local-currency swap agreements, started a trial in April 2009 to use renminbi to settle cross-border trade accounts in Shanghai and four cities in Guangdong Province.

7.3 The Financial Crisis Reveals Conflicts in the Current International Monetary System

The current international monetary system is fraught with potential unstable factors which could trigger national, regional, or even global crises when external conditions are ripe.

7.3.1 *A brief review of the financial crises under the current international monetary system*[11]

Since the 1980s, the world has seen several major financial crises. In 1982, the Latin American financial crisis hit Mexico, Brazil, Argentina, and Venezuela. The European currency crisis of 1992 affected Britain and Italy. Other financial crises include the Mexican financial crisis of 1994, the Asian financial crisis of 1997 (which caused the collapse of the "East

---

[9] www.xinhuanet.com (2008).
[10] Zhou Xiaochuan (2009).
[11] Li Ruogu, *Quanqiuhua de Zhongguo Jinrong* (*Chinese Finance in Globalization*), Social Sciences Academic Press, April 2008, pp. 7–8. Parts of the content have been supplemented and revised.

Asian miracle"), the Brazilian financial crisis of 1999, the Turkish financial crisis of 2000, the Argentinean financial crisis of 2001, and the Vietnamese financial crisis several years later. The 2007 U.S. subprime crisis has escalated into a global financial crisis.

The above mentioned crises can be classified as follows: (1) Debt crisis, in which the government of a country failed to repay foreign sovereign debt. Examples include the Latin American financial crisis in 1982 and the Argentinean financial crisis in 2001. (2) Monetary crisis in which exchange rate regimes and currency values were attacked. Examples include the European Monetary System crisis in 1992, the Russian financial crisis in 1998, and the Brazilian financial crisis in 1999. (3) Banking crisis — the Turkish financial crisis of 2000 was a credit crisis triggered by bank-run. (4) General crisis which covered the currency, stock exchange, and bond markets. They include the Mexican financial crisis in 1994, the Asian financial crisis in 1997, and the Vietnamese financial crisis in 2008. The U.S. financial crisis is the most serious and extensive international financial crisis since the collapse of the Bretton Woods system. It has not only covered all sectors of the financial industry such as banking, securities, insurance, but has also severely hurt the real economy and created huge negative impacts on the global economy.

The frequent outbreak of financial crises has greatly undermined the harmonious development of all countries in the world. These crises have created the following serious consequences:

First, the economy of countries hit by crisis has been damaged. Economic growth slowed down and even dropped to negative zone. Foreign exchange, stock exchange, and real estate markets suffered. Prices fluctuated drastically, and unemployment surged. Foreign exchange reserves decreased rapidly and were even completely depleted. A large number of people fell into poverty. According to IMF statistics, the Asian financial crisis caused the growth rate of many Asian countries to plummet. From 1997 to 1998, it dropped from 4.7% to −6.9% in South Korea, from 4.5% to −13.1% in Indonesia, from 7.3% to −7.4% in Malaysia and from −1.4% to −10.5% in Thailand. The Japanese financial sector was also severely hit, with bad debts increasing, the stock market bubble bursting, and the real estate market crashing down. Japan's economy suffered from deflation and sluggish growth and experienced a decade-long stagnation. The recent U.S. financial crisis has also seriously damaged the U.S. economy. According to data released by U.S. Department of Commerce in April 2009, the annualized U.S. GDP dropped by 6.1% in the first quarter, which was slightly lower than the 6.3% drop in the fourth quarter of the previous year. The drop in U.S. GDP lasted for three consecutive quarters.

Second, development of the global economy has been affected. International trade declined, economic growth slowed down, trade protectionism mounted, trade clashes intensified, and the world economic imbalance spread. With the deepening of the U.S. financial crisis, trade protectionism rose in the country. In early 2009, the U.S. Congress passed a heavily protectionist trade act. The major Asian economies that had close ties with the United States were soon affected. As shown in Table 7-3, in January 2009, the year-on-year growth of export for major Asian economies all saw sharp decline. In January 2009, the year-on-year decline in export for Japan, the Philippines, Singapore, etc. was close to and even surpassed 40%. The drop for Malaysian export was the lowest, but it still reached 14.9%. Since the East Asian economies have long relied on the U.S. market, decline in their export soon affected their economic growth. As Table 7-3 shows, in the fourth quarter of 2008, with the exception of China and the Philippines which maintained robust growth, all other Asian economies saw declining growth, and Malaysia had virtually zero growth.

Third, serious social and political unrest have been caused. Countries in crisis have generally experienced political turbulence and social disturbance, causing loss of lives and properties. For instance, Indonesia saw a nationwide turmoil in May 1998, with more than 500 people killed in Djakarta and its surrounding areas, and the country's economic loss reached US$ 1 billion.[12] The impact of 2008 global financial crisis is more widespread. Economic depression forced prime ministers of Latvia, Iceland, and Hungary to leave office in early 2009. Heads of governments in the Czech Republic and Bulgaria were also under tremendous pressure. In countries with prolonged crisis, governments changed

---

[12] Hu Guangyao and Yu Qianliang (1998).

Table 7-3   **Export and GDP Growth of Major Asian Economies in 2009**

(Percent)

	China	Japan	South Korea	Singapore	Philippines	Hong Kong	Vietnam	Thailand	Malaysia
Export Year-on-year Growth*	−17.50	−43.06	−32.30	−37.80	−40.40	−21.80	−24.20	−21.37	−14.90
GDP Growth**	9.0	−3.8	−3.4	−4.2	4.5	−2.5	−2.4	−4.3	0.1

Note: *The export data of Philippines is of December 2008; for other countries the export data is the year-on-year standard of January 2009.
**All GDP growth data are the year-on-year standard for the fourth quarter of 2008.
Source: Official Statistical Departments of respective economies.

frequently. Presidents and prime ministers were forced to resign, and the crisis caused defeat of incumbent governments in general elections.

Fourth, national credit and economic sovereignty of the crisis countries have been threatened. The outbreak of a financial crisis and particularly the debt crisis has severely damaged the sovereign credit and international standing of affected countries. After the outbreak of the crises, many affected countries had to accept international assistance schemes undertaken by Western countries. Financial grants provided by international financial institutions usually had strict lending conditions attached, causing recipient countries to lose much of their economic sovereignty. For example, the South Korean media and public called December 3, 1997, when the South Korean government signed an assistance agreement with the IMF, a day of national humiliation.

7.3.2 The linkage between financial crisis and the current international monetary system

International financial crises broke out not only in developing countries or countries on the periphery of the international monetary system, but also in the core countries of the international monetary system. The frequent occurrence of international financial crises in a country or region and their escalation into a global ones shows that the current international monetary system is quite weak in sustaining a stable international financial order.

In general, both internal and external causes can be traced when a financial crisis breaks out in a particular country or region (Li Ruogu, 2008).

Uncoordinated economic development is the major internal cause, which includes an unbalanced economic structure, excessive dependence on foreign capital, and the lack of both experience and ability to prevent crisis in the process of opening up the financial market. For instance, the 1994 Mexican financial crisis was caused by Mexico's excessive dependence on foreign capital, and the premature opening of its capital accounts. When its currency fluctuated after official devaluation, huge sums of short-term overseas capital were promptly withdrawn, triggering the crisis. The Asian financial crisis occurred because some Asian countries had blindly pursued rapid development while ignoring scientific and technological progress and the improvement of productivity. This created a mismatch between speed and efficiency and caused a structural imbalance and bubble boom. At the same time, excessive dependence on foreign capital and the premature opening up of the financial market put these countries in a vulnerable situation, when their economies were still small and weak and with no ability to resist crisis. Under an inequitable international monetary system crisis will erupt, due to either external or internal factors, or a combination of both, causing bubbles to burst.

The external causes include factors such as the impact of international speculative forces and inadequate international assistance. The international speculative forces, to a varying degree, were involved in many crises. And some such forces even directly caused the crisis. For instance, George Soros and his Quantum Fund successfully forced the GBP to devalue and triggered European Monetary System crisis. In just one day, Soros made billions of dollars.[13] During the 1997 Asian Financial Crisis, international speculative forces represented by Soros attacked the currencies of Southeast Asian countries, triggering a currency crisis that eventu-

---

[13] *George Soros, the Bad Boy of Global Finance*, www.webtrade-USA.com, March 30, 2003.

ally evolved into a regional financial crisis. The effectiveness of international assistance was a key factor in controlling the crisis. Thanks to timely international assistance, the financial crises in Mexico, Russia, and Brazil were put under control, and their damage was limited. During the Asian financial crisis, however, the Western-led international assistance was slow in coming. Western countries took action only when the crisis worsened and threatened both global stability and their own interests. Consequently, the assistance failed to stop the spread of the crisis which caused far greater losses. These problems reveal the inadequacies in the international monetary system and the West-dominated IMF, World Bank, and international coordination mechanism.

In reality, the aforementioned financial crises, although different in cause and manifestation, were all related to the operation of the international monetary system to varying degrees. These financial crises were closely associated with either the inadequacy of the international exchange rate regimes, or the hot money generated by the global surplus liquidity, or deficiencies in international coordination institutions. They also showed the subordinate position of weak countries and unequal treatment they receive in the monetary system. The unjust international monetary system has played a major role in the emergence and spread of these crises.

The 2008 global financial crisis has originated in the United States, which is at the very core of the international financial system. The causes and impact of this crisis are different from those of the more common international financial crises mentioned above. Under the dollar standard, by issuing currency without any check, the United States could make foreign payment and meet domestic consumption demand without undertaking any liability. In the course of promoting export-led economic growth, developing countries have accumulated huge amounts of United States backed dollars and then use those dollars to purchase U.S. financial assets. As a result, a global circulation chain between trading (real goods and services) and financing (capital) has emerged. This is what the international monetary system was like before the U.S. financial crisis erupted. The dollar's core position in this system had sustained the United States' trade deficit for years and accumulated huge risks. These risks were greatly exacerbated by blind trust in and excessive dependence on free market mechanisms.[14] The eventual result was the outbreak of a highly destructive global financial crisis (Li Ruogu, 2008).

The unjust and unequal dollar-based international monetary system is not only a systemic factor that harms countries on the periphery, it is also a bitter pill for the United States itself. Historically, each major crisis provided an opportunity to create a new system. Similarly, the severe crisis of the current international monetary system has placed on our agenda the issue of addressing the unsustainability of this system and reforming it.

---

[14] Li Ruogu,"Global Financial Crisis: Impact on China and the World", a presentation at the 5th Global Conference of Beijing International Finance Forum, November 2008.

Part Three

Global Financial Crisis and the International Monetary System

Triggered by subprime lending in the U.S. real estate market, the financial turbulence has developed into the most serious global financial and economic crisis since the Great Depression. In tracing the causes of the crisis, people will naturally point to principles underlying the American style free market economy and the fundamental flaws of the existing international monetary system. Against the backdrop of the relative weakening of the United States' power after the crisis, adjustment of the international monetary system has become a pressing issue confronting the international community. This section will first take a brief look at the emergence and evolution of the 2008 financial crisis and then analyze its root causes and impact. Secondly, this section will discuss the crisis' profound impact on the international monetary system, particularly on the dollar and dollar assets. It will proceed to discuss plans for rebuilding the international monetary system after the financial crisis. Finally, this section will discuss three possibilities for reforming the international monetary system: unilateral adjustment, multilateral adjustment, and international cooperation, and analyze the strength, weakness, and feasibility of these three options.

Chapter 8

Causes, Development, and Impact of the Global Financial Crisis

The 2008 global financial crisis, with its huge destructive force, originated in the United States, and its impact had both spread from the financial sector to the real economy and from the United States to the whole world. Forces triggering its outbreak included changes in monetary policy, excessive financial innovation, inadequate financial supervision, and the unsustainable growth model featuring borrowing supported consumption. In the final analysis, the 2008 global financial crisis was a systemic one and the result of unscrupulous and blind pursuit of the free market tenets. The crisis was also a massive financial market adjustment caused by the building up of conflicts within the current international monetary system. This crisis has made reforming the current international monetary system increasingly urgent.

8.1 Emergence and Development of the Global Financial Crisis

During the five years leading up to 2006, the U.S. housing market, propelled by low interest rates, was booming and the subprime lending market expanded rapidly, from US$ 65 billion in 1995 to US$ 1.3 trillion by the end of 2006, and its share of home mortgage lending grew from 6% in 2002 to 20% in 2006.[1] During this process, financial institutions sought profit by engaging in subprime mortgage lending through financial innovation and derivatives. To increase profit, American banks packaged subprime loans into a series of subprime mortgage securities such as MBS[2] and CDO[3] by using asset securitization. Such subprime mortgage securities were then sold to different investors after their credit ratings had been upgraded by rating agencies. Issuing and trading of subprime products and their derivatives became popular among global investors because of high profitability. All major investment banks rushed into the business, using financial leverages as high as 30 times.

Credit Default Swap (CDS)[4] is another type of financial innovation. Insurance companies take fees by providing insurance for the huge subprime-based securities market but at the same time run enormous default

---

[1] Mortgage Finance (2009).

[2] MBS refers to Mortgage-backed Security, which is an instrument for financing by issuing bonds in the financial market, based on such credit assets as housing mortgage loan, with the cash flow from repayment of loans by borrowers as support. It is essentially the same with Asset-backed Security (ABS), but the basic assets for ABS are other assets than housing mortgage loans.

[3] CDO refers to Collateralized Debt Obligation, which is the securitization based one or more types of distributed collateralize debt loans. Its basic assets can be bank loans, government or corporate bonds as well as such securitized assets as ABS and MBS, or their combination. It is actually the further securitization based on MBS and ABS. But, it is different from MBS or ABS in the following aspects: (1) different backing assets: backing assets of MBS and ABS need to be of homogeny, with similar maturity, which can appropriately control the cash flow, while CDO requires the backing assets to have different natures, different sources, with less correlation so as to distribute risks; (2) purpose of establishment is different: lending companies establish MBS mainly to raise funds, while investment banks establish CDO mainly to transfer risks and extract price difference.

[4] CDS is equivalent to a kind of insurance for the credits of creditors. By selling CDS, CDS sellers guarantee for the performance of a corresponding credit, while the buying creditor transfers the credit default risk to the CDS seller, and, in case of any "credit event" (when the default rate of credit products rises), can still gain the expected income and profit, because upon occurrence of such "credit event", CDS seller will pay, for CDS, cash equal to the face value of guaranteed bond. However, under the condition without any "credit event", if the guaranteed bond is performed as per schedule, CDS seller will gain regular

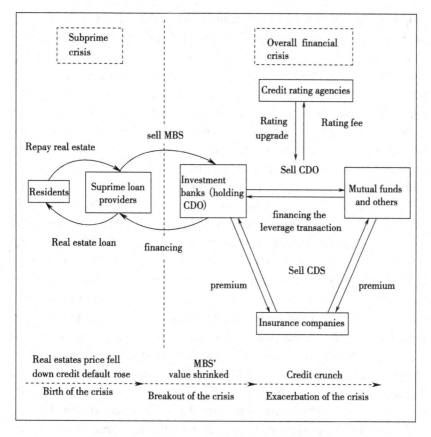

Figure 8-1   Scheme of the U.S. Financial Crisis

risks. During the boom time of real estate market, however, such risks were totally ignored. Attracted by high returns, almost all financial institutions, including commercial banks, investment banks, hedge funds, and insurance companies flocked to this market.

However, with the cooling of the U.S. housing market and an increase in the short-term interest rate, the boom soon ended, and the conflict between soft assets and real debt came to a head. For example, suppose a

premium income from the buyer as well as profit there from. But, as a whole, in case of any "credit event", CDS sellers will bear a rather huge loss.

property is purchased for US$ 1 million. When the real estate market rises by 50%, that property is valued at US$ 1.5 million, a soft and moving asset value. Debt, on the contrary, is hard and real. If one takes a mortgage loan of US$ 1.2 million for a house valued US$ 1.5 million at the time of purchase, regardless of how the price of the house changes — even if it falls to US$ 1 million, the amount of debt will not drop. Therefore, when the market interest rate increases and real estate prices fall, homeowners' burden will be greatly increased, and they will face insolvency as their debts exceed their assets. This means that a large number of borrowers will not be able to repay their loans on time. This was the trigger of the 2007 U.S. subprime crisis. Soon afterwards, MBS and CDO securities on the financial market, either directly or indirectly linked to subprime loans, were also devalued. This caused huge losses to financial institutions which owned a large amount of these securities. In September 2008, several U.S.-based transnational financial giants, led by Lehman Brothers, Citibank, and Merrill Lynch, were trapped. Eventually, they faced either bankruptcy, restructuring, or became target of merger and acquisition. The subprime crisis thus escalated into a full scale financial crisis (see Figure 8-2).

The financial crisis subsequently triggered the global economic crisis. Major developed economies including the United States, Europe, and Japan fell into the most serious economic recession they had ever seen in six decades. The global financial turbulence and the slowing down of global economic growth also severely hurt the economy of developing countries and emerging markets. China, India, Brazil, Mexico, Indonesia, and other countries experienced their greatest economic difficulties in a decade. China's economic growth slowed down significantly after the third quarter of 2008. The International Monetary Fund (IMF) predicted that the global economic growth would fall 1.4% in 2009, and developed countries would see a decline of 3.8% in economic growth (IMF, 2009).[5] The World Trade Organization (WTO) forecasted that global trade would contract by 9% in 2009 (WTO, 2009).[6]

---

[5] IMF, *World Economic Outlook Update* (July 2009).
[6] WTO (2009).

8.2 Causes of the Global Financial Crisis

The 2008 financial crisis was the result of a combination of many factors. The loose monetary policy pursued by United States between 2001 and 2004 led to a significant increase in dollar liquidity. Both these pushed up real estate prices and encouraged financial institutions to relax requirements for home mortgage loans. Excess liquidity also caused a large amount of capital to rush into the financial market in pursuit of profit, giving rise to various financial instruments. When the economy was doing well, this type of operating model could work, with home buyers, lenders, investment banks, and rating agencies all gaining profit, and the regulatory authorities would assume that the self-adjustment function of the market would correct excesses. It was only after the drastic change on the market and the outbreak of the crisis that people came to see that it was just an illusion.

8.2.1 *Loose monetary policy*

Generally speaking, both monetary policy and fiscal policy are means to promote economic growth and regulate the economy. However, government intervention is often attacked in the United States because of blind worship of free market. Expansionist fiscal policy is generally frowned upon because it is associated with big government and high taxes. The Republican administration was unwilling to intervene in the market even when negative signals emerged. On September 11, 2001, the United States suffered from September 11 terrorist attack, the first external attack against the continental United States in 230 years since its founding and during a time of peace. Much damage was sustained and the whole country was caught off guard. The U.S. government promptly adopted new fiscal and monetary policies to stabilize the market. The Federal Reserve lowered U.S. interest rate 13 consecutive times to 1%, the lowest in 46 years, and kept it for one year. The European Central Bank also lowered interest rates four times by a total of 150 basis points in 2001 and maintained a low interest rate of 2% for two and a half years starting from June 2003. To stimulate economic recovery, the Bank of Japan adopted a loose monetary policy in 2001 and held the benchmark interest rate at nearly 0 for 5 years. These monetary policies were designed to stimulate the economy but actually caused more problems than resolved. Yet, such adverse effects were just ignored. Excess international liquidity caused by the loose monetary policies pursued by the United States and other major economies was a fundamental factor causing a new round of U.S. financial crisis.[7]

Excess liquidity meant that financial institutions had easy access to greater amount of capital, which allowed them to leverage fund operation. Market sentiment became over-optimistic, risks to financial products were underestimated and investors and financial institutions became unscrupulous. Trading on the financial market was over-extended. Excess liquidity also brought down home mortgage interest rates, attracting borrowers with lower credit rating. All this created a huge potential default risk.

8.2.2 *Excessive financial innovation*

The United States has the most developed financial infrastructure in the world. Its sound legal system, developed market, advanced technologies and a huge talent pool has made the United States the center of global financial innovation. Almost all the financial innovations made after World War II originated in the United States. Relying on its strength, the United States vigorously developed the financial market to maintain its leading position in the world economy. Financial innovation, however, is a double-edged sword. The negative impact of excessive financial innovation has been fully exposed in the current financial crisis. It is fair to say that financial innovation accelerated the escalation of the subprime crisis into a full scale financial crisis and the spread of the U.S. financial crisis to the rest of the world.

(1) Potential Risks of Subprime Mortgage Loans
Subprime mortgage lending, in contrast to general home mortgage lending, made it possible for medium- and low-income groups to purchase home property, and it thus promoted market boom. But relaxing lending

---

[7]Li Ruogu, *China Today* (2008).

requirements sowed the seeds of crisis. First, as those receiving the loans were in the medium- and low-income group and were even people with poor credit rating, subprime mortgage lending itself had inherent risks. Second, the interest rate structure of subprime mortgage loans increased credit risk at the later stage. Particularly in the case of adjustable-rate mortgages (ARM), borrowers had to repay their loans based on the benchmark interest rate plus risk premium when they later needed to repay loans at floating rates. Pressure for their loan repayment went up as a result. Thus, credit risk of individual borrowers and systemic risk of the real estate mortgage market both increased, and losses thus caused were far greater than that of normal consumption lending.[8] Third, it was extremely difficult for subprime mortgage lending to protect itself against systemic risk. These home mortgage loans were granted when the U.S. real estate market was booming with low interest rates. Once interest rates went up or housing prices came down, not only borrowers were unable to repay their loans, the chain of capital flow of financial institutions also broke.

(2) Excessive and Irrational Development of Asset Securitization
A financial instrument to diversify risks, asset securitization was one of the most important financial innovations of the 20th century. Through securitization, financial institutions shifted default risks of home mortgages to the capital market, where buyers of MBS (commercial banks, public funds, pension funds, etc.) bore default risk. Securitization to some extent was innovative. But subprime lending related securitized products soon became targets of wild market speculation. Without necessary supervision and regulation, these products became increasingly separated from their underlying assets. The extensive use of mathematical model and quantitative analysis in the financial sector created increasingly complicated financial derivatives. Through the use of complicated mathematical models, subprime mortgage loans were turned into complicated and mind boggling structural products: a CDO could be the end of a value chain of SB–MBS–CDO–CDS–synthetic CDO–CDO. Most institutional investors, unable to understand the pricing mechanism behind those securitized products, relied on credit ratings, and inflated credit ratings led

---

[8] Sun Lijian and Peng Shutao (2008).

institutional investors to blindly put their faith into securitized products. Risks mounted as a result and eventually erupted into a financial crisis.

(3) Systemic Risks Heightened by High-leverage Capital Operation
Financial leverage is widely used by commercial banks, investment banks, and other financial institutions and its proper application could increase earnings. However, excessive leverage inevitably leads to crisis. The current crisis was caused by high leverage ratio used by financial institutions. Under the asset and liability management mode based on Value at Risk (VaR), financial institutions were forced to begin the process of deleveraging when asset value dropped. They could either sell risk assets to repay debts or increase their paid-up capitals by attracting new equity investment (Zhang Ming, 2008). If institutional investors simultaneously sell risk assets on a large scale within a short period of time, this would naturally push down prices of assets and cause market chaos. The book value of risk assets they still held would drop further as a result. On the other hand, raising capital requirement would tighten liquidity available in the market and eventually lead to a systemic credit crisis of the entire market.

Table 8-1 shows that major U.S. investment banks raised their leverage ratio from 2003 to 2007. In contrast, being subjected to capital adequacy ratio requirements, commercial banks were less leveraged, and levels of their leverage even declined slightly in recent years. Accordingly, their losses were relatively small. It is the investment banks that were hit hardest.

8.2.3 *Insufficient financial regulation*

At a time when American financial industry expanded rapidly with the extensive introduction of financial innovations, U.S. financial regulatory authorities' inadequate regulation was another important factor contributing to the financial crisis. The current model of an umbrella of regulating agencies centered around the Federal Reserve had proved ineffective in alerting and preventing financial risks. The Federal Reserve was not really at the center of regulation. At least, it had not played the role of a core regulatory body.

Table 8-1   Leverage Ratio of U.S. Financial Institutions (2003–2007)

	2003	2004	2005	2006	2007
Commercial Banks					
Citibank	9.1	9.3	9.6	12.4	14.3
Bank of America	14.0	11.3	11.7	10.2	10.7
JP Morgan Chase	15.7	10.0	10.2	10.7	11.7
Wachovia	11.4	9.4	9.9	9.1	9.2
Investment Banks					
Lehman Brothers	22.7	22.9	23.4	25.2	29.7
Merrill Lynch	15.6	19.0	18.1	26.2	30.9
Morgan Stanley	23.3	25.5	29.8	—	—
Goldman Sachs	17.7	20.2	24.2	20.6	25.2

Note: Leverage ratio = liabilities/equity.
Source: Annual reports of each financial institution.

It was difficult for specialized regulatory agencies to individually assess the systemic risk of the overall financial market as they all had limited scopes of responsibilities. For instance, by means of securitization, commercial banks could transfer risk assets out of the balance sheet and thereby dodge the Federal Reserve's limit on their capital adequacy ratio. At the same time, because the securitized assets were created by commercial banks, the Securities and Exchange Commission (SEC) had not paid sufficient attention to them. Securitized products transferred credit risks from credit market to the capital market. As credit market and capital market were under separate regulation, it was difficult to adequately identify and control the risks of securitization. The lack of effective regulations and even the absence of regulation in certain areas, particularly on structural products such as MBSs, CDOs, plus the inefficient regulations governing those institutions involved exposed financial product innovation and the financial market to high risk.

More importantly, under the influence of the prevailing free market sentiments in the United States, the regulatory authorities represented by the Federal Reserve tended to adopt a "detached" attitude, expecting market self-regulation to resolve problems. This is the fundamental reason for the worsening of the subprime lending problems and the outbreak of the financial crisis. Alan Greenspan, former Chairman of Federal Reserve, claimed that it was easier to clean up after a bubble bursts than to discover and deflate the bubble in advance.[9] Such *laissez-faire* attitude has proved highly destructive as it only led to a loss of control over the market and "violent" correction.

8.2.4 *Consumer credit based growth model in the age of globalization*

Personal consumption has long been the main force driving economic growth in the United States. This was particularly the case when, after the September 11 attacks, the U.S. government pursued expansionist monetary and fiscal policies which boosted the American consumption culture that had thrived since the late 19th century and further stimulated both personal and government consumption. Private consumption's contribution to U.S. GDP growth reached 217.5% and 118.8% in 2001 and 2002 respectively, the first two years of interest rates cut. Its contribution to GDP growth was above 70% in the following years, with the exception of 2008.[10] Private consumption thus greatly promoted U.S. economic growth.

The excessive growth of consumption created a savings–investment imbalance. During the 14 years between 1994 and 2007, real consumption demand grew at a high average annual rate of 3.5% in the United States, while the average annual growth of real personal disposable income was only 3.2%.[11] At the same time, government expenditure grew at a higher rate than that of government revenue. This widened the gap between government revenue and expenditure, which reached nearly US$ 40 billion in 2003, and it caused a continued decline of the U.S. savings ratio in recent years. Net savings as a proportion of gross national income dropped to –0.9% in 2008 from 8% in the 1970s. Government net savings were always negative throughout those years, which exacerbated the problem (see Figure 8-2).

---

[9] Martin Wolf (2009).
[10] Calculated as per data of BEA.
[11] Stephen Roach (2008).

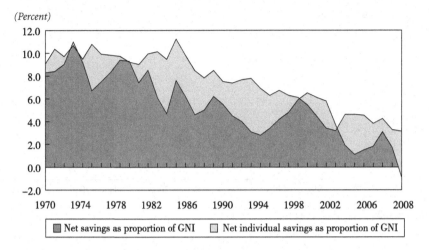

Figure 8-2   U.S. Net Savings as Proportion of GNI (1970–2008)

Source: U.S. Bureau of Economic Analysis.

Internal imbalance led to external imbalance. The Unites States' over-consumption is the inherent cause of the growing savings–investment gap and balance of payments disequilibrium, and globalization has also made this possible. On the one hand, as globalization deepens, progress made in the use of capital, labor, and science and technology has greatly stimu-lated the growth of productivity. Global economy entered a golden period of high growth and low inflation which lasted for nearly two decades. This provided the United States a good climate to use interest rate to stimulate consumption and regulate its economy. On the other hand, since the 1980s, the emerging economies represented by East Asia seized the opportunity of economic globalization. Drawing on their advantages such as low labor costs, they attracted substantial amount of foreign capital and expanded trade. They continuously provided the United States and other developed countries with huge quantities of quality but low-cost goods. This met the United States' booming consumption demand. An outlet was also found for these countries' comparatively high ratio of savings. The huge U.S. market enabled these countries to develop export-led economic growth when they were still facing the problem of inadequate

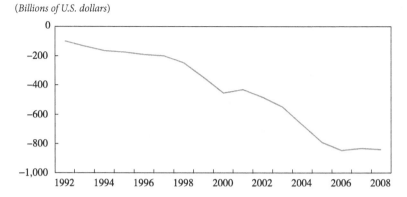

(*Billions of U.S. dollars*)

Figure 8-3   U.S. Trade Deficit

Source: Bureau of Economic Analysis.

internal demand. Owing to these two factors, the U.S. commercial trade deficit has continued to grow, and at a particularly high rate since 2000. By 2008, such deficit amounted to US$ 840.25 billion, accounting for 5.8% of the U.S. GDP.[12]

This means that the United States had to seek financial support to sustain its large consumption. Since the beginning of the 21st century, stimulated by the increasingly loose monetary policy, U.S. real estate market and financial market surged. With the continued appreciation of the value of their collateral, people could acquire new loans to foot consumption or to sustain consumption through realizing capital gains. American consumers found that it was no longer necessary to save on the basis of income; rather, they turned to a new savings strategy based on assets appreciation which was, in fact, home mortgages. Consumer credit began to expand rapidly after 2000, and a new economic growth model supported by capital inflow and credit consumption took shape. According to the U.S. Department of the Treasury, resident debt reached 100.3% of GDP (Figure 8-4) in 2007.[13] This growth model was based on adequate liquidity, sustained capital inflow and continued rise of asset prices. If any

---

[12] Calculated based on Bureau of Economic Analysis data.
[13] Calculated as per data of US Department of Treasury.

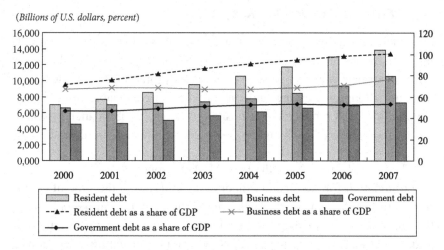

Figure 8-4   U.S. Debt Outstanding by Sectors (2000–2007)

Source: U.S. Department of the Treasury.

external shock occurs, such as loss of foreign investors' confidence in the U.S. market, declining asset price, or liquidity shortage, the foundation of U.S. economic growth would collapse. The 2008 financial crisis was actually a penalty against the American growth model in the age of globalization.

8.3 Origin of the Global Financial Crisis

The causes of the 2008 global financial crisis are far more complex than stated earlier. The current crisis is referred to as a "once in a century" crisis, one that is as severe as the 1929 Great Depression, if not more so. It has deep-seated systemic causes. Loose monetary policy, excessive financial innovation, and inadequate supervision are merely symptoms. The main culprit for the crisis is the blind faith in the *laissez-faire* market economy. Additionally, the U.S. growth model of excessive consumption supported by the existing international monetary system has become unsustainable, which is another underlying cause of the current financial crisis.

8.3.1 *Free market economic system*

Objectively speaking, practices such as stimulating the economy through monetary policy and developing market potential through financial innovation are normal. They can all serve as tools for promoting economic development as long as they are undertaken within a reasonable limit. Going beyond limit will produce the opposite result. The 2008 financial crisis is a natural outcome of applying the free market philosophy to the extreme.

(1) Theory and Practices of the Free Market Economy
The foundation for free market theory was laid during the time of Adam Smith. In his classical work *Wealth of Nations*, Adam Smith emphasized the importance of *laissez-faire* economy, namely, free operation, free trade, and free competition, as necessary factors contributing to economic growth. He also advocated that governments should minimize interference in economic activities. According to Smith, individual pursuit of self-interest would naturally guide one to use capital at one's disposal in the way most beneficial for society, that is, one would inevitably be led by an "invisible hand" to maximize social interests. Therefore, government functions should be limited to a role of being a "night watcher", providing citizens with a peaceful and safe economic environment for free competition.

Smith lived before the Industrial Revolution took place. At that time, capitalism had developed from infancy to youth, entering a stage of free competition. It was competitive enough and needed no further support from the state. Therefore, economic liberalism, reflecting the interests of industrial capitalist class, met the need of development of the capitalist economy at the time. Adam Smith's theory and policies enabled Britain to become the first country in the world to complete the Industrial Revolution, and boosted the economic development of other European countries and the United States. It had a great influence on the subsequent evolution of economic thinking. Over a period spanning more than a 100 years, liberalism became the dominant theory guiding the development of market economy in various countries.

However, the 1929 Great Depression broke the myth of perfection of market self-regulation. The fundamental flaws in the *laissez-faire* system were exposed, and the system was replaced by state intervention based on Keynesianism. This period is referred to as the New Deal. Keynesianism also played an important role in rebuilding the global economy after World War II. Under the influence of state interventionism, state monopoly capitalism registered unprecedented growth. This plus the advent of the third technological revolution ushered in a period of rapid growth and prosperity between 1950s and 1970s for the Western world.

The two oil crises during the 1970s ended this golden age. For the first time, developed capitalist countries were confronted with stagflation characterized by low growth and high inflation. Keynesianism fell into a dilemma. Neo-liberalism, represented by monetarism and supply-side economics, became the trend. Neo-liberalists called for abandoning state intervention, pushing economic liberalism to an extreme. Moreover, since the 1970s and 1980s, neo-liberalism has become heavily politicized and ideologically oriented, being used as an important tool for American and British monopoly capital to maximize their interests globally. Washington Consensus represents the theory of neo-liberalism. Influenced by Washington Consensus, Latin American, former Soviet Union, and Eastern European countries started to transition into market economic system, a process that was accompanied by privatization, liberalization, and economic globalization. Movement towards free market thus became a basic trend underlying the global economy. It cleared the systemic obstacles to global expansion of international monopoly capital and its control of the global economy. In this sense, economic marketization and globalization advocated by U.S.-led Western countries have linked the interests of all countries in the world closely together, making them share a huge common stake.

(2) Free Market and Government Intervention
The history of modern global economic development is the history of the development of the capitalist system, and the history of fighting for supremacy and mutual influence between the theories and practices of free market and state intervention. In practice, both two theories have worked, but they have also encountered enormous difficulties. It is hard to say which of the two propositions is better and should replace the other

one. Rather, they should be appropriately integrated and adopted according to different conditions and stages of development of different countries. The former Soviet Union and China, before its reform and opening, practiced planned economy that depended excessively on state regulation. Both countries experienced rapid growth, but the flaws of their growth model also became increasingly prominent. The United States, Britain, and other developed countries, on their part, practice free market economy. This growth model can allocate resources more efficiently, but it also has deep-rooted problems such as monopoly, being exposed to external impact and lack of clear goals in economic development. In particular, free market economy is unable to strike a balance between efficiency and justice, resulting in imbalanced development. The fact that the two most serious economic crises in the human history broke out in a period dominated by free market theory shows that the basic flaws of free market economy could be highly destructive.

(3) Free Market Capitalism and Financial Crises
As the market is the source of profits, it meets the inherent needs of the development of the capitalist world, but market is often abused in this process. Since its birth, capitalism has gone through stages of liberal capitalism, private monopoly capitalism, state monopoly capitalism, and international monopoly capitalism. Its growth has been driven by the pursuit and opening of market. During the infant stage of capitalism, the opening of new sea routes created huge overseas market. Today, as the economy has become globalized, the expansion of transnational companies and the establishment of international cooperation organizations and regional integration organizations aim to make profit by increasing the market capacity in a particular area. When market capacity reaches its limit, the development of capitalism will break and push the "new free market economic model" to an extreme. Since the second half of the 20th century, a new virtual market has been created through the development of financial instruments and products. "Financial assets" thus increased stimulated consumption and economic growth. Under the free market economy, deregulation and globalized operations have been vigorously pursued in Western countries' financial sectors. Thanks to the use of electronic technologies, internet, and other information technologies, numerous new

financial products were created, accelerating the development of a virtual economy and a rapidly expanding financial asset bubble. At the same time, major Western countries have used the free-market-based Washington Consensus to absorb transitional economies, emerging economies, and numerous developing countries into the Western liberal economic system so that they would become part of the Western virtual prosperity in the "free" and "transparent" market environment.

Over the last three decades, Western countries such as the United States and Britain have spared no effort to advocate free market economic theory. During the long period of prosperity in the Western world, potential problems associated with the free market were concealed, and opportunities to address these issues were missed. After the eruption of the financial crisis in 2008, governments of the United States and Britain which had long advocated free market economy had to intervene forcefully to save their economy. This has caused some people to jokingly comment that the United States was marching towards "Socialism with U.S. Characteristics". The myth of the omnipotent market has exploded.

8.3.2 *The unjust international monetary system*

In terms of the mechanisms involved, the outbreak of the 2008 financial crisis was closely linked to the imbalance in the international monetary system. The characteristics of the reserve currency pattern, exchange rate arrangements, international coordination mechanisms, and international payment adjustment have been discussed in the previous sections. However, in order to reveal the unjust nature of this system and its linkage with the financial crisis, it is necessary to further study the non-equilibrium of the international monetary system.

First, there is imbalance between the dollar's position as the main reserve currency and U.S. economic strength. After World War II, the establishment of the Bretton Woods system gave the dollar the position of close-to-gold and an international currency. The United States actually became the bank of the world because of its control of the issuance of the international currency, and this created the condition for the United States to become a dominant global power. Although the double linkage system is gone and the euro and other currencies have grown in strength, the

Table 8-2   Status of Major Economies and their Currency Usage

	U.S.A.	Japan	Europe
Proportion of World GDP (PPP)	21.2	6.4	15.7
Proportion of Total World Export	8.1	4.9	28.6
Share of Global Foreign Exchange Reserves	64.9	2.9	25.9

Sources: IMF, *World Economic Outlook Database* (April 2009); World Trade Organization, Statistics Database.

dollar remains the most important settlement currency in global trade. The United States is still undeniably the world's greatest power, and the dollar is even more important in settling international business transactions. In other words, the international balance of payments depends heavily on a single sovereign currency, the dollar, while there is still a long way to go before reserve currencies can become diversified. This status quo is determined by economic strength but, more importantly, it is the inertia created by the network effect (see Table 8-2).

The central position of the dollar has created numerous problems. The key problem is that only the United States can issue dollars, while no other country can intervene, and this has created a serious imbalance between the benefits and responsibility in the international monetary system. The United States can finance its trade deficit by printing dollars. It has thus pursued a growth model featuring high consumption, low savings and high deficit, and exacerbated global economic imbalance. In the course of economic expansion, the United States has long pursed an easy monetary policy, and the huge amount of dollars issued created excessive global liquidity. At a time of economic and financial globalization, this has made the international financial market more volatile and encouraged financial speculation. Excessive liquidity has made the financial system more fragile and triggered continued global crises.

M2 is generally used to measure a country's domestic currency supply, but M3 is a most suitable index for measuring the issue of an international currency like the dollar. The U.S. M3 includes M2, certificates of deposit (CDs, valued at over US$ 100,000), the balance of money market mutual funds (MMMFs), short-term repurchase agreements, and the Eurodollar. After the Bretton Woods system collapsed, the U.S. M3

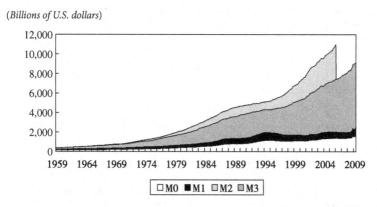

(Billions of U.S. dollars)

Figure 8-5   Composition of the U.S. Money Supply (January 1959–June 2009)

Source: Federal Reserve, http://www.federalreserve.gov/releases/h6/hist/.

increased continually. The gap between the U.S M3 and M2 was only US$ 2.2 billion in 1959. It exceeded US$ 100 billion for the first time in 1973, increased further in the late 1990s, and exceeded US$ 3.5 trillion by February 2006. This shows that more dollars had flowed into the world (Figure 8-5). However, the Federal Reserve stopped releasing the M3 figure in March 2006, and the reason given was that M3 did not contain more information than M2. This was criticized by U.S. Congressman Ron Paul, who said that M3 was the best index to measure the speed of Federal Reserve's currency issuance.

This shows that the U.S. government not only failed to rein in the excessive issuance of the dollar, but also tried to conceal it. The Federal Reserve stopped releasing the M3 right before the subprime lending problem erupted. While one cannot tell if there was any connection between the two, it is an irrefutable fact that there is excessive global liquidity and that the market is flooded by financial innovation products. They are major factors triggering the 2008 financial crisis.

Second, on the strength of the core position of the dollar in the international monetary system, the United States is able to pursue its monetary policy only to meet the needs of domestic political agenda without living up to its responsibility of adjusting imbalance in international payments and accommodating the economic conditions of other countries affected. Unlike other countries, the United States does not need to maintain the

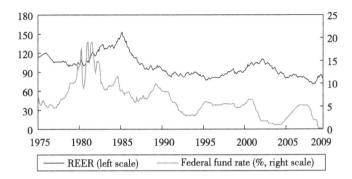

Figure 8-6   Federal Funds Rate and USD Real Effective Exchange Rate (January 1975–June 2009)

Source: Bloomberg, Federal Reserve Board of Governors.

stable value of the dollar. On the contrary, the dollar exchange rate can even become an instrument for the United States to adjust its domestic economy. A strong dollar can reduce the costs of import and export. On the other hand, when the current account deficit and fiscal deficit continue to rise, a strong dollar is not the best choice. In such a case, devaluation of the dollar increases imports and reduces the cost of foreign debt repayment. Therefore, by adjusting the federal funds rate to influence the dollar's exchange rate, the United States can achieve its desired policy target. The dollar has experienced three devaluation–revaluation cycles since the breakdown of the Bretton Woods system (Figure 8-6).

The dollar exchange rate adjustment cycle has made it possible for the United States to relieve, to a certain extent, its sustained current account deficit caused by the strong dollar. At the same time, it has led to transfer of value and wealth. Under a strong dollar, U.S. trade deficit starts to build up and other countries gradually accumulate dollar assets at higher cost. When such dollar assets reach a certain level, the dollar is devaluated, and the value of the dollar assets shrink as a result. The United States, with a reduced trade deficit, will be able to buy back the dollar at a lower price (Xia Bin and Chen Daofu, 2006).[14]

More importantly, as the U.S. economic cycle and that of other countries do not occur at the same time, the other countries have to adjust their

---

[14] Xia Bin and Chen Daofu (2006).

policies according to the U.S. macro-policy and face the risk of external shock to their economic and financial security. Under the condition of open economy, adjustment of U.S. interest rate and exchange rate will impact significantly and even would be an assault on the peripheral countries, and particularly those that have close economic and trade relations with the United States. For instance, in the mid- and late-1980s, Japan was forced to appreciate yen, and the Japanese government consequently eased monetary policy to reduce loss suffered by the export industry, thus resulting in domestic surplus liquidity. This created bubble in the Japanese economy. Later, increase of the U.S. federal funds rate in 1989 drove the Western developed countries into a cycle of interest rate hike, leading to the reverse flow of speculative capital. This, along with the tightening of Japanese domestic land and financial policy, caused the Japanese economic bubble to burst. The Mexican, Southeast Asian, and Russian financial crises were, in one way or another, connected with the adjustment of U.S. monetary policy and frequent cross-border flow of capital. All this brought catastrophe to the peripheral countries under the dollar standard.

Third, the free floating exchange rates regime is not fair. Regarding the justification of free floating exchange rates, there have been no convincing explanation, but only the preaching of Western market fundamentalism. While the free floating exchange rates regime has been accepted since the breakdown of the Bretton Woods system, it has failed to play a positive role in improving the balance of payments and stabilizing the world economy. First, there is a lack of benchmark in the regime. What is the reference in floating? If everyone floats, which one should be the benchmark? For instance, major industrialized countries led by the United States all take the position that floating exchange rates are a market-based regime which means that market can determine the relative prices of two currencies. But how does market price a currency? What pricing method is used? How is the price of the dollar determined by the market? Second, the free floating exchange rates work against developing countries. Currencies of developing countries are floating against major international currencies such as the dollar and the euro, but neither one of them is a stable anchor. And there is no policy to ensure the stability of the dollar, especially its purchasing power. Fluctuation of the dollar exchange rate inevitably leads to fluctuation of developing countries' currencies, thus causing speculation. During the 2008 financial crisis, the first shock developing countries confronted was currency devaluation, and some developed countries faced the same problem. This proves that at a time of financial crisis, floating exchange rates will intensify conflicts instead of showing so-called elasticity. The free floating exchange rates regime has showed little effect in regulating developing countries' balance of payments. Since developing countries mainly export primary products but import capital and manufacturing goods for economic development, there is little elasticity in either their exports or imports, which can hardly meet the Marshall–Learner condition. Devaluation will not do much to improve balance of payments of developing countries. Also, renminbi appreciation will not help cut China's trade surplus with the United States but could only boost China's domestic asset prices. Finally, evidences show that following the Asian financial crisis, Asian, Latin American, and other emerging markets have successively turned to pegged exchange rates (Li Yang, 2009).[15] This also demonstrates that stable exchange rates is a natural choice for developing countries.

Fourth, disequilibrium in the balance of payments has persisted, and the distribution and the use of reserve assets is not equitable. Theoretically speaking, if the floating exchange rates regime could effectively regulate balance of payments, it would not be necessary for countries, especially those from Asia, to accumulate a huge amount of foreign exchange reserves. However, in reality, disequilibrium in the balance of payments is constant due to the special status of the dollar. To prevent risk, many countries, particularly Asian countries, have to hold a huge amount of dollar assets. This has resulted in *de facto* unfairness. The assets these countries hold are actually a credit, namely, the dollar's purchasing power and its reliable liquidity. As many countries pursue dollar assets, a huge amount of dollars flow back into the United States, causing the interest rate of the dollar to decline. This not only makes up for the U.S. trade deficit, but also reduces the cost for the United States in pursuing an expansionist monetary policy. But developing countries as a whole and particularly the most underdeveloped countries have long been in deficit. While this situation has slightly improved in recent years due to rise in resources and energy

---

[15] Li Yang (2009).

prices, their balance of payments still faces difficulty. With inadequate inflow of direct foreign investment and aid, they have to borrow in huge amounts, which not only incur heavy debts, but could also trigger debt crisis. This stands in sharp contrast with the huge flow of capital into developed countries, showing a huge imbalance in the use of reserve assets.

Under this system, the United States can finance its current account deficit and budget deficit with low interest and ensure high domestic consumption. Those trade surplus countries at the low end of international division of labor, while being able to boost growth and employment through sustained export drive, can only purchase overseas financial assets with surplus dollars due to lack of investment channels, and such dollars invariably find their way back into the United States. What is more, this system is unable to exercise control over the United States. As a result, U.S. credit expands excessively, eventually growing into a serious solvency crisis, which in turn results in losses to the export countries through trade. So the current financial crisis is actually a penalty against this unfair growth model and unjust international monetary system.

8.4 The Impact of the Global Financial Crisis

The global financial crisis triggered by the U.S. subprime lending crisis has grown into the most serious financial and economic crisis since the Great Depression, in which both the financial sector and the real economic sector have been hard hit. Growth in developed economies sharply declined, and so did their total demand, and this caused slowing down of growth in emerging economies, including China.

8.4.1 *U.S. economy will not recover any time soon*

Since the eruption of the current financial crisis, the U.S. government has taken all possible actions including pursuing extremely loose monetary policies and large-scale fiscal assistance programs to prevent its economy from falling into a long depression. The effect of these steps so far have been limited.

The U.S. Federal Reserve lowered the benchmark interest rate to 0–0.25% and injected over US$ 1 trillion into investment and commercial banks through several innovative channels. However, the tight credit market was not significantly improved. In September 2008, as the financial crisis deepened, the United States began to inject liquidity into the financial system. The year-on-year growth of base money rose close to 10% in September 2008, against the previous level of within 2%. From December 2008 to 2009, the growth of money supply increased significantly to about 100%. Yet, the increase in base money only brought about a slight increase in the year-on-year growth of M2 money supply from less than 7% in 2008 to about 9% in 2009. Financial institutions' unwillingness to lend hindered money creation and turned the liquidity injected by the U.S. Federal Reserve into a sharply increased reserve deposit. The year-on-year growth of the deposit reserve for financial institutions jumped to 141.0% in September 2008, from −1.0% the month before. It then rocketed to a surprising level of 1,942.4% in May 2009 (see Figure 8-7).

The U.S. economy depends heavily on its financial sector. American consumption is to a large extent credit driven and investment is mainly

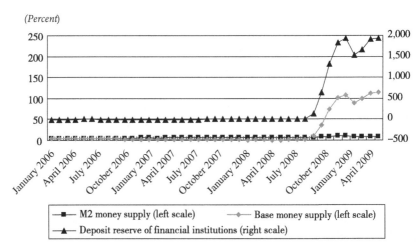

Figure 8-7   Year-on-Year Growth of U.S. Base Money, Deposit Reserve, and the M2 Money Supply

Source: Bloomberg.

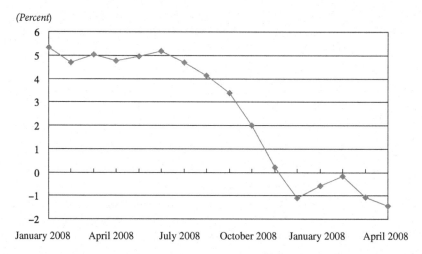

(Percent)

Figure 8-8   Year-on-year Growth of U.S. Personal Consumption Expenditures
Source: U.S. Bureau of Economic Analysis.

financed by equity and bond markets. Thus, it is difficult for the U.S. economy to recover when its financial sector remains unstable. Currently, growth of U.S. consumption is weak. According to data from the U.S. Bureau of Economic Analysis, U.S. personal consumption expenditure continued to decline between December 2008 and April 2009, suffering a negative growth of –1.1%, –0.6%, –0.2%, –1.1%, and –1.5% over the same period the year before. This stands in sharp contrast with the average monthly growth of 5% from January to September in 2008 (Figure 8-8). Growth in investment has been weak since 2007, with negative growth in four consecutive quarters since the second quarter of 2008 (see Figure 8-9).[16]

The U.S. financial institutions are still in the process of writing off bad assets and deleveraging has not been completed. When the financial market, especially the derivatives market are sluggish and financing required for growth is hard to come by, it will take more time for U.S. consumption and investment to recover. Recovery of investors' confidence and rebuilding trust in credit will also take a long time. Therefore, the U.S. economy is unlikely to experience a "V" shape rebound. The time needed

---

[16]Calculated as per data from the U.S. Bureau of Economic Analysis.

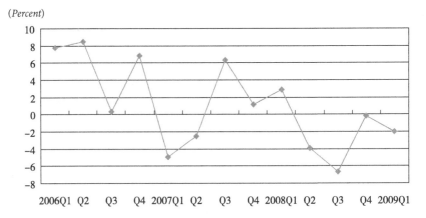

(Percent)

Figure 8-9   Growth of U.S. Domestic Investment

Source: U.S. Bureau of Economic Analysis.

for the American economy to recover might be as long as that of the 1929 Great Depression, although the decline might not be as deep.

8.4.2 *The global financial crisis has caused slowing down of the global economy*

The 2008 financial crisis has an unprecedented impact on the global economy. When the crisis began, it was not taken too seriously by many market analysts. However, as the crisis intensified, market sentiments quickly changed. Losses suffered by financial institutions in various countries since the beginning of the crisis have totaled US$ 2.6 trillion, and the global stock market has lost US$ 16.22 trillion in value. From the third quarter of 2008 to the second quarter of 2009, U.S. GDP fell at an annual rate of 12.5%, registering the largest continual fall since the Great Depression (the previous record was an accumulative slide of 10.6% from the third quarter of 1953 to the first quarter of 1954). In the July 2009 updated edition of the *World Economic Outlook*, the International Monetary Fund forecasted that in 2009 global economic growth would decelerate by –1.4%. If this were the case, it would be the first negative growth since World War II. The crisis' impact on the economy is no less severe than that of a war.

By fall, 2008, confronted by stressed liquidity and credit risk, major economies have adopted numerous rescue policies at unprecedented scale. However, as financial institutions were still in a state of panic about the uncertainty of the market, huge funds accumulated within the banking system, unable to be used as liquidity. Chaos and contraction of the international financial market can hardly be reversed within a short period of time. The dysfunction of the global credit market has seriously affected consumption, production, and trade. Sharp declines in real estate and stock prices were shaking market confidence worldwide. Consumption and investment could remain sluggish for a long time to come. In late May 2009, Standard & Poor's lowered the UK sovereign credit rating from"stable"to"negative"because its debt was approaching 100% of GDP. Investors were concerned that the United States, with a growing fiscal budget deficit, could face the same fate. Such downgrading was rare and the public was shocked by it. It shows that despite expanding expenditure and injecting huge financial resources, Western governments have made little progress in their efforts to save the economy.

As major developed countries fell into the financial crisis around roughly the same time, the global economy fell into negative territory as a result. Even if government intervention could effectively recover the normal function of the financial market and the fiscal and monetary policies adopted could play their expected role, it was still difficult for developed economies to achieve fast recovery. Emerging economies and developing countries were not close to the epicenter of the financial turbulence, and the economic fundamentals of some of them were sound which enabled them to be in a better position to cope with the crisis. Still, their trade, financing, and growth will also face great difficulties. Trade and financial protectionism could rise and emerging economies could face even higher trade barriers. Sharp increase of public debt, exchange rates, and interest rates in many emerging markets could also affect them and their private sectors could be deep into trouble as they are less capable to obtain adequate external financing. All this lead to loss of momentum in their economic development. The emerging economies which depend heavily on external financing and demand to power economic growth saw their financial markets and trade sector fall into great difficulty.

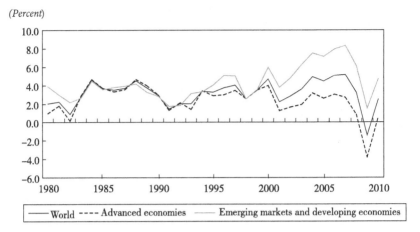

(Percent)

Figure 8-10   Trends of World Economic Growth (1980–2010)

Note: Forecast value for 2009 and 2010.

Sources: IMF, *World Economic Outlook Database* (April 2009, July 2009).

8.4.3 *The reform of the international monetary system could accelerate*

Over the last two decades, the general pattern of the international balance of payments is as follows: East Asian countries exported physical goods and oil-exporting countries exported resources, while the United States exported dollars in exchange for such goods and resources. Thus, the East Asian Countries and oil exporting countries maintained growth through export, and the American consumers benefited from inexpensive imports. All this was possible because of the status of the dollar as an international currency, although it is just credit money without any obligation to exchange for gold.

However, the 2008 financial crisis has changed this arrangement. Devaluation of dollar-based financial assets makes their holders around the world suffer heavy losses. A huge amount of wealth has evaporated. U.S. consumers who now only have negative assets were unable to maintain their previous level of consumption, dragging a large number of logistics and manufacturing enterprises to the brink of bankruptcy. This has led to high unemployment which further affected growth. Export surplus countries are also affected. As the U.S. financial crisis spreads, there is growing concern over the trustworthiness of the dollar and the U.S. economy. There is even market concern that the sovereign rating of the United States would also be downgraded, like that of Britain.

Thus, the 2008 crisis has exerted a serious negative impact on the dollar's status as the core currency of the international monetary system, the pivotal role played by the U.S. financial market globally and the functioning of the U.S. economy as a global growth engine. The loss of confidence in them by the international community will inevitably cause the United States' status as a global financial leader to decline. There is now heated global debate about the need to reform the current international monetary system, and this call has gained the support of the United Nations, some European countries (including Russia), and Brazil. It is true that there are yet no alternatives to the dollar, the U.S. financial market, and the U.S. economy. But the eruption of the current financial crisis certainly has speed up the process of reforming the existing international monetary system, no matter how long and arduous this will be.

Chapter 9

Global Financial Crisis' Impact on the International Monetary System

The 2008 financial crisis has caused great damage to the world economy. It has also posed a major challenge to the integrity of the international monetary system and put its sustainability into question. The financial crisis has made it possible for the international society to place the reform of the international monetary system on the agenda, although such reform takes time to achieve.

9.1 Global Financial Crisis' Impact on the Dollar

During the two decades when Alan Greenspan was Chairman of the Federal Reserve, the "Greenspan Put" dominated: whenever a crisis occurred on the financial market, the Federal Reserve would lower the federal funds rate and inject liquidity into the market to fence off its impact on the real economy (e.g., inflation and employment). While such rescue could lessen the impact of the crisis in the near term, it also caused two major problems. First, surplus liquidity flooded the market and persisted, thus making the dollar weak. Second, as the Greenspan Put was a one-way and asymmetric incentive, it bred new moral hazard by encouraging market participants to engage in investment with higher risk. The moment the market crashed, the government would act speedily to bail it out, which reduced the overall cost of high-risk investing. During the current financial crisis, developed countries have responded in the same way by immediately injecting liquidity into the market and drastically lowering interest rates.

However, the big issue is how will the U.S. government be able to raise fund for such rescue. It is obvious that raising taxes is not a feasible option because of the heavy debts already incurred by American households. The only way left for the U.S. government is to raise funds by issuing treasury bonds which are guaranteed by U.S. tax revenue. With American households heavily in debts, the United States naturally turns to overseas buyers. From 2002 to 2007, the United States issued about US$ 400 billion of treasury bonds each year, about half of which were purchased by foreign investors.

Greenspan admitted that this unprecedented financial crisis would severely threaten the position of the dollar. And this would affect the U.S. economy and other economies which rely on demand and investment opportunities in the U.S. market.

Starting from 1995, the U.S. government maintained a strong dollar policy, causing global capital flowing into the Wall Street, thus consolidating the core position of the dollar. Around 2002, the U.S. Dollar Index (USDX) reached as high as 120 points. However, after 2002, due to the impact of factors such as interest rate cut, the USDX started to slide. After falling below 80 points in September of 2007, it continued to fluctuate sharply. In March 2008, when Bear Stearns was acquired by JP Morgan Chase, the USDX fell below 71 points. However, despite the fact that the United States was at the epicenter of the financial turbulence and suffered huge losses, the dollar then reversed course and registered an unusual upwards trend, something known as the dollar paradox (Figure 9-1). But many economists considered this a temporary phenomenon. Japanese economist Joi Ito believed the strong status of the dollar could not be sustained (2009). The reason is that during the financial crisis, U.S. companies and financial institutions sold their overseas assets to make up for inadequate liquidity. Such huge funds, priced in foreign currencies, had to be converted into the dollar to be repatriated

Figure 9-1   USDX (June 2008–June 2009)

Source: http://stockcharts.com/h-sc/ui?s=$USD&p=D&yr=1&mn=0&dy=0&id=p03166912098.

back to the United States. This increased demand for the dollar and thus boost its value. But such capital inflow would stop once the U.S. financial system becomes stabilized and U.S. companies and financial institutions regained their strength. It would again weaken the dollar. In July 2009, the USDX has again fallen below 80 points, and the international foreign exchange market has seen more fluctuations. In the 10 months following September 2008, the USDX has fluctuated in a range of about 14 points, which was rare in the last decade. It reflects the increasing instability of the dollar.

However, the dollar will not immediately lose its leading position. The United States could indeed fall into a recession due to the financial crisis, and the dollar could also slide if central banks from other countries sell it. But what other currency could take the place of the dollar? One alternative would be the euro. However, the eastward expansion of the European Union has not been completed, and the core EU countries are yet to find ways to integrate the less developed new members into the Union. Delay in structural reform will also prevent the euro from becoming a global currency. Another alternative is the Japanese yen. But because of Japan's domestic and foreign policies, the yen's influence is confined to East Asia. Additionally, as long as the currency of one country is used as an international currency, the Triffin Dilemma will be unavoidable, and such a currency would not be sustainable. One other alternative is the Special Drawing Right of the International Monetary Fund. But it will take quite a long time before SDR could be put into use. Therefore, despite its increasing weakness, the dollar's leading status will not change in the near future. Still, the financial crisis will speed up the reform of the international monetary system.

9.2 Global Financial Crisis' Impact on Dollar Assets

Since the subprime lending crisis broke out, the prices of major assets in the United States such as real estate, corporate stocks and bonds plummeted. Most importantly, as market confidence has not yet recovered, both private and foreign investors are reluctant to buy these assets. Thus, the prices of dollar assets will remain sluggish for quite some time.

9.2.1 *The real estate market*

The 2008 financial crisis originated in the U.S. residential housing mortgage market. As the crisis spread and escalated, the U.S. real estate bubble got squeezed. In late May, 2009, the S&P/Case–Shiller Home Price Indices of 20 U.S. cities dropped to 139.84 points, one-third below its peak of 206.52 points in July 2006, and the drop exceeded 50% in some regions. In the first quarter of 2009, the price index of these 20 cities saw a year-on-year drop of 19.1%, a historical record. This trend is continuing. In the second quarter of 2009, the average U.S. home price is basically at the same level as that at the end of 2002 (Figure 9-2).[1]

A rebound in the U.S. real estate market depends on increased effective demand. But at a time of persistent recession, sluggish real economy and increasing unemployment, the U.S. real estate market will remain bearish for some time to come.

---

[1]http://www2.standardandpoors.com/spf/pdf/index/CSHomePrice_History_052619.xls.

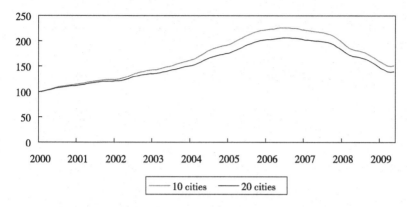

Figure 9-2   S&P/Case–Shiller Home Price Indices Trends (2000–2009)
Source: Standard & Poor's.

9.2.2 *Stock market*

As the U.S. subprime lending crisis escalated, the U.S. stock market responded accordingly. In the summer of 2007 when the U.S. subprime lending crisis emerged, the U.S. stock market responded immediately, with three major indices, namely, Dow Jones, Standard & Poor's, and NASDAQ, each showing drastic fluctuation. Still, the U.S. financial market believed that since the subprime mortgage market was relatively small and the U.S. and world economy were experiencing robust growth, the problems in subprime lending would soon be absorbed in the course of rapid economic growth. By the end of 2007, however, the subprime lending problem was quickly deteriorating, with increasing cases of home foreclosure. The real estate development agencies were facing shortage in funding. Once again, the stock market responded accordingly. In March 2008, the Bear Stearns incident caused the three major U.S. stock indices to fall by about 10%. But, as it was assumed that the U.S. subprime lending crisis had hit the bottom, and particularly because JP Morgan Chase acquired Bear Stearns with the backing of the U.S. government, the market regained confidence. Yet, during August and September of 2008, the United States was struck by the Fannie Mae & Freddie Mac crisis and within two weeks Merrill Lynch was acquired, Lehman Brothers went bankrupt, and AIG became nationalized. People began to realize that the

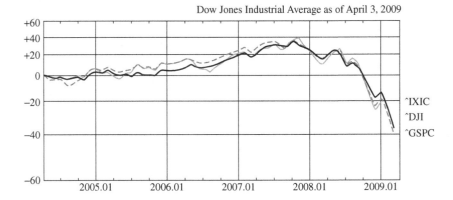

Figure 9-3   Index Trends of US Major Stock Exchanges

Source: Yahoo Finance.

subprime lending crisis was far more serious than expected, thus causing all the three major stock indices to plummet.

From the end of 2007 to the end of March 2009, the three major indices dropped from their peak level by more than 50%, the most drastic dive since the Great Depression. The value of U.S. listed companies also fell significantly. During this period, stock prices of blue chip giants such as AIG and Citibank fell to less than US$ 1, a share, becoming junk stocks. Citibank was even kept out of Standard and Poor's stock index. Although the U.S. stock market has recently taken a turn for the better, is was mostly a technical rebound after the sharp slide rather than a signal of improvement in the stock market (Figure 9-3).

9.2.3 *The U.S. treasury bond market*

U.S. fiscal deficit and government debt increased sharply as a result of the current financial crisis, putting the sustainability of U.S. debt into question. Tax revenue fell while rescue expenditure went up sharply, and this would cause U.S. fiscal deficit to reach a historical record of US$ 1.8 trillion in 2009. Such deficit was expected to increase from 3.2% in 2008 to 13% in 2009 as a share of GDP and would be at a level of 9.9% and 6.5% in 2010 and 2011 respectively.[2] In 2008, the U.S. government's total

---

[2]Congressional Budget Office, Economic Projections for 2009–2019 (March 2009).

accumulated debt amounted to US$ 10 trillion, accounting for 70.2% of GDP, including public-held debt (net debt) of US$ 5.8 trillion that accounted for 40.8% of GDP. It was predicted that by 2011, the U.S. government's total debt and public-held debt would increase to US$ 15.7 trillion and US$ 10.9 trillion, respectively, accounting for 101.1% and 70.1% of GDP, the highest in six decades.[3]

In the short term, the challenge facing the United States is to how to make up the 2009 deficit by making a net issue of US$ 2 trillion in treasury bonds without sharply increasing its cost. Due to the impact of the financial crisis, however, this target could hardly be achieved. First, market concern about the U.S. economy and the value of the dollar caused U.S. bonds yield to rise. Compared to the low points in December 2008, the yield of a 10-year U.S. bond increased by about 2% points by the end of July 2009.[4] Borrowing cost would go up by approximately US$ 100 billion for each per percentage point increase in average government bond yield. Second, U.S. bonds might encounter inadequate demand. Tightened liquidity might result in shrinking demand from U.S. domestic investors. And the sharp decline in export growth caused corresponding decline in the foreign exchange reserves of East Asian emerging market economies. Caused by depressed prices of the global energy and commodities markets, growth in the foreign exchange reserves of resource export countries would also be sluggish. The balance of payments surplus in Germany and Japan would fall as well. All these factors would contribute to the decline of surplus savings and funds available for lending worldwide, thus making it difficult for the United States to borrow at a low cost.

In the mid and long term, the sustainability of U.S. debt borrowing is worrisome. Fixed expenditures such as social and medical insurance will continue to increase. The United States' basic fiscal balance (i.e., the balance of payments before repayment expenditures are excluded) will be in deficit for a long time to come. In other words, the United States must borrow to repay old debts, including payments on interest. This means that as such debt accumulates, its share of GDP will also continue to increase.

---

[3] Office of Management and Budget, http://www.whitehouse.gov/omb/budget/Historicals/.
[4] Bloomberg.

(*Percent*)

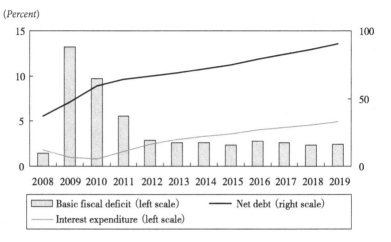

Figure 9-4 Proportions of U.S. Basic Fiscal Deficit, Net Debt, and Interest Expenditure in GDP

Source: IMF, *World Economic Outlook Database* (April 2009).

9.3 The Global Financial Crisis Serves as a Catalyst for Reform of the International Monetary System

The dollar-based international monetary system emerged over two decades ago following the end of the World War II. Because of the dominant power of the United States, despite the collapse of the Bretton Woods system, the global monetary system has remained dollar-based, and no other currency can yet take the place of the dollar in the near term.

After suffering the impact of the financial crisis in the late 1990s, East Asian countries began to accumulate a huge amount of foreign exchange reserves, mostly in dollars, in order to prevent against future external impact. At the same time, the United States became the sole superpower after the Cold War. Therefore, for nearly two decades after 1990, the international monetary system was actually an extension of the Bretton Woods system and is known as the Post-Bretton Woods system[5] (Dooley, 2003).

---

[5]The existing international monetary system is known as the Jamaica System or Dollar Standard, with such credit money as the dollar acting as a global currency. Dollar Standard is essentially an extension of the Bretton Woods System, also known as Post-Bretton Woods System.

However, what is different is that, under the current system, the U.S. government no longer bases the value of the dollar on gold as in the Bretton Woods system. The United States levies seigniorage for international use of the dollar but does not bear any responsibility for balancing international current account deficit. In other words, a major feature of this system is that U.S. monetary policy is pursued to meet the domestic needs of the United States rather than adjusting balance of international payments equilibrium (Byrant, 2008). The seigniorage privilege has caused the continued growth of the U.S. current account deficit, giving rise to "New Triffin Dilemma" (McCauley, 2003). In studying the capital flow mechanisms of the United States and of East Asian countries, McCauley pointed out that given the unsustainable U.S. current account deficit, there is an irreconcilable conflict between the United States' intermediary status in international finance and its absorption of other countries' international investment. By issuing treasury bonds (liabilities), the United States absorbs the foreign exchange capital of East Asian countries and other trade surplus countries and thus acquires financing for its current account deficits. Because of this process, East Asia countries and other trade surplus countries have become a "quasi bank" of the United States. However, the key problem is that the capital supply (i.e., the dollar backflow) of this "quasi bank" is met by foreign direct investment from the United States and its current account deficits. Once U.S. investment decreases and its current account deficit shrinks, the money supply for the East Asian "quasi bank" will drop. It will then affect the U.S. financial market and threaten the intermediary status of the United States in international finance.

Back in the 1980s, I wrote about the unjust nature of the international monetary system in which the country that issues the reserve currency is unable to balance the conflict between the need of internal policies and the need of global economic development (Li Ruogu, 1986). The 2008 financial crisis occurred because the loose U.S. monetary policy resulted in liquidity flooding the global market, which drives down interest rate in the U.S. financial market and thus generated rarely seen bubbles in the real estate market and derivatives. The United States arbitrarily pursues any policy that is beneficial to itself without giving any consideration to its impact on the world economy, while other countries have to bear the consequences of flawed U.S. economic policies. "Crises are not necessarily the intended result of the issuing of reserve currency, but they are the inevitable systemic outcome".[6] Therefore, the emergence and escalation of the new financial crisis has much to do with the global economic imbalance and the "Post-Bretton Woods System".[7] Right after the East Asian financial crisis, I wrote about the need to accelerate the reform of the international monetary system in order to prevent a similar financial crisis from occurring.[8] Unfortunately, nothing much has been done.

The outbreak and spread of the 2008 global financial crisis fully show that the "New Triffin Dilemma" is still an unsolvable problem within the current international monetary system. Therefore, in order to improve the performance of the international monetary system and address the balance of payments balance in a steady, effective and safe manner, it is imperative to carry out a major reform of the foundation of the current international monetary system, namely, the dollar standard.

On November 15, 2008, G20 leaders held a summit on "Financial Markets and the World Economy" in Washington DC. It was the first summit held between major developed countries and developing countries in the world after the outbreak of the U.S. subprime lending crisis. The summit reviewed both the domestic factors in the United States and international factors which led to the subprime lending crisis. It examined major issues like global economic imbalance, the dollar and the international monetary system dominated by the International Monetary Fund, and explored various ways to deepen the reform of the international monetary system.

Afterward, on April 2, 2009, G20 leaders held another summit in London during which they committed themselves to work together to fight the global financial crisis. The declaration released after the summit shows that the world leaders were confident in meeting the crisis, promoting economic recovery and carrying out reform. The summit leaders reached broad consensus on the need to promote global economic recovery, enhance financial supervision, consolidate global financial institutions, increase global

---

[6]Li Ruogu (1986).

[7]Li Ruogu (2006), p. 22.

[8]Li Ruogu (2002).

trade and investment, and ensure fair and sustainable economic recovery for all countries. British Prime Minister Gordon Brown pointed out that the summit and its declaration marked the emergence of a "new world order".

Commitment to rebuild the international monetary system is considered one of the five major outcomes of the London Summit that will have a major impact on the reform of international monetary system. Since the collapse of the Bretton Woods system, the role of the International Monetary Fund (IMF) has been severely weakened. As a result, it can neither coordinate international currency cooperation nor maintain and protect the integrity of the international monetary system. A heated and extensive international debate on the current international monetary system and the functions of the IMF is going on.

Some members of the U.S. Congress and scholars like Charles K. Rowley believe that the rebuilding of the international monetary system is a false proposition and that the IMF should be abolished altogether. They hold that through self-regulation, the market can resolve problems in the international monetary system. However, most people consider it necessary to deepen the reform of the international monetary system and strengthen the function of the IMF. At the London Summit, reform of the international monetary system was put on the agenda, and important progress was made in this respect. The participating leaders agreed to contribute US$ 750 billion to the IMF to enhance its function. It was also agreed to increase funding for other international financial institutions so as to extensively enhance their roles in promoting growth. The summit also agreed to put in place a mechanism of international monetary supervision with its focus on the IMF.

Chapter 10

Adjust Global Economic Imbalance and Reform the International Monetary System

Since the eruption of the current financial crisis, the U.S. government has taken unprecedented steps to contain it. These steps included a dramatic lowering of benchmark interest rates, direct injection of liquidity, tax exemption, economic stimulus programs, financial stabilization programs, and troubled assets relief program. The European Union, Britain, Japan, and emerging economies have all adopted large scale relief and stimulus programs. It must be pointed out, however, that 2008 financial crisis was triggered by both global economic imbalance and the accumulated inherent conflicts within the international monetary system. Measures taken by these countries were mostly a response to the crisis. As long as the systemic causes of such imbalance remain, a new crisis cannot be avoided.[1]

In 2006, I already pointed out that the increasing global financial imbalance had become a major factor affecting global economic and financial stability. Imbalance in international capital flow, the international capital market, international trade and the international monetary

---

[1]Li Ruogu (2006), p. 41.

system, as well as the dysfunction of the international coordination mechanisms together would make global finance and economy a fragile one. To resolve this issue requires a common global response. In the opinion of Aheame (2007), there are two ways to correct the global economic imbalance and address distortions in the international monetary system. One is for major countries to implement adjustment through policy coordination. The other is just letting the financial market's self-correction mechanism to address the international economic imbalance and the international monetary system distortions. The former is an incremental and non-destructive adjustment, while the latter is an eruptive and destructive adjustment. Unfortunately, the second adjustment is what has been happening over the years.

The eruption of the financial crisis is a way to address economic imbalance. But the cost is contraction of global financial activities, while problems in a twisted international monetary system still remain. To avoid such a situation, it is necessary for countries to pursue proactive and coordinated adjustment policies. Using the core country (the United States) vs. peripheral countries (East Asian and oil-exporting countries) model, we can classify adjustment of global economic imbalances and the international monetary system into three types — unilateral adjustment, multilateral adjustment, and regional and international monetary system adjustment. As each type of adjustment involves different participants and different approaches, the feasibility of these adjustments and their impact on the international monetary system and balance of payments vary greatly.

10.1 Unilateral Adjustment

10.1.1 *Unilateral adjustment made by trade surplus countries*

The East Asian countries and oil-exporting countries could take initiative to reduce dependence on the dollar. First, they could reduce the share of the dollar assets in their foreign exchange reserves by selling dollar assets. Secondly, they could use other currencies or a basket of currencies to settle transactions in international trade. Thirdly, they could use other currencies, or a basket of currencies, in commodities pricing. Fourthly, they could adjust growth model and transition from export-led economy to domestic demand driven economy to reduce dependence on the U.S. market.

If the East Asian countries and oil-exporting countries were to make such adjustments, it would be the worst choice for both the U.S. economy and the global economy. Since there is no agreement between the United States and other countries on their respective obligations of sharing the job of correcting the international economic disequilibrium, there would be no coordinated adjustment, and this would leave adjustment in the hands of the financial market. Collective selling of dollar assets by East Asian countries would result in a sharp devaluation of the dollar and a plunge in the price of the U.S. treasury bonds. This would also lead to a long-term rise in U.S. interest rates and thus would be a heavy blow to the U.S. real estate and stock markets. The U.S. economy would be dragged into a severe recession. This means that the engine for global economic growth would stop and that there would be a decline in demand for global import, thus triggering a recession in the global economy.

However, such proactive adjustment cannot be pursued in a practical sense. Because by holding a huge amount of dollar assets, the East Asian and oil-exporting countries have to some extent become hostages of the United States (Guan Zhixiong, 2006). These countries are unlikely to sell their dollar assets on a large scale. A falling U.S. dollar exchange rate caused by collectively selling would lead to a severe shrinking of their respective foreign exchange reserves. Therefore, the most they could do is to sell out a small portion of their dollar assets to give a warning to the United States. Also, the decline of the U.S. economy would cause a corresponding decline in U.S. demand for global import. This, in turn, would trigger reduction in export, decrease in GDP growth, and hit the export sector of East Asian countries. This would also hurt employment in these countries. Such adjustment is therefore not feasible.

10.1.2 *Unilateral adjustment taken by trade deficit countries*

As the source of 2008 financial crisis, the United States is responsible for the eruption and the spread of the crisis. Theoretically, if the United States can shift its growth model which depends on excessive borrowing and consumption, and if the American consumers can increase personal savings, the size of the U.S. current account deficit would be reduced. The United States would not need massive capital inflow, and its net foreign debts would be reduced accordingly. Thus, the amount of the dollar issued would be smaller and the dollar's exchange rate would remain at a relatively stable level, making the Triffin Dilemma less an issue for the dollar standard. Such an outcome would be a desired one for both international trade and the stability of the international monetary system.

In reality, however, the United States is unwilling to make such adjustment. After the financial crisis broke out, the U.S. personal savings rate increased significantly from 0.4% in 2007 to 3.2% by the end of 2008.[2] It was a natural response to the financial crisis, and it is too early to say that the U.S. consumption model has changed. Obviously, it does not serve its best interests for the United States to make the above mentioned adjustment. The current international monetary system is based on the dollar. The United States can purchase overseas goods and services by printing bank notes. By means of currency devaluation, it can also evade part of its responsibility for debt repayment. As the current international monetary system best serves the interests of the United States, it is unlikely that the United States will take the initiative to change it.

10.2 Multilateral Adjustment

Multilateral adjustment refers to agreement reached by both trade surplus and trade deficit countries on correcting disequilibrium in international payments and on sharing the cost of reforming the current international monetary system. Additionally, parties involved need to adjust domestic policies so that they are in keeping with the above mentioned agreement reached. Here, whether a country is a surplus or deficit country is determined by its overall balance of payments rather than by its specific surplus or deficit with a single trade partner. Adjustment in both trade surplus and trade deficit must be made by all the countries involved at the same time,

---

[2]U.S. BEA.

not only between two countries. One country may be in trade deficit with Country A, but can be in surplus with Country B. So, bilateral adjustment is a one-sided approach. Disequilibrium in international payments should be considered as a whole. For instance, trade imbalance between China and the United States has attracted a lot of attention. But China only accounts for 20% of the total U.S. trade deficit. Even if adjustment is made between China and the United States, it will not solve all of the United States' problems. Therefore, to prevent the market from once again correcting global imbalances by means of financial crisis, it is necessary for all the major countries in the world to adjust their respective domestic policies in a coordinated way so that they can make a unified adjustment internationally.

First of all, the United States which has trade deficit and countries with trade surplus such as East Asian countries need to carry out synchronized adjustment. The rebalancing of consumption and savings between the United States and East Asia is beneficial to the whole world. It will reduce the dependence of the East Asian countries on trade of goods and balance of payments, and it will also strengthen the foundation of global economy and its stability. As a country in trade deficit, the United States should reduce its fiscal deficit and raise government savings, and it should adjust the structure of individual expenditure and increase personal savings. This will promote the growth of its real economy and stop economic hollowing. Secondly, East Asian countries in surplus (especially China) should increase public expenditure, increase dividend payment of state-owned enterprises (listed companies) so as to reduce governments' savings. The distribution of national income should shift towards all those who work to raise individual income. All this plus improved social security system can cause personal savings to drop, and domestic demand can be boosted as a result. However, developing countries must strike a balance between transition and development. Due to their limited domestic markets and the weak purchasing power of their population, many developing countries, especially small and medium ones, will find it difficult to break away from the export-led development model overnight. It takes time for them to make such adjustment.

Other countries, especially the European countries and Japan, should accelerate their respective structural reform, speed up GDP growth, and open their markets wider. In short, all the parties involved should live up to their responsibilities for adjustment and share their due cost, and this would benefit both the United States and the global economy.

10.3 Regional and International Monetary Cooperation

It should be pointed out that even if major countries in imbalance could reach agreement on a multilateral adjustment, it would only bring about partial improvement of the current system. It could help relieve global economic imbalance, but it could not resolve the core issue, namely, one country's currency acting as the main global reserve currency. At a time when no single country can challenge the position of the United States and the dollar, strengthening regional economic, financial, and monetary cooperation should be a feasible approach in the short- to mid-term, while long-term efforts should be made to create a unified international currency.

In the case of Asia, because of cultural differences and historical reasons, there is no effective monetary coordination among Asian countries, and it will be difficult to create a unified monetary union as that has been achieved in Europe. But this does not mean that Asia cannot carry out regional monetary cooperation. Enhancing the mechanism for regional crisis warning, relief, and reconstruction, further developing the Asian bond market, steadily promoting the multilateral arrangement of the Chiang Mai Initiative (CMI) and accelerating the setting up of an Asian reserve pool, all these steps can serve as both preventative and remedy measures and means to strengthen monetary cooperation (Li Ruogu, 2001). In other words, the formation of a unified Asian currency can only take a natural course. It could be a country's currency, or using the currency of a country as benchmark, or even a unified Asian currency similar to the euro. Whatever form it should take, such a currency should evolve in a natural way instead of being imposed upon the Asian countries. Such regional monetary cooperation, transitional in nature, could serve as a base for enhancing global monetary cooperation.

From a global perspective, international monetary cooperation can reduce uncertainty of the market and exchange rates. The so-called free floating exchange rate regime of the current international monetary system is detrimental to a country's domestic macroeconomic regulation and price stabilization. While floating exchange rate regime does help maintain a country's independent monetary policy, such independence is only a means to an end. The goal should be stabilization of macro-economy and currency value, a foundation on which growth is based. In an open economic environment, unusual domestic capital market fluctuation of one country can affect the international market. Likewise, an international capital market crisis will quickly spread the domestic market of individual countries. In other words, an independent monetary policy cannot fully shield the spillover effect of the capital market, and frequent fluctuation in the capital market weakens the effectiveness of a country's monetary policy. Therefore, by conceding partial monetary sovereignty to enhance international cooperation, countries can reduce uncertainty of foreign exchange markets and exchange rates and eventually benefit from such cooperation.

To build consensus and pursue in-depth cooperation between countries is crucial in advancing the reform of the international monetary system and address the root of the imbalance and turbulence in international finance. First, it is necessary to establish a global currency (not based on a sovereign currency) to avoid the Triffin Dilemma (Li Ruogu, 2006). The currency basket designed for the new international currency should accurately reflect the new global economic composition. The United States should undertake the responsibility to address imbalance of international payments and be mindful of the external effect of its domestic policy. The next step should be to reform the institutional vehicles of the international monetary system, especially the IMF (Li Ruogu, 2004, 2006). The governance structure of the IMF should be strengthened, and the IMF should be given more funding and more authority. It should be able to effectively monitor whether the United States and other relevant countries have lived up their respective responsibilities. Additionally, it should monitor closely risk factors in both individual economies and the international economy as a whole, so as to lower systemic risk and to conduct relief and reconstruction when necessary. The third step should be to establish a mechanism for managing risks in the international financial market. An enhanced Financial Stability Board (FSB) should have the authority to regulate large-scale financial institutions, mutual funds, and hedge funds of systemic significance. International capital flow, especially hot money flow, should also be closely monitored to defuse their risks. These steps will create necessary conditions for reforming the international monetary system. These points will be discussed in greater detail in the following chapters.

Part Four

Reform of the Current International Monetary System

Following the disintegration of the Bretton Woods system, in addition to the dollar, the euro and the Japanese yen have gradually become the main international reserve currencies, but the International Monetary Fund (IMF) has remained the primary institution of supervision and coordination. Since the 1990s, economic globalization and financial sector has faced continued instability. Financial crises have plagued Mexico, Southeast Asia, Argentina, Brazil, Russia, and Turkey. Western scholars, government officials, and experts from international institutions like the IMF place blame for these crises on the countries hit by crises, and few people have seen the underlying cause, namely, the flaws in the current international monetary system. The 2008 global financial crisis triggered by the subprime crisis in the United States has caused huge losses to the world economy. This has made the international monetary system and thus created an important opportunity to restructure this system (Li Ruogu, 2008). On the basis of discussing various proposals for reforming the international monetary system (Part Four, Chapter 11), this section explores feasible reform option (Part Four, Chapter 12) and the role China can play in the reform process (Part Four, Chapter 13).

Chapter 11

Proposals for Reforming the International Monetary System

The dollar-based international monetary system, which has failed to adapt to changes in the world economy, has become the single most important cause of the current problems in the international financial system, and urgent reform is called for (Li Ruogu, 1986, 2002, 2008). Reform proposals put forward fall into the following four categories.

11.1 Returning to Keynesian Plan and Establishing a New Bretton Woods System

Prior to the Bretton Woods conference in 1944, John Maynard Keynes, representing Britain, proposed a monetary cooperation plan ahead of the United States. This plan included the following elements: (1) creating an international currency unit, (2) coupling sovereign currencies with the international unit, (3) sharing responsibility by trading parties to correct imbalance of payments, and (4) forming an international clearing union. In this plan, Keynes designed the "Bancor", a neutral unit for use as the international currency and proposed the establishment of a basket of currencies based on 30 commodities such as gold, grains, petroleum, copper, etc. as the basis for defining and stabilizing the currency's value. In addition, he proposed that a new financial institution called the International

Clearing Union should take responsibility for issuing and managing the Bancor. With the Bancor serving as the standard, central banks would link the value of their currencies to the Bancor through fixed but adjustable exchange rates. All international trade would be settled in Bancors. Countries that exported more than they imported were termed "Creditor Nations", and those that imported more than they exported were termed "Debtor Nations".

According to the Keynes Plan, both creditor and debtor nations would have equal obligation to maintain balanced trade. The International Clearing Union would charge debtor nations a small amount of interest on their overdrawn account to press these nations to adjust domestic policies by conducting currency devaluation and export promotion. For creditor nations, the International Clearing Union would charge a fee on their surplus account so as to encourage them to spend their excess Bancors and reduce their surplus. If a nation could maintain its balance of trade, its national Bancor trade account surplus in the International Clearing Union would be minimal or even zero. Such interest and fees were intended not so much as a penalty, but as a benign feedback mechanism. Keynes' hope was to promote balance of trade between countries through this system.

Some economists call for a return to the Keynes Plan, proposing that major economies should reach an international monetary cooperation agreement on creating a world currency unit. Sovereign currencies should be linked with the world currency unit, and the International Monetary Fund (IMF) should be turned into a world central bank. This proposal was first made by Robert Mundell, who, as early as in 1968, proposed the substitution of the dollar with a world currency. In 2005, he proposed the establishment of new world currency unit called the DEY[1] based on the dollar, euro, and yen. Mundell pointed out that the current crisis could enable people to reach consensus, and 2010 would be a good time to launch a world currency.

Scholars such as Ronald McKinnon and Peter Kenen also believe that under certain conditions, a monetary union or a unified global currency could be the best choice. Morrison Bonpasse, President of Single Global Currency Association which is a non-governmental organization in the

---

[1] First letter of Dollar, Euro, and Yen.

United States, called for establishing a global central bank. At the beginning, this institution would play the role of an international supervisory body. He proposed a target date of 2024, the 80th anniversary of the Bretton Woods system, as a timeline for establishing a unified global currency.

Cooper holds similar views (2007). In his opinion, the only way to stabilize exchange rates is to establish an institution with international authority to issue a special currency for international trade, and all countries should pursue a unified monetary policy. He calls for a step by step approach, namely, setting up an exchange rate target system in the first few years, followed by forming a single currency system between America, Japan, and Europe in a decade, and ultimately transitioning to a single global currency system.

In the political circle, former British Prime Minister Gordon Brown is the most active one in calling for the establishment of a new Bretton Woods system. Japan does not explicitly endorse this idea, but has indicated that it prefers a basket of currencies composed of dollar, euro, and Japanese yen.

11.2 Special Drawing Rights as the International Currency and IMF as the World Central Bank

Some scholars believe that if the global economy is to be viewed as an integral whole, the IMF should play the role of the central bank and it should adopt a quasi inflation targeting system to ensure stable global growth in a low inflation environment and maintain stability of the international financial system.

Schneider and Tornell (2000) proposed to strengthen the core role the IMF should play within the international monetary system: it should to some extent function as the global central bank. It should set up a comprehensive mechanism to maintain relative stability of exchange rates among major international currencies, assume responsibility in maintaining the stability of overall international price levels, defuse global inflation risk, supervise banks which issue major reserve currencies, and issue a new international currency for valuation and settling international accounts, for global investment transactions, and as reserve assets.

In the opinion of Egyptian economist Samir Amin, the IMF should be converted into a global central bank with the authority to issue a world currency to replace the dollar. This currency should ensure stability of exchange rates and provide developing countries with the solvency needed for "adjustment in growth".

Some other scholars propose to expand the functions of Special Drawing Right (SDR) so that it could become a fully-fledged global currency unit. In the opinion of Li Ruogu (2001, 2002), the way to reform the unjust international monetary system is to create a new international currency or currency unit not based on the currency of any single country. This currency would be used as the international reserve currency and for exchange and settling accounts. Soon after the founding of the IMF, this type of proposal was discussed but not adopted. For example, the IMF in the 1960s created the SDR, commonly regarded as a feasible substitute for the dollar. But the SDR was not allocated on a large scale due to the opposition of major developed countries. The international community should study ways to replace the current system which relies heavily on the currency of one country with a new one. However, the composition of the SDR should be changed to reflect due changes in the current international economic system.

In the opinion of Greenwald and Stiglitz (2006), to reform the international monetary system, a kind of international reserve assets, more stable than the dollar and other reserve currencies, should be available. One effective way would be to issue a substantial amount of SDR, which would be valued on weighted average of a basket of convertible currencies and would thus be less sensitive to fluctuation of individual currencies. The SDR could become a more extensive foreign exchange reserve as well as a measuring unit for commodities and raw materials.

11.2.1 The SDR has many benefits as an international reserve asset

Since the international reserves grow annually at a rate of about 7%, an amount of SDR valued at US$ 200 billion would be sufficient to meet such demands. With the SDR serving as the international reserve, the United States will not be able to unscrupulously increase its trade deficit and debt by taking advantage of the dollar's status as the primary international reserve currency. The SDR would thus play an important role in maintaining stability of both the value of the dollar and dollar assets. Competition for external liquidity, especially for relief funds during crisis, and beggar-thy-neighbor exchange rate policies would be greatly reduced, which should help stabilize balance of payments and exchange rates. Taking the SDR as the single international currency will not only put an end to various abuses of the multi-currency monetary system; more importantly, it could simplify the process of foreign currency exchange. Additionally, with its relatively stable value, the SDR would create a favorable environment for promoting global growth.

11.2.2 Some conditions should be met for the SDR to act as the main reserve asset

Theoretically speaking, the viability of the SDR hinges on two major factors: (1) For the SDR value to be determined by a basket of currencies, it is necessary to establish trade weights for currencies concerned at a reasonable level. (2) Since the SDR's role is based on multilateral coordination and not on state sovereignty, the functions and power of the IMF as an international multilateral agency should be further strengthened.

On the technical level, to substitute the SDR for multiple reserve currencies, the following steps should be taken: first, the SDR should be used in international trade as the currency to price all commercial products so as to enlarge the scope of its application. Secondly, a market for SDR trading should be opened to increase its liquidity. Furthermore, mandatory trade clearing should be conducted in the SDR. Allocation of the SDR should be expanded so that foreign exchange reserves of all member countries should be converted into the SDR within a specified period of time. In other words, all countries should convert dollars, euros, and other currencies in their foreign exchange reserves into the SDR. Finally, countries should reach consensus on time needed for the transition.

11.3 The Dollar Serves as the Sole World Currency and the Federal Reserve Serves as the World Central Bank

It is proposed that the dollar could be turned into the sole international currency, and the Federal Reserve could be restructured as a world central bank. Thus the world would have a single currency system.

This proposal is based on the Optimum Currency Area theory. According to this theory, under certain conditions, a monetary union or single currency regime would be more stable than a multi-currency regime. The institutional arrangements of the euro have shown that the system of monetary union has changed people's attitude towards floating exchange rates and monetary zone.

Since the creation of the euro, growth within the euro zone has been relatively stable, policy coordination between economies has been strengthened, and both trade and financial flow within the zone has increased.

However, over the last decade, both the IMF and the United States have tried hard to preach the importance of the floating exchange rate to the international community and especially to China in recent years. They claim that if a fixed exchange rate system were adopted, there would be increased risk of imbalances, both domestic and international, and this could trigger economic crisis. The outbreak and spread of the global financial crisis, however, shows the opposite: adoption of floating exchange rates exacerbates the impact of a financial crisis upon the financial sector and the real economy. In addition, there is no convincing definition of the so-called floating exchange rates system, which has been viewed as a concept relative to fixed exchange rates. In reality, "float" should have a benchmark. Because of the difficulty to identify such a benchmark, the dollar-based exchange rate system has become one of the root causes for the frequent crises in the current international financial system (Li Ruogu, 2008).

There are several barriers to the dollar becoming the sole international currency and the Federal Reserve becoming the world central bank. First, would the United States be willing to give up its monetary sovereignty? In pursuing its monetary policy, the United States would have to take into account the world economy, not just its domestic economic situation. How could a unified global monetary policy coordinate policies pursued by economies with different structures in different stages of development? Secondly, being the world central bank, would the Federal Reserve be immune to U.S. political influence? Instead of having an exclusive American staff, would it be possible that staff of the Federal Reserve be composed of people from all the countries? Thirdly, how could other countries participate in the management of this system? How should seigniorage be distributed? Could the euro zone management system be adopted, or could the United States remain the sole manager? As the European Commission and the Council of European Central Bank (which consists of central banks of countries of all European Union (EU) members) have authority over the European Central Bank, which super-state government body would supervise the Federal Reserve? Could the United Nations play this role? What would be the internal governance structure of the Federal Reserve? Fourthly, being the currency of the United States, the dollar would still face the Triffin Dilemma (BIS, 2003). On first look, for the dollar to serve as the sole world currency and the Federal Reserve serve as the world central bank would be the easiest reform proposal. In reality, however, this proposal would be hard to carry out due to lack of technical and systemic arrangements.

11.4 Enhance Regional Monetary Cooperation and Build Three Islands of Stability Consisting of the U.S. Dollar, the Euro, and the Asian Dollar

It has been proposed that regional currencies could be used to stabilize both exchange rates and market and prevent and defuse crisis. A diversified international monetary system or regionalized monetary regime could be formed through enhancing regional monetary and financial security systems through bilateral or multilateral coordination. For instance, through internationalizing the Chiang Mai Initiative, Asia could establish a regional reserve fund for fending off financial crisis and to be used as relief funding. Deepening the development of bond markets in Asia could resolve issues such as high proportion of indirect financing, currency mismatch, and maturity mismatch. Such an approach would remove the root cause of financial crisis. When conditions are ripe, the Asian dollar could be launched. Thus, the international monetary system would consist of "Three Islands of Stability" supported by the U.S. dollar, the euro, and the Asian dollar.

Under the regionalized international monetary system, there would be unified monetary unions and currency zones in the three regions. Within each region, internal exchange rate fluctuation and speculation between member economies would then be eliminated. Additionally, a comprehensive exchange rate stabilization system could be set up between the "Three Islands of Stability". For instance, by means of monetary agreements, exchange rates among the three currencies could be maintained within a certain range but with some elasticity. Technically, this approach is workable: the dollar would still act as the pivot currency, while the euro, and the future Asian dollar would maintain exchange rate stability through international coordination. A mechanism could be put in place on sharing seigniorage. This system would be similar to the single currency union, which are currency unions with fixed exchange rates for major economic regions in the world (Mundell, 2000).

Chapter 12

Realistic Choice for Reforming the International Monetary System

Each of the proposals mentioned earlier has both its rationale and uncertainty. Realistically, none of them can be fully adopted in its own right. The reform of the international monetary system involves both parties of vested interests and those whose interests are hurt. This process will be one of hard bargaining between countries. At the same time, it will also be a process of evolution of the global economic order, a complex process fraught with conflicts. As no new pole has emerged in the international financial arena, the road towards reforming the international monetary system, international coordination mechanisms, and international financial institutions would be a long and twisted one. Reaching a compromise would be the only realistic choice.

12.1 Reform of the International Monetary System Takes Time

History of the evolution of international currencies shows that the evolution of the international monetary system is a long process from quantitative change to qualitative change. As the relative strengths of countries involved vary greatly, the dollar-based international monetary system will not change any time soon. The reform of this system takes time.

12.1.1 *Lessons learnt from the evolution of international currencies*

Fighting for monetary power has been an important part of great power rivalry. Along with military power, monetary power has always been a key part of a country's overall state power. Monetary power was behind the expansion of major powers, and military power paved the way for these countries to realize even greater monetary and financial gains. The history of relations between major powers is one of fight for monetary supremacy. Major powers sought to internationalize their respective currencies and resultant political dominance and huge economic benefits. At the same time, they all did their utmost to prevent others from making similar gains. As Eichengreen (2006) pointed out, the international monetary system had always been dominated by a power structure composed of financial interests. Zhang Yuyan termed this as unannounced fierce rivalry between major powers.[1]

According to Modelski's Long Cycle Theory, a world war occurred every 100 years and resulted in the rise of a new global hegemonic power. Another hegemonic power would take over after a century. From the start of the 16th century, Portugal, Holland, Britain, and the United States successively acquired that position and became the dominant global power. After the emergence of a unified global market, British pound sterling and the dollar one after another became the hard currency for international payments and settlement. The rise and fall of a big power ultimately finds expression in changes in its monetary power.

In 1821, Britain introduced the gold standard, with each pound valued at 7.32238 grams of gold. This stablized the value of the pound. The Bank of England Regulation issued in 1844 gave the Bank of England sole authority of issuing the pound. Functioning as the central bank, the Bank of England maintained the strong position of the pound. Following the Crimea War in 1856, Britain's economic power swelled. With its

---

[1]Zhang Yuyan (2009).

economic and military strengths, Britain made Portugal, Germany, France, Holland, and Spain accept the gold standard. As a result, the international gold standard took shape in the 1870s, and the pound became the international currency for close to 100 years.

After World War II, changes in the relative power of countries led to the emergence of a new international financial and monetary system, as reflected in the Bretton Woods Agreement reached in July, 1944. By carrying out the Marshall Plan, the United States flooded Europe with the dollar and turned it into the most important pricing, settlement, and reserve currency. This established the dollar's dominant position in the international monetary system.

The historical evolution of the international monetary system from a British pound-dominated one to a dollar-dominated one shows that a country needs to meet several basic conditions for its currency to become a major international currency: first, it should have a strong economy, which is the foundation for the internationalization of any currency. Second, timing is important. For instance, World War I weakened the position of the pound, the 1930s Crisis led to the collapse of the existing international monetary system, and World War II turned the United States into the world's only superpower. Under the current global political and economic system, drastic change in the United States and European-dominated political and economic governance structure is not likely, while developing countries, whether individually or collectively, are not yet able to compete with developed countries in the political, economic, and military spheres. Therefore, the fundamental reform of the global economic order and the international financial system cannot take place overnight.

12.1.2 *The dollar will remain dominant in the near future*

The dollar, as a major currency, is the most important vehicle of American economic power and represents the U.S. national interests. Therefore, the United States will do everything to protect its position and the dollar-based monetary system.

The United States is still the strongest economic power in the world, and the dollar will remain a major global currency. Despite the severe impact exerted by the financial crisis on the American economy, it is expected that the American economy and its financial system are still able to retain resilience after the crisis, and it will continue to lead in science and technology. All these factors have ensured the strength of the dollar. In the short term, there will be no fundamental change in the dollar's position in international trade, foreign exchange reserves, and financial market transactions.

When a country's currency becomes an international currency, it will encounter the Triffin Dilemma. As such a currency needs to play the role of conducting international settlement, to ensure that other countries will have sufficient amounts of currency for making international transactions, the currency issuing state needs to ensure a steady supply of its currency to the international market through either trade deficit or large-scale overseas investment. On the other hand, serving as the international reserve currency, such a currency should maintain both stability and its strength. And this calls for the currency issuing state to maintain long-term trade surplus. This conflict is irreconcilable.

It is difficult for countries with different interests to agree on a monetary system acceptable to all. To protect its own interests, the United States will not yield the dollar's position as an international currency. The EU's political and economic integration process is a long-term one, and the EU cannot take over the U.S. leadership any time soon. While still an economic power, Japan's influence in the global economy is declining, and the Japanese yen's role as an international currency is diminishing. All this makes it difficult for Japan to play the role of a global economic power.

In short, the dollar-based international monetary system is not likely to change in the short term. Despite the numerous flaws of this system, it is difficult to replace it with another one soon, and the reform of the international monetary system will be a long-term endeavor.

12.2 A Realistic Pathway for Reforming the International Monetary System

The 2008 global financial crisis has provided an opportunity to reform the international financial and monetary systems. Although the American and European financial sectors were hard hit by the crisis, the global configuration of political, economic, and financial power has not been fundamentally changed. To overhaul the current international monetary system in the short term is therefore not feasible. A more realistic choice would be a step-by-step approach.

The reform of the international monetary systems could be carried out in two phases (Li Ruogu, 2008). Phase one is a transitional period during which the stability of the dollar-based international monetary system should be maintained. The euro and other currencies which are qualified as international currencies should play their due role in this system. At the same time, the United States' macro-economic policies and its currency issuance should be kept in check to prevent the United States from reverting to the practice of using loose monetary policy to stimulate economic recovery and thus sow the seed of economic bubble. Major economies should reach consensus and make compromises. The United States should curb the growth of dollar supply and consumer spending, while other countries should boost domestic demands and reduce dependence on export. This transitional period could last 5 to 10 years or for a longer period.

The goal of the second phase is to restructure the international monetary system and build a fairer and more equitable international financial order. The core issue involved is the selection of currency as the standard of international reserves. Proposals raised so far include the following: returning to the gold standard, restoring the dollar standard, establishing a commodity reserve standard, and turning the SDR into the basic international reserves.

Returning to the gold standard would avoid excessive issuance of currency and prevent a few countries from collecting inflation-based taxes and seigniorage and make it hard to practice protectionism by changing normal exchange rates. However, the gold standard has a fatal flaw: the gap between finite supply of gold and the infinite nature of economic growth. Thus, the gold standard which was abandoned over half a century ago is not a feasible option. Because of the inherent defect of using a single currency as the reserve currency, the dollar standard has been proved unstable, as 2008 financial crisis has shown. A commodity reserve standard is not realistic. The last proposal, namely, turning the SDR into a real currency for payments, is a practical choice. The SDR, based on a basket of currencies, could replace the dollar. This means establishing a new Bretton Woods system based on a basket of currencies. The choice of currencies to be included should be based on factors such as share of global GDP, trade, reserves, and population of countries of candidacy currencies.

12.3 Concrete Proposals for Reforming the International Monetary System

Considering the flaws of the current international monetary system and on the basis of evaluating various proposals and years of experience in international financial research and work, this author proposes to take concrete steps to reform the international monetary system in three areas: international currency, international coordination mechanism, and international financial institutions.

12.3.1 *International currency reform*

(1) Establish a mechanism for stabilizing exchange rates of major international currencies and strengthen supervision over the issuance of major reserve currencies.

For the current international monetary system to play its basic role of stabilizing exchange rates, it is important to set up a mechanism that stabilizes exchange rates between major reserve currencies such as the dollar and the euro without affecting their flexibility. Flexibility certainly does not mean sharp fluctuation. What should be achieved is relative stable exchange rates through policy adjustment and full consultation (Li Ruogu, 2006). As to weaker currencies, their issuing countries should be allowed to choose from among pegged, managed floating, and floating exchange rate systems in accordance with their respective national conditions such as the size and openness of the economy, level of inflation, flexibility of labor market, level of development of domestic financial markets, credibility of decision makers, and capital liquidity.

To reform the international monetary system, it is also necessary to strengthen supervision over the issuers of major international currencies. The United States and Europe should be stopped from printing excessive amounts of their currencies and thus shifting risks onto developing countries. For instance, as the issuer of the international reserve currency, the United States not only derives huge profit from collecting seigniorage, but also issues debts unscrupulously over a long period of time to support excessive domestic consumption in disregard of economic laws. At the same time, taking advantage of its leadership position in the international financial institutions, the United States has long evaded the supervision and check of both the international community and international organizations. As a major international currency, the dollar is unable to meet the United States' international obligation and responsibility to promote global growth and correct international imbalance. This is the core issue that must be faced in reforming the current international monetary system (Li Ruogu, 2006).

Therefore, in the short term, it is necessary to establish a mechanism for stabilizing major international currencies. As a long-term goal, it is imperative to create a non-sovereign global currency so as to set up a stable, effective and just international monetary system.

(2) Expand the functions and usage of the SDR (Li Ruogu, 2008).

Currently, the value of the SDR is based on a basket of four currencies — the dollar, euro, British pound sterling, and Japanese yen. This basket of currencies can no longer reflect the weight of various economies in the current world and would not be able to represent a future global currency. The issuance and use of the SDR is linked with the total contributions made to the IMF and the share of such contributions by its member countries. For instance, if a member country needs to use the SDR to manage crisis, it can only use the amount of the SDR equivalent to its contribution. The additional amount it can use is quite limited which can hardly meet the need to manage the crisis.

As no currency issued by any sovereign country can resolve the imbalance between risk and benefit, the only way to solve the problems in the current international monetary system is to create a global currency not based the currency of any particular country. As a basket of currencies, the SDR can serve as a prototype of this global currency. The international society should work towards this goal and increase the composition currencies of the SDR. For example, the currencies of countries that hold more than 2.5% of world exports such as China, Canada, Korea, Russia, etc. should be included. Weighting of each composite currency could be adjusted periodically in line with changes of their respective shares of the world economy and trade. Using a more diversified basket of currencies to serve as the basis of the international monetary system would better reflect the latest changes in the international economic environment, and it would be more stable than the dollar standard.

12.3.2 *Reform of international coordination mechanisms*

Both international coordination mechanisms and international financial institutions are important components of the international monetary system. These coordination mechanisms work through communication channels between various economies. After World War II, the key institutions for the coordination of economic policies were the IMF, the World Bank, and the General Agreement for Tariffs and Trade (GATT). At that time, the United States and Europe played the leadership role in these coordinating mechanisms, as the share of developing countries in the global economy was insignificant. Later, due to the recovery and development of European and Japanese economies, coordination mechanisms such as Group of Five (G5) and Group of Seven (G7) came into being. But they were exclusive clubs for developed countries, and developing countries were kept out. Within the IMF, developing countries, with less than half of the voting rights, could hardly influence the decision-making process. As developing countries needed funding support, they could only do as required by the IMF. But the IMF requirements were not necessarily in keeping with the actual conditions of many developing countries, and many of their proposals failed to work. The international economic decision-making process should focus on issues vital to developing countries. Developing countries should have a greater voice in such process so that they can decide their own future, instead of listening to the preaching of a small number of developed countries.

The viability of an international monetary system hinges on whether it serves the fundamental interests of most countries and peoples. Controlled by developed countries, the current international economic coordination and decision-making mechanisms represent the interests of these countries, not those of the developing countries. Such mechanisms are therefore not viable. If developing countries cannot benefit from global growth and remain marginalized, such global growth is not sustainable. History has shown that the existing coordination mechanisms have failed to play their due role in the past decades. At a time of increasing globalization and growing mutual interdependence, cooperation between developed and developing countries should be strengthened. Developed countries should increase assistance to developing countries so that they can share in the benefits of global growth. Only when the gap between developed and developing nations is narrowed can our world be a safe and prosperous one. Several thousand years ago, Chinese philosopher Laozi said, "The big state should show modesty". Big powers and strong countries should treat smaller and weaker ones with modesty. Regardless of size and strength, all countries should respect and cooperate with each other. This is the sure way to promote world peace and development (Li Ruogu, 2002).

Changes in the relative strengths among various countries have led to corresponding changes in the structure of international economic coordination mechanisms. Thanks to persistent efforts made by developing countries, the Group of Twenty (G20) which consists of major developed and developing countries was established in 1999. The London financial summit held in April 2009 affirmed changes in the relative strengths between developed and developing countries. To a certain degree, it recognized the international position of emerging economies. G7 used to dominate global economic governance. But this global economic governance structure is obviously outdated, and its legitimacy, representation, and effectiveness are all called into question. Participation in global economic governance by emerging economies is a natural choice for the international community. John Williamson of the U.S. Institute of International Economy (IIE) pointed out that the London Summit showed the direction of global trend. Without the participation of China, India, and Brazil, the decisions adopted would have little value.

However, there is still a long way to go before G20 could replace G7 as the main body for conducting global economic coordination. Representing the vested interests of the existing global economic order, G7 will try hard to maintain its influence in international economic affairs despite the fact that its representation and effectiveness have been greatly weakened. The opening of the G20 summit shows that the United States has realized that G7 and other mechanisms can no longer resolve the current financial crisis and the global issues created by this crisis. The trend towards close international economic coordination is thus inevitable. But developed countries will try to prevent G20 from taking over the role of G7. Only after the further rise of the overall strength of developing countries, especially the growth of relative strength of major developing countries, can G20 become the leading coordination mechanism for both international economy and global governance.

12.3.3 *Reforming international financial institutions*[2]

The Bretton Woods institutions and other existing international economic institutions were mostly established in the 1940s. As the world economy today is totally different from what it was 50 or 60 years ago, the guiding philosophy of these institutions, their organizational structure, and operational guidelines are incompatible with the present reality. Their reform therefore should be placed on the agenda.

The reform of international financial institutions mainly involves the IMF and the World Bank, the two most important international financial institutions which have the responsibility of maintaining global economic and financial stability and security. If these institutions are not reformed, it would not be possible for them to respond to both the need of economic globalization and the changes of relative strength in the global economy. Of course, this does not mean other financial institutions such as the Bank for International Settlement and regional development banks need not be reformed.

The Bretton Woods institutions have indeed gone through several rounds of reform in the past 60 years, and these institutions have made due contribution to promoting the development and stability of the global economic and financial system. In the age of increasing globalization, the task facing the IMF now is to coordinate relations among different countries in

---

[2]On reforming both international financial institutions and the Bretton Woods institution citing from Li Ruogu (2006).

growth. In particular, it should focus on supervising and coordinating economic reform and development of developed countries having major influence on the global economy to ensure stable growth of the global economy.

The World Bank's mission is to eliminate poverty, narrow the gap between developed and developing countries, ensure that gains derived from global economic development benefit all countries and people, thus achieving sustainable development. In other words, the IMF's task is to maintain macro-economic stability, while that of the World Bank is to promote micro-economic stability. These tasks are now different from the ones these institutions had 60 years ago, thus making reform necessary.

(1) Reform the IMF to keep the international monetary system stable:
In the process of restructuring the international monetary and financial systems, the function of the IMF, as a core institution, should be enhanced, and its governance structure should be reformed. It should strengthen its function of monitoring and supervising the economic policies of reserve currency issuing countries. This is an important goal of the international monetary system reform (Li Ruogu, 2008). Truman (2005) emphasized that the IMF should play a pivotal role in the global economic system, and should be empowered to monitor and control the flow of international capital. The IMF's core position in the international monetary system should be strengthened so that it will become a real pillar of the system.

The IMF should reform its governance structure in relation to basic voting rights, fund quotas, and composition of the executive board. Doing so will make it more representative of changes in the global economic system and enhance the legitimacy of the international monetary system. At present, the allocation of both quotas in the IMF and seats in its executive board are lacking in terms of representation, independence, and authority. Its operation and management have deviated from the principles of fairness, objectivity, and reciprocity, thus causing the inequitable nature of the international monetary system (Li Ruogu, 2006).

The allocation of the IMF's voting rights and quotas are not fair. Basic voting rights exist in name only, as they have given way to fund determined voting rights. Since the IMF was established, its total voting rights has increased 37 times, but the share of basic voting rights has fallen from the original 11.3% to the current 2.1%. The principle of "one country, one vote" has been replaced by the principle of "one vote per 10,000 SDRs". Basic voting rights have thus lost their original function. The fund quota which serves as the basis for allocation of voting rights is incompatible with the current global economic structure. This is shown in the fact that developed countries maintain a dominant position in the decision-making body, while the growth of economic strength of China, Brazil, and other developing countries is not fully reflected in the allocation of quotas. Hence, it is necessary to reallocate quotas, expand basic voting rights, increase the proportion of voting rights of developing countries, and prevent any country or group (e.g., EU) from having veto power (Li Ruogu, 2008). The simplest and most equitable solution is to divide voting rights between developed and developing countries, with each holding 50%; and the United States and the EU should not have veto power. The votes needed for making major decisions should be reduced from the current 85% to a more reasonable level, thus making the IMF's decision-making process a more democratic one. In April 2008, after the IMF launched the second stage of reform, the proportion of voting rights held by developing countries increased from 40.5% to 42.1% (IMF, 2008). But they are still in the minority. Moreover, there is no direct link between the reform of the composition of IMF's executive board and the reform of quotas allocation. The allocation and the number of executive board seats are actually decided by the proportion of fund quotas and voting rights held by individual countries, also a result of the IMF's operations and decision-making process. In April 2008, IMF separated the reform of the executive board from the reform of quotas and voting rights, thus sowing the seed of uncertainty in subsequent reforms. On April 2, 2009, at the London Financial Summit, leaders of the attending countries agreed that heads and senior management of international financial institutions should be selected through an open and transparent process.

The IMF should fully play its role of stabilizing exchange rates. A major defect of the current international monetary system is exchange rates volatility. Major economies pursue floating exchange rates and float their currencies independently or jointly as called for by their own interests, while the currencies of the majority of developing countries are pegged to major currencies and their exchange rates fluctuate accordingly.

The floating exchange rate itself is difficult to define. First, what kind of exchange rate system is the floating exchange rate system? The fixed exchange rate refers to the fixed value between a currency and gold. As gold is no longer the basis of value, against what benchmark does a currency float? Next, should a currency pegged to the dollar, the euro or any other currency be considered a floating one if the latter float against other currencies? Finally, adopting monetary policy is the sovereign right of a country. A country has the right to pursue its exchange rate policy and no other country should intervene. If the IMF which is controlled by developed countries has such power of intervention, it means that developed countries can order other countries about. As both the United States and the EU have veto power in the IMF and can veto any decision they do not like, the IMF is reduced to a tool used by them against developing countries. In fact, developing countries with poor ability to defuse risks are victims of floating exchange rates. What floating exchange rates have brought them is monetary crisis or financial crisis. Cyclical and non-cyclical instability between major reserve currencies can only hurt balanced and orderly growth of the global economy.

The exchange rates of international reserve currencies are determined by many factors. As the primary organization for safeguarding the international monetary system, the IMF has the duty and responsibility to promote exchange rates stability (for details, see Articles of Agreement of the IMF). Unfortunately, the IMF has failed to diligently promote the relative stability of major currencies, and it even urges developing countries to adopt floating exchange rates and open their capital accounts. Because of the hazardous nature of fluctuations in exchange rates, the IMF should commit itself to maintaining exchange rates stability. It should increase supervision over major countries' exchange rates and international capital flows and work for the establishment of a stable but flexible international exchange rate regime.

At the same time, to maintain stability of international prices and guard against the risk of global inflation should also be one of the major functions of the IMF. It should strengthen supervision over the issuance of base money by countries that supply major reserve currencies in the world. The supervision it exercises over the member states should have binding force. For instance, although Article 4 (Negotiation) of the IMF covers major developed countries, the IMF has little influence over the policies pursued by these countries. As the global economy can grow only in an equitable and just environment, the reform of the IMF's voting rights, quota allocation, or binding agreements should address the interests and concerns of all parties, and such reform should be feasible and enforceable (Li Ruogu, 2008).

The IMF should make the SDR assume the role of international reserve currency. Lack of stability in international reserve currencies is a major flaw of the current international monetary system. A desired reserve currency should be independent of the issuing agency of the government of a particular country, and it should be adequate in amount to facilitate international trade and financial transactions. But obviously this is not the case with the current international reserve currency. What should be done is to create a global currency and establish an international settlement mechanism based on institutional arrangements and using this global currency as the vehicle. The SDR could be such a global currency. As the monetary unit created by the IMF, the SDR already has some basic features of a global currency, but it still has a long way to go before it can perform the function of a global currency. The IMF needs to adopt effective measures to promote the use of the SDR, put in place due institutional arrangements, and create a stable international reserve currency as soon as possible so as to lay the foundation for building a stable international monetary system (Li Ruogu, 2006).

The IMF should strengthen its role of supervision. Maintaining the long-term stability of the international monetary system has always been a primary responsibility of the IMF. It should adopt and carry out supervisory standards widely accepted by the international society. Such supervision should cover not only major economies, but also small but important open economies in the global economic chain, not just macroeconomics, but also microeconomics (Eichengreen, 2006). This supervisory function should be exercised at global and local level, both bilaterally and multilaterally (Schneider and Tornell, 2000).

In terms of risk supervision, the IMF should first strengthen supervision of short-term accounts, particularly short-term capital flows. According to Little and Olivei (2002), from the long term point of view, an open capital markets should be promoted as it effectively allocates resources and defuses risks. However, in view of the volatility of short-term capital flows and such volatility's role in recent financial crises, short-term capital flows should be the primary target of monitoring and supervision by the international monetary system and the IMF. The IMF calls for liberalization of capital accounts. But such liberalization can only be carried out in a phased way and under conditions of open current accounts, an elastic labor market, and having prudent fiscal policies in place.

The IMF should strengthen its function of preventing and controlling monetary crisis. In summarizing the academic view of the East Asian financial crisis's rescue efforts, Yuntong Wang (1999) pointed out that a tailored approach should be taken in addressing the crisis. If a member country's crisis is due to inadequate short-term liquidity caused by frenzied international speculation, then IMF should immediately inject liquidity into that country. The IMF's current lending conditions which require a borrowing country to implement tight macroeconomic policies and to reform its economic structure are only applicable when a crisis is caused by moral hazard and structural problems. Of course, in most cases, a country's problem is mainly caused by internal factors, but external factors are also at work from time to time. The IMF should be clear about whether the economic crisis in a country stems from internal or external factors. If the crisis is triggered by internal causes, the IMF can place strict conditions for lending as called for. Schneider and Tornell (2000) believed that in most situations, the international monetary system and the IMF should follow a non-relief principle. Otherwise, some member countries could pursue irresponsible fiscal policies with the knowledge that they could always expect relief (this is the so-called moral hazard). Fischer (1999) cited Bagehot's Rule[3] and pointed out that market disciplinary mechanism is the most effective means of preventing moral hazard. Yuntong Wang (1999) had the opinion that since some countries' crises were caused by external shock rather than internal moral hazard, the IMF's application of the conventional Bagehot's Rule was inappropriate. The IMF should differentiate between different cases and refrain from taking a sweeping

---

[3]Bagehot's rule holds that the lender of last resort should follow three principles when engaging in lending activities in a crisis: (1) provide solvent borrowers with unlimited liquidity, (2) adopt punitive interest rates, and (3) attach other conditions.

approach. In order to effectively prevent and control crisis, it should assume the role of an independent central bank as called for during a particular period of time.

There are many different views regarding the reform of the international monetary system and the IMF. The international society should fully explore all these proposals and set a timeline (which should not be too long) for reaching consensus on such reform. Dragging feet on reaching consensus is not acceptable. An implementation system should be put in place and it should be steadily improved. Exchange rates and markets should be kept stable, but this does not mean that fluctuations are not allowed. Actually, fluctuations are the norm while stability is relative. It is through fluctuations that economy grows and opportunities are created. Thus, focusing on stability does not mean eliminating fluctuations, which should be kept under control. Fluctuations and crises are inevitable since crises arise in the course of economic development. Then why should there still be an emphasis on stability? This is because nothing should be allowed to go to extreme. Excessive fluctuations and the resultant crises are highly detrimental to economic development. Therefore, stability implies that in most circumstances fluctuations should be allowed to exist within a controllable scope. In my view, this should be the goal for IMF reform.

(2) Reform the World Bank to promote harmonious global development
The main task of the World Bank is to eliminate poverty and promote economic development of developing countries. In order to achieve this goal, the World Bank should take the following two steps:

First, it should raise adequate funds and use them effectively. Low-income developing countries need international assistance in pursuing development. Back in 1970, the United Nations set 0.7% of developed countries' GNI as the target for official development assistance. Over 30 years have passed, but most of the developed countries have failed to meet this target. According to data published by the Development Assistance Committee (DAC) in 2009, in 2007, only Norway, Denmark, Luxembourg, Holland, and Sweden met the target, while the overall level of DAC members was 0.28%, far below the 0.7% target. The World Bank is an important channel for supplying funds to developing countries. But its funding resources are limited. In recent years, the annual funds provided by the World Bank to developing countries amounted to US$ 20–25 billion. In fiscal year 2004, the World Bank provided US$ 11 billion for 87 programs in 33 countries. The International Development Association (IDA) provided US$ 9 billion for 158 programs in 62 countries. In fiscal year 2008, the World Bank provided loans totaling US$ 13.5 billion, and the IDA provided US$ 11.2 billion of loans (for details, see the annual report of the World Bank). This is utterly inadequate for 153 low and mid-income economies and is unable to stimulate flow of private capital into them. Hence, the World Bank should improve its financing mechanism, expand the size of funding, and increase support for developing countries. Due to limited supply of funding, the World Bank should not overreach itself. It should focus on key areas and strive to solve one to two major problems within a specified period of time. For instance, the World Bank should give priority to upgrading the transportation sector in Africa, and bring about interconnectivity of railways, aviation, and ports. Doing so would not only improve Africa's infrastructure, but also attract the inflow of private capital.

Second, it should ensure that there is a clear-cut division of labor among development financial institutions. Over the past decades, the international society has established international, regional, and bilateral development financial institutions. However, these institutions lack effective coordination and clear-cut division of labor, resulting in both surplus and shortage in funding and both overlapping and vacuum in areas of development. This has greatly affected the efficient use of development aid. Therefore, development financial institutions should strengthen coordination, have clearly defined strategic goals and areas of operation, allocate aid in a balanced way, and cover all areas of development. As an international development institution, the World Bank should focus on upgrading infrastructure so as to help developing countries pursue development (Li Ruogu, 2006). To achieve this goal, the most important thing is to ensure that international financial institutions should have the right guidelines. Development financial institutions should give top priority to promoting development. Development is the prerequisite for solving all other problems. Thus, development financial institutions should focus their energy on helping developing countries grow instead of getting involved in democracy and human rights related issues. Democracy is a tool, not an end, while development is the ultimate goal. Human rights are not the prerequisite for development; rather, they derive from development. If this principle is not adhered to, the reform of the World Bank and the IMF cannot be achieved.

Regarding the governance structure of these institutions, it is necessary to change the established practice of a European serving as the managing director of the IMF and an American serving as the World Bank governor. It is necessary to change the operating culture of these international institutions that is divorced from the reality of developing countries. The quotas and voting rights of developing countries should be increased. Specialists familiar with the conditions of developing countries should be hired, and the staff from developing countries should be increased (Li Ruogu, 2006).

In the declaration of the London Summit, the G20 committed itself to carrying out the reform of the World Bank agreed upon in October 2008. Leaders attending the summit also agreed to appoint the World Bank's senior management through an open selection process.

(3) Reform the Financial Stability Board (FSB) to maintain global financial stability

The leaders of the G20 London Summit agreed to strengthen regulatory systems in their respective countries, pursue consistent and systemic international cooperation, and put in place a unanimously recognized financial regulatory framework based on high standards. The participating leaders believed that strengthening financial regulation would accelerate economic prosperity, improve operating systems, and increase transparency. This would stem the spread of systemic risks, shorten financial and economic cycles, reduce dependence on risky financing, and discourage excessive risk-taking. The regulatory bodies should protect individual consumers and investors, maintain market discipline, and avoid adverse impacts on other countries. They should also reduce the scope for "regulatory arbitrage", support competition and keep pace with market innovation (G20 London Summit Communique).

With this in mind, the G20 will implement the Action Plan agreed upon at the Washington Summit. It also issued a declaration of "Strengthening the Financial System" which established FSB to replace the Financial Stability Forum (FSF).[4] The FSB consists of all the G20 members, FSF members and the European Commission. Together with the IMF, the FSB will constitute an important mechanism for international financial cooperation and supervision to protect the stability and growth of global economy and finance.

The leaders at the G20 summit admitted that major failures in the financial sector and financial regulation and supervision were fundamental causes of the crisis. All countries should adopt a stronger and more globally consistent regulatory framework for the future financial sector, thus supporting sustainable global growth and development. The Summit also decided to strengthen and improve global financial regulation and supervision. It is expected that this will lead to major changes in the global financial regulatory order and system.

First, the new regulatory system will be global in nature and have consistency in financial regulation and supervision. While individual economies should enhance regulatory supervision, a high standard global regulatory framework with supervisory and regulatory system, regulatory standards and institutional arrangements should be established. As these systemic arrangements will determine how the financial sector in various countries and regions should be regulated and supervised, full consideration should be given to the views and interests of developing countries in adopting such systemic standards.

Second, global financial regulation and supervision will be enhanced. The new regulatory framework will cover all systemically important financial institutions, instruments and markets, and will strengthen supervision over big financial institutions and different innovative financial instruments to make these institutions and products more transparent. In addition, the framework will take steps to check the operation of "tax havens" by classifying them as black or grey. When established, the new global regulatory framework will have a major impact on the financial sectors and financial regulation of all economies.

---

[4]The FSF was founded by the G7 in 1999, and was composed of international financial institutions and G7 governmental authorities responsible for financial stability. The FSF's responsibility was to evaluate the problems affecting global financial stability and research and monitor countermeasures that needed to be adopted to solve these problems.

Lastly, accounting standards will be improved. The London Summit called on bodies responsible for setting accounting standards to work closely with regulators and supervisors to improve standards for valuation and setting reserve capital and adopt a single set of high quality global accounting standards. After the Summit, the U.S. Financial Accounting Standard Board (FASB) immediately changed the fair value accounting standard from "mark to market" to "self-assessment". Relaxing of this particular standard, primarily aimed at rescuing big financial institutions who were subject to market on a daily basis, will change the accounting basis for asset pricing and asset management. Such relaxation implies that "self-assessment" is the most reasonable pricing method. However, this could well create a new and bigger problem in trying to solve an old one. No matter what will happen, these changes in accounting standards will produce a major impact on the stability of financial markets and international monetary system and should be watched closely.

It should be pointed out that in establishing standards for the global financial regulatory system and setting up relevant institutions, and particularly in developing unified standard, full attention should be paid to the reality of developing countries. First, as developed and developing countries are at different stages of development, the regulatory standards for financial institutions of developed and developing countries should not be the same. The needs of developing countries for economic development should be taken into account. Second, developing countries should participate fully in the process of formulating regulatory standards and rules, which should not be dominated by developed countries. Developing countries should participate in the operation and management of the regulatory bodies. Finally, it is quite clear that prior to the crisis, the rather lax regulatory standards and norms as well as decentralized regulatory system in developed countries, especially in the United States, were all based on the belief of free market economy. Hence, failure in the regulatory system was due to the failure of the belief of free market economy. If this belief is not changed and is still pursued as the basis for establishing a new regulatory framework and standards, failure will still be inevitable.

Chapter 13

China and Current International Monetary System Reform

As China is the largest developing country, has the largest foreign exchange reserves and is the third largest trading country in the world, the operation and changes of the international monetary system invariably affect its vital interests. China and many developing countries are inactive participants of the existing international monetary system, and the 2008 global financial crisis inflicted severe damage on China's development. Therefore, China should actively participate in the building of a new international monetary system to ensure that the new system will be in the interest of its development. The global economic growth calls for a new international economic and financial order. With China's growing economic strength, increasing openness in trade and finance as well as the steady improvement of its financial environment, conditions have emerged for the renminbi to become a regional or international currency. Indeed, it can be expected that the renminbi will sooner or later become an important currency in the international monetary system; and China will more actively participate in the reform of the international financial system and make its due contribution to the stable growth of the global economy (Li Ruogu, 2008).

13.1 China's Role in Reforming the International Monetary System

A country's overall strength determines the role it can play in formulating international rules. China is not in the position to play a leadership role in adopting these new rules. However, it can actively involve itself in this process to make sure that these rules facilitate the growth of China and other developing countries.

13.1.1 *China is not in a position to lead the reform of the international monetary system*

At present, over 60% the international reserve, foreign exchange transactions, and international trade settlement are based on the dollar, which has come about as a result of historical evolution. The U.S. economy grew rapidly in the 50 years before the end of World War II. Its GDP surpassed that of Britain in 1894, making the United States the leading global economic power, and the dollar became an international currency. The creation of the Bretton Woods system after World War II turned the dollar into the only international currency. In the two decades and more that followed, the value of the dollar was linked with gold. Because the U.S. economy was strong and the momentum created in the international monetary system before 1971, the collapse of the Bretton Woods system did not significantly weaken the international position of the dollar. As Jim Rogers pointed out (2009), the rise and decline of big powers is a historical process. Before the end of World War I, Britain was the most powerful country in the world, and its decline took place over a period of 50 years. Similarly, the decline of the United States and other big powers will be a long historical process.

In their article published in the March/April 2009 issue of *Foreign Affairs*, Brooks and Wohlforth (2009) pointed out that the relative political, economic and military strengths of the United States and other countries determine that the global power equation will be one of "1+X" for some time to come, in which the role of the dollar and a U.S. led international monetary system will not be fundamentally reversed.

In 2008, China's GDP reached RMB 30 trillion Yuan, equivalent to US$ 4.4 trillion based on the exchange rate of that year, ranking the third in the world. But its per capita GDP was only 3,266.80 dollars, ranking behind the 100th place in the world. China's per capita share of basic resources such as land, water, and forest, is also behind the 100th place. The use of the renminbi in international economy was insignificant. Obviously, China is not in a position to lead the reform of the international monetary system.

The dollar's dominance reflects the dominance of the U.S. economy in the world. So long as the latter does not change, the dominance of the dollar in the international monetary system will largely remain unchanged. To maintain the dollar's dominance is important to the dominance of the U.S. economy in the world. The United States will naturally do everything possible to maintain the dollar's position as an international currency. If the dollar can no longer serve as an international reserve currency, the United States will not be able to purchase goods and services from overseas and raise funds to cover its budget deficit by printing dollars. The loss of the dollar's position as an international currency is unthinkable to the United States whose growth is mainly driven by consumption. To the United States with a growth model featuring trade deficit, budget deficit, and saving deficit, this would be a disaster. To achieve economic recovery and growth, the United States will resort to all means, perhaps even war, to defend the dollar's position as an international currency.

I also need to point out that the outbreak of the current crisis underscores the unsustainability of the dollar-based international monetary system. Whether the United States likes it or not, the reform of the current international monetary system is bound to take place. However, as it came into being along with the rise of big power, the current international monetary system can only change along with the relative change in the status of big power. Owing to changes in its relative strength in the past 60 years since the end of World War II, the United States is no longer the only dominant global economic power, and both Europe and Japan have become leading powers in the global economy. Developing countries have become an important force in the global economy in the past 30 years. China, in particular, has become the third largest economy, the country with the largest foreign exchange reserve and the third largest trading country, as well as the largest producer of several hundred products.

All this has given China greater prominence in the international economy. The current global financial crisis has moved China to a leading position earlier than expected. People have reason to believe that the world will be different after the crisis. The pre-crisis global growth model in which the United States and other western countries' consumption demand is met by saving and products provided by China and other developing countries will not be the same again. The global economy will go through fundamental change. It will be jointly governed by the West, China, and other developing countries rather than dominated by U.S.-led West.

13.1.2 *China and the reform of the international monetary system reform*

Having the largest amount of foreign exchange reserves, over US$ 2 trillion, and also the largest holder of U.S. debt, China should play its due role in the next round of reform of the international monetary system. As discussed previously, changes in the international monetary system reflect changes in economic strength. In 2008, global GDP was US$ 60 trillion, with that of the United States being US$ 14 trillion, approximately 23.5% of the global total. The figures for other economics are: the EU: US$ 18.4 trillion, approximately 30.3%; Japan: US$ 4.9 trillion, approximately 8%; and China: US$ 4.4 trillion, approximately 7.3%. Since the GDP of these four economies added up to US$ 42 trillion, approximately 70% of the world's GDP,[1] they should play a major role in reforming the international monetary system.

As we know, it has taken several decades for the European monetary unit to develop into the euro, a common currency for the EU. This is a major achievement in both the history of global economic development and the history of European development. It is also a contribution to the reform of the international monetary system. But developments of the past few decades also show that for Europe, which have over 40 countries that are quite different in level of development, cultural tradition and history, to pursue common monetary, fiscal, economic, as well as social development policies is extremely difficult, something that cannot be achieved

---

[1] WEO Database (2009).

soon. This makes the euro inherently unstable. This plus the fact that the dollar is used to price major products in the world means that the euro will not replace the dollar in the foreseeable future. The renminbi and Japanese yen are even less able to become the main international currencies. All this means the dollar's position as the main international currency cannot be replaced in the near future. On the other hand, the dollar-based international monetary system must be reformed. What is the way out? This author believes that the reform of the international monetary system should be pursued in phases. There should be both short-term and long-term goals. In the short run, the position of the dollar as the main international currency should be conditionally maintained, while preparation should be made now for achieving the long-term goal of reforming the dollar-based international monetary system.

What does conditional maintenance of the dollar's position as an international currency mean?

First, the consumption driven U.S. growth model must change. Such change, however, will take time. Therefore, if the dollar were to hastily relinquish its role as an international currency, neither the United States nor other countries would be ready for such transition. In other words, it takes time for the United States and other developed countries to boost the real economy with their advanced technologies. It also takes time for other countries to shift their export-led growth model to one driven by domestic demand. So maintaining the dollar's current position is also maintaining the pre-crisis model of global growth. However, this should not be to maintain the *status quo* just for its sake. The aim should be to gain time for reform.

Secondly, the position of the dollar would only be maintained with conditions attached. The United States should be required to pursue responsible monetary and fiscal policies and change its growth mode. In other words, in adopting monetary and fiscal policies, the United States must consider whether such policies would have adverse effect on the global economy and the economy of other countries.

Thirdly, the international community should reach consensus on reforming the U.S. dollar-based international monetary system and on how to transition to a new system.

Only on the basis of reaching consensus on the above three conditions can the position of the dollar as an international currency be maintained.

Only on these conditions should China continue to purchase an appropriate amount of U.S. treasury bonds, help the dollar to maintain its position and stability. This is what China can, should, and must do.

13.2 How China Should Involve Itself in the Reform of the International Monetary System

It is necessary for China to have both a short-term objective and a long-term objective. What should be done now? As a Chinese saying goes, one must first give in order to take. We must start to build an international monetary system based not on any single sovereign currency but on multiple sovereign currencies with joint responsibilities and obligations. In other words, the use of the euro and other internationally acceptable currencies, including the renminbi, should be promoted.

13.2.1 *Promote the internationalization of the renminbi in an orderly way*

The internationalization of the renminbi is bound to occur. The current global financial crisis has made it possible for the internationalization of the renminbi, and we should explore ways to promote this goal.

The renminbi's internationalization is not something new. About 20 years ago, a Federal Reserve Board governor predicted that both the euro and the renminbi would become international currencies. This process did not just start with the Asian Bond Market agreements based on local currencies signed by the People's Bank of China (PBC) and the central banks of China's neighboring countries. Around 2004, the PBC already reached agreements for cross-border trade settlement in local currencies with Russia, Vietnam, and Nepal. When the Closer Economic Partnership Arrangement (CEPA) was made between China's central government and Hong Kong, Hong Kong residents and account holders were allowed to use the renminbi, though the amount was limited to RMB 20,000. Thus, by being convertible to the Hong Kong dollar and U.S. dollar, the renminbi is already semi-internationalized. Moreover, the renminbi is being used in numerous places overseas (e.g., UnionPay cards which use the renminbi to settle accounts). When working at the PBC, I conducted surveys at airports in Chicago, Vancouver, and Europe, and found that the renminbi could easily be converted. Being used in China's border areas and for cross-border trade, the renminbi is already semi-internationalized, whether this is recognized or not.

Two things are important in promoting the internationalization of the renminbi. First, this is a natural process, which means one cannot artificially advance it when others are not yet ready to accept it. A currency's international acceptance has come about as a matter of natural choice. However, when conditions are ripe, we should lose no time to promote it. For example, some countries around China are now willing to use the renminbi, and it is not necessary to stop them. Second, the internationalization of the renminbi must be based on economic strength. Without such strength, it would be futile to promote its internationalization.

Many countries around China have started to accept the renminbi and even use it as reserve currency. Although the renminbi is only a partially convertible currency, many countries have confidence in it, as the renminbi has kept stable in the past few decades, even during the Asian financial crisis. Since it started the reform and opening-up program 30 years ago, China has maintained robust growth, and the international community is optimist about its future. As a result, the renminbi has become increasingly attractive. Holders of the renminbi have benefited from its increased value. All this has both laid a good foundation and created a good opportunity for the internationalization of the renminbi. Moreover, as the dollar is unstable, it would be better for China to provide international aid directly in the renminbi during a global financial crisis. It would be too complicated if China's aid were to be priced in dollars.

The renminbi should not follow the path of the dollar in its course of internationalization, and it will not become the sole international currency. Although more countries are willing to use the renminbi, it does not mean that the renminbi has become an international currency. China should not be reluctant about promoting the internationalization of the renminbi because of what has happened to the dollar. The process of internationalizing the renminbi should be in keeping with China's economic growth and the progress in its market-oriented reform. China does not seek financial domination. China only hopes that its currency can be used internationally as a means to stabilize and regulate its economy.

The internationalization of the renminbi has both advantages and disadvantages. Its greatest advantages include improved economic stability, less economic uncertainty, and less exchange rate risk. Both importers and exporters can benefit from lower foreign exchange hedging needs and reduced remittance procedures and costs. In macro terms, the internationalization of the renminbi will increase stability of the international monetary system, reduce currency mismatch, give China more say in coordinating international economic and financial policies, and share Seigniorage collected.

New checks imposed on the making of China's domestic economic policy would be the major disadvantage brought about by the renminbi's internationalization. In adopting macroeconomic policies, China would have to balance domestic and external policies. The impact of its monetary policies on the international market and other renminbi assets holding countries would have to be taken into consideration. Conflict between international macroeconomic policy coordination and protection of China's domestic interests would also need to be addressed.

There is no need to rush for the internationalization of the renminbi. It is not an opportunity that must be seized at one particular point of time before it is lost. Rather, it should evolve as a natural and continuous process, and we should seek solid and incremental progress.

China still lacks experience and is not yet ready in many aspects. For instance, its domestic financial markets are not fully developed, and there is a shortage of qualified financial personnel. At present, we should make good preparations for promoting the internationalization of the renminbi. First, the value of the renminbi should be kept stable. If the value of an international currency which serves as value standard and exchange medium on the international market fluctuates excessively, it could only increase market uncertainty and undermine the international monetary system. Secondly, China's capital market should be opened in a phased way. Currently, China's capital market is not open enough for the renminbi to become freely convertible. Thirdly, the management of China's financial institutions and the competence of financial personnel, which are important for the free convertibility of the renminbi, should be improved. Fourthly, control over interest rates should be relaxed gradually. Market-based interest rates are a common feature of convertible currencies. China has moved in this direction but still has much to do to meet this goal.

13.2.2 *Strengthen regional monetary cooperation*

First, a regional financial security system should be set up. A regional mechanism for monetary and financial cooperation will assist the international monetary system in stabilizing interest rates and market and in preventing and controlling crisis. The International Monetary Fund (IMF), as the leading institution in the international monetary system, should enhance cooperation and coordination with regional financial organizations. And regional financial security systems should be put in place through bilateral and multilateral coordination. In Asia, for example, multilateralization of the Chiang Mai Initiative (CMI) has made it possible to establish a regional reserve fund to prevent financial crisis. It can also provide assistance when member countries encounter liquidity shortage. The further development of Asia's bond market can address problems such as high ratio of indirect financing and mismatch in both reserve currencies and maturities. This will help address the root cause of financial crisis (Li Ruogu, 2006).

In addition, currency swap should be fully implemented. By April 2, 2009, bilateral currency swap agreements had been concluded between China and six other economies, with amount totaling RMB 650 billion Yuan.[2] Another important development in this regard is that the PBC has made inter-operative arrangements for a multi-currency payment system with Hong Kong, which is a multiple currency cross-boundary payment and clearing mechanism. Although this system is currently used for handling transactions only, Hong Kong is likely to become an offshore renminbi clearing center, allowing overseas renminbi to flow back to China. China is also working to turn Shanghai into an international financial center, and Shanghai could very well become an international renminbi clearing center. These steps will lay a solid foundation for the internationalization of the renminbi.

---

[2] Summed up by the author according to the data of www.pbc.gov.cn.

Finally, China should strengthen financial cooperation with neighboring Asian economies. Owing to historical reasons, progress in monetary cooperation between Asian countries has been relatively slow. Japan's economic development is a case of full Westernization. Due to its history of aggression and lack of geopolitical advantage, Japan cannot play a leading role in Asia's economic integration. However, Asian economic cooperation has gained momentum in the past decade, and such momentum should be sustained. I believe that a unified Asian economic zone and monetary zone will ultimately emerge.

13.2.3 *Promote the creation of non-sovereign currency and the reform of international financial institutions*

As the author pointed out earlier, returning to the Keynesian plan and taking several basis commodities as the basis of the international currency are both unrealistic options. Reforming the current SDR to turn it into a real settlement currency, which is a basket of currencies acceptable to all countries, to replace the dollar could be a feasible alternative. Zhou Xiaochuan (2009) made an in-depth analysis of this possibility. China should actively promote and participate in the reform of the IMF and the World Bank. Proposals made should be feasible and take into account the interests of all the parties involved.

13.2.4 *Guard against risks China faces in the process of reforming the international monetary system*

China must guard against risks as it is becoming a key member of the international monetary system. Three conditions need to be met for a country to become such a member: (1) The size of its economy should be big enough to have substantial influence in global economy and trade and in the international monetary system. China has basically met this condition. (2) It should be an engine driving global growth. China has to a fair extent met this condition. (3) Its trade and capital markets should be open to the world. It will take a long time for China to meet this third condition, especially in opening the capital market. The economic conditions in China are not yet ripe for it to fully open the capital market, and it lacks the capacity to manage an open capital market. We need to be on high alert for potential risks in the course of opening the financial sector. But this does not mean closing the door to the outside world or slowing the pace of reform and opening-up. What we should do is to identify risks and defuse them. Damage to China caused by the current financial crisis is controllable because China's capital market is not fully open, and because of lack of derivatives trading in China. But this does not mean that slowing the pace of opening is correct. Development opportunities would be missed if the pace of opening slows down. We should strike a balance between risk management and market opening.

Part Five

Regional Currency Cooperation

Regional currency cooperation or regional currency integration means monetary and financial coordination and particularly the common monetary and exchange rate policies carried out by countries of a certain region. The highest level of regional currency cooperation is the forming of a regional currency union, with unified monetary currency management authorities issuing a single currency and pursuing a single monetary policy, such as the European Monetary Union (EMU). Regional currency cooperation is a choice made by geographically close countries with close economic contact to tap the strengths of economic integration and overcome some inherent defects in the international monetary system. Regional currency cooperation itself is a reform of the international monetary system.

Chapter 14

Regional Currency Cooperation Theory

The theory of optimum currency area (OCA) is the theoretical basis of regional currency cooperation. According to the New Palgrave Dictionary of Economics, the optimum currency area is an "optimum" geographical area. Within this area, the general means of payment is a single common currency, or there is full convertibility among over a dozen currencies with mutually pegged exchange rates that remain unchanged in daily transactions and capital transactions, while their exchange rates with currencies of outside countries remain floating.

The optimum currency area theory, first proposed by Mundell (1961) to challenge the floating exchange rates system, has developed over the years. Studies on the theory and application of optimum currency area mainly focus on three areas: (1) economic criteria necessary for countries to enter into a currency union; (2) cost-benefit analysis on whether a country should join a currency union; and (3) endogeneity of an optimum currency areas. The first two areas of analysis are known as the first-generation theory of optimum currency area, or theory of static optimum currency area, while the third area is also known as the second-generation theory of optimum currency area, or the theory of dynamic optimum currency area.

14.1 Economic Criteria for Countries to Enter into a Currency Union

Mundell raised a question in 1961: If the floating exchange rate system has so many advantages, why has it not been used among different regions of a single country? What costs will arise from the use of multiple currencies in one country? Mundell's answer was that the choice between fixed exchange rates and floating exchange rates is, in fact, a choice between minimal transaction cost and the macro-stabilization mechanism provided by floating exchange rates. If different factors of production (including labor, capital, and raw materials) flow freely between two countries, then when one of them experiences a deficit, the flow of factors of production from the country with a surplus to the deficit country will rebalance its payments so that adjustment by means of currency devaluation will not be necessary. Therefore, as long as factors of production can flow completely freely between two countries, it is unnecessary for them to use different currencies. This is because the stabilization mechanism provided by the flow of factors of production can substitute for the stabilization mechanism provided by fluctuation in exchange rates (Mundell, 1961).

Later, more economists explored economic criteria necessary for countries to enter into a currency union from different angles. Ingram (1962) maintained that if a regional financial market is highly integrated, a temporary imbalance in international payments can be adjusted by financial transactions. Even in the case of a long-term structural disequilibrium, financial transactions can be used to provide a necessary buffer mechanism to reduce the cost of actual adjustment. Therefore, integration of financial markets reduces the need to adjust the regional balance of payments by changing exchange rates.

McKinnon (1963) pointed out that a high degree of openness of an economy should be one criterion for joining an optimum currency area, as small open economies cannot balance international payments through change in exchange rates. For instance, if a country tries to improve its trade deficit by devaluating its currency, it will cause the country's domestic prices to rise provided its prices and wages are highly flexible. The rising prices will result in a decline in real wages and thus create pressure for an increase in nominal wages. Therefore, changes in exchange rates will be offset by changes in price and will thus be unable to change terms of trade. Therefore, the adoption of fixed exchange rates among highly open economies will be more conducive to ensuring stability of the macro economy.

Kenen (1969) argued that countries with greater diversity in products should join an optimum currency area, because if the structure of exported products is adequately diversified, the impact of demand and technological change on a particular product can be offset.

Willet and Tower (1970) proposed that policy integration should be considered a criterion for joining an optimum currency area. For a currency area with an imperfect internal adjustment mechanism, its eventual success hinges on whether its member countries can take a common position towards inflation and unemployment and have a common understanding of alternation between inflation and unemployment. For instance, it is extremely difficult for a country that does not tolerate inflation and a country that does not tolerate unemployment to pursue the same policy. If policy cooperation is to act as a mechanism for balance of payments, it is necessary to form a supranational and unified monetary and fiscal policy based on the consensus of member countries.

Fleming (1971) believed that member countries of an optimum currency area should have similar inflation rates. If there is a great, continuous difference between the inflation rates of two countries, this will eventually cause a big difference in the two countries' purchasing power and will thus damage the existing foundation for fixed exchange rates. In addition, different inflation rates of different countries will impact short-term capital flow by influencing interest rate differential and thus leading to a new disequilibrium in the international balance of payments.

The aforementioned studies on economic criteria necessary for countries to enter into a currency union have provided ideal criteria for practicing monetary integration. Yet, these criteria have the following shortcomings: (1) There are differences among various standards. Thus, optimum currency areas based on different standards can be quite different in scope. (2) Different standards may be inconsistent with each other. For instance, small open economies may have a high degree of openness, but a low degree of product diversity. (3) Many of the criteria cannot be analyzed quantitatively (He Fan and Qin Donghai, 2005). Just as Tower and Willett (1976) pointed out that criteria are important for joining an optimum currency area. As there is a lack of unanimously agreed-upon quantitative indicators, more empirical studies should be conducted.

14.2 Cost-benefit Analysis for Joining a Currency Union

Starting from the 1970s, the focus of the theoretical study of optimum currency area shifted to evaluation of costs and benefits for a country joining an optimum currency area.

Corden (1972) pointed out that, once joining a currency union, a country abandons its independent monetary and exchange rate policies. If it experiences an imbalance of international payments (trade deficit) because of the impact of external demands, it may restore external equilibrium by carrying out a tight fiscal policy or tolerate a decline in real wages and prices and restore external equilibrium by means of exchange rate depreciation.

Ishiyama (1975) emphasized that differences in preferences of different governments and societies and significant differences in demand management policy of different governments create barriers to the establishment of optimum currency areas and make it difficult to use a single criterion to determine whether a country should join an optimum currency area. Therefore, different countries should evaluate costs and benefits of joining an optimum currency area according to their respective national conditions.

Tower and Willett (1976) believed that the main benefit of joining a currency area lies in increase in currency efficiency, and the main cost is increase in external constraints on the use of demand management policy to achieve internal balance. Because of this, a member country that has no independent monetary and exchange rate policies has to regulate by means of fiscal policy. As monetary policy helps to stabilize the economic cycle, the loss of independent monetary policy may create greater fluctuation in output. If a country has low elasticity in wage and price and poor labor mobility, the cost of losing control over exchange rate policy could be high when asymmetric shock occurs.

Giavazzi and Giovannini (1989) pointed out that for a country with a history of high inflation, the greatest benefit of joining a currency union is the introduction of an external anchor for its currency. For example, for

Italy, joining the euro zone meant it could benefit from the Deutsche Bundesbank's good reputation in anti-inflation. Therefore, the optimum currency area in fact creates credibility sharing for monetary policy. A country with a history of high inflation benefits most by giving up its own currency and joining an optimum currency area.

Fischer (1982) stated that after a country joins a currency union, it gives up the right to issue its own currency and seignorage, or that seignorage now belongs to a different entity. Allocation of seigniorage between different entities is a difficult bargaining process.

Krugman (1990) derived the famous GG–LL curve from his analysis of the costs and benefits for Finland to join the European Union (EU) His main conclusions were: (1) The monetary efficiency gains (MEG) for a country joining the currency union lie in the uncertainty and complexity that the country could avoid related to floating exchange rate as well as costs of foreign exchange settlement and trade losses. The greater the degree of economic integration a member country has with other member countries of a currency union, the more frequent are cross-border trade and flow of resources, and the greater the benefits of joining a currency union. (2) The cost a country faces in joining a currency union lies in economic instability caused by price and employment fluctuations as it abandons independent monetary and exchange policies. The greater degree of economic integration a member country has with other member countries of a currency union, the lesser the costs of joining it. An area of economic integration formed through frequent international trade and flow of production factors is most suitable for the establishment of an optimum currency area.

Tavlas (1993) focused the efficacy of a currency union in coping with the impact of fluctuation and speculation on the financial market. A currency union can pool the foreign exchange reserve of its member countries to jointly and effectively cope with the speculative shock in the exchange market, and accordingly reduces the foreign reserves held by a single member country. A unified currency can also reduce price fluctuation in the foreign exchange market and makes it difficult for speculators to influence prices and weaken monetary policy.

Obstfeld and Rogoff (1996) analyzed in greater detail the cost and benefits for a country joining a currency union. The four costs include the following: (1) the country gives up the right to manage macroeconomic shocks through the use of monetary policy; (2) it gives up the right to reduce real public debt by creating inflation; (3) political disputes in determining the allocation of seigniorage among the member countries of a currency union may cause loss to a member country; (4) the country may suffer speculative shock during the transitional period in which it gives up its own currency and joins the currency union. The four benefits include: (1) reduction in currency exchange related transaction costs; (2) reduction in clearing costs and enhanced price stability in business activities; (3) alleviation of fluctuation of real exchange rates caused by monetary policy or speculative shock; and (4) less political pressure such as trade protectionism.

Fukuda (2002) discussed the costs of both joining and leaving a currency union. The costs of joining the currency union include costs of coinage, creating the monetary authorities and other regulatory costs required for creating a new currency. In terms of the costs of leaving a currency union, the costs a member country will have in returning to its original currency are extremely high.

Cost-benefit analysis provides an analytical framework for a country to judge the positive and negative effects of joining a currency union. However, these positive and negative effects often cannot be directly weighed against each other, mainly for the following reasons: (1) costs and benefits are often vaguely defined and cannot be precisely evaluated, so indirect targets and estimates need to be used; (2) different units of measurement are often used for evaluating costs and benefits, and there is the need to assign weight to different factors. This is usually subjective and even depends entirely on the personal belief of politicians (He Fan and Qin Donghai, 2005).

14.3 The Endogeneity of Optimum Currency Areas

A lot of empirical studies have examined whether a particular region constitutes an optimum currency area according to the evaluation standards for the optimum currency area theory, particularly the European Monetary Union (EMU). Such studies have also discussed whether a country meets the criteria for joining an optimum currency area based on these standards.

However, just looking at the historical data of a country to judge whether it meets the criteria for joining an optimum currency area could be misleading, because an optimum currency area has the characteristic of endogeneity (Gao Haihong *et al.*, 2008).

The endogeneity of an optimum currency area refers to some prerequisites for the establishment of a currency union that can be satisfied after its establishment. Failure to take this into consideration in judging whether an optimum currency area can be formed could result in setting conditions which are too harsh for forming an optimum currency area. Endogeneity thus implies relaxing pre-establishment criteria with the expectation that post-establishment criteria will be strengthened. If such dynamic change is ignored, it could mean a wrong policy choice (Zhu Dantao, 2005).

The European Commission pointed out that upon its establishment, the euro area was not an optimum currency area, but economic and monetary integration made the euro area an optimum currency area after its establishment (Commission of the European Community, 1990).

Frankel and Rose (1996) examined the correlation between the degree of integration of trade of a currency union and the economic cycle among its member countries' economies. Using historical data from 20 industrialized countries spanning three decades, they pointed out that there is a positive correlation between bilateral trade integration and the bilateral synchronization of economic cycles. The greater the integration of trade between countries, the stronger the synchronization of their economic cycles. The stronger the synchronization of countries' economic cycles, the lower the cost of giving up the right to pursue independent monetary and exchange policy, and the greater their willingness to form a currency union.

Artis and Zhang (1997) study showed that European countries and the United States experienced similar economic cycles between 1961 and 1979 and that after the EU introduced the Exchange Rate Mechanism (ERM), European countries and Germany experienced similar economic cycles. This shows that regional currency cooperation helps strengthen synchronization of member countries' economic cycles.

Garnier (2003) analyzed data from 1962 to 1979 and from 1979 to 2001 and reached the following conclusions: (1) there was a clear positive correlation between the progress of monetary integration and business cycles; (2) in terms of European monetary integration, the synchronization of economic cycles among the core countries (Germany, France, Austria, Luxembourg, and Holland, etc.) was strong; (3) the heterogeneity of economic cycles among peripheral countries (particularly Spain, Belgium, and Greece) was stronger.

The major cost a country faces in joining an optimum currency area is giving up the regulatory power over monetary and exchange rate policies in coping with asymmetric external shocks. But Zhu Dantao (2005) pointed out that the formation of a currency union can reduce the asymmetric shocks that member countries face. After the formation of a currency union, mutual dependence among member countries in terms of trade increases, their financial integration deepens, and their economic cycles tend to occur at the same time. This lessens asymmetric shocks generated by different sources. Empirical studies have also found that the formation of a currency union will strengthen the correlation between prices and output among its member countries. Strengthened policy coordination and cooperation means a significant reduction in asymmetric shocks originating from different policy preferences and paces. If different countries' monetary and exchange rate policies are the sources of asymmetric shock, the establishment of a currency union could directly remove these sources.

Chapter 15

European Currency Cooperation

Currently, the fairly developed currency unions in the world include the European Economic and Monetary Union (EMU), the West African Economic and Monetary Union (UEMOA), and the Central African Currency Union. The EMU, also known as the European Monetary Union, is thus far the most successful currency union in operation. Some EMU countries are already using the euro, which has become the second biggest global reserve currency after the dollar. This chapter provides an overview of the evolution of European currency cooperation and summarizes its experiences and lessons.

15.1 European Monetary System: Predecessor to the EMU

The predecessor to the EMU was the European Monetary System (EMS). In 1957, France, the Federal Republic of Germany, Italy, Belgium, Holland, and Luxembourg signed the Treaty Establishing the European Economic Community (EEC) and the Treaty Establishing the European Atomic Energy Community (collectively referred to as the Treaty of Rome) to accelerate European reconstruction after World War II. The treaties proposed the establishment of the European Communities on January 1, 1958, with six member countries, namely, Belgium, France, Italy, Luxembourg, Holland, and the Federal Republic of Germany. In 1962, the

European Council (EC) proposed the establishment of a currency union. In March 1979, with the support of France and the Federal Republic of Germany, the EC countries — excluding Britain — established the EMS.

The EMS had three core elements: the Exchange Rate Mechanism (ERM), the European Currency Unit (ECU), and the credit mechanism. The ERM required member countries to maintain exchange rate parity among their currencies and allowed exchange rates to fluctuate based on this parity without exceeding the agreed margin. The initial allowable floating margin was ±6%. Two commitments regarding the exchange rate mechanism were made: (1) When the exchange rate reached the upper or lower limit of this floating margin, member countries must intervene in the foreign exchange market. (2) Only upon collective agreement could the central exchange rate parity be adjusted, and no member country could unilaterally change it. This shows that the ERM was an exchange rate arrangement with an adjustable margin and finite elasticity. The ECU was a basket of currencies according to which the EMS determined the central exchange parity and the allowable margins for each currency, and the responsibility for changing the exchange rate when these margins were exceeded. The ECU should identify which currency in the ECU basket had the excessive exchange rate deviation, and the currency country involved was required to adjust its exchange rate. Under the credit mechanism, member countries committed themselves to take monetary cooperation measures and provide assistance when a member's currency came under pressure (Giancarlo Gandolfo, 2006).[1]

The EMS went through three stages of operation. The first stage was from March 1979 to January 1987 during which the exchange rate parity was frequently adjusted. Thus, the system resembled an updated version of the Bretton Woods system based on the European Community. The second stage was from January 1987 to August 1992, during which the exchange rates of member countries were quite stable. When the Italian lira (ITL) joined the EMS in 1991, the exchange rate floating margin was narrowed from an initial range of ±6% to ±2.25%. The third stage was from September 1992 to 1999, when the EMU was officially established. The EMS currency crisis broke out at the beginning of this stage.

---

[1] Giancarlo Gandolfo (2006).

The Italian lira was the first to devaluate, falling by 7% in September of 1992. Soon afterwards, the Italian government decided to leave the EMS and allowed the lira to float freely. Britain also soon withdrew from the EMS, allowing the British pound sterling to float freely. One factor contributing to the EMS currency crisis in the early 1990s was that the Danish public voted against signing the Treaty of Maastricht, which caused market concern about lack of progress of European currency unification. Another factor was that the German Central Bank refused to reduce interest rates in order to control the flow of speculative capital into Germany. The speculative capital then assaulted the weaker currencies within the EMS, namely the Italian lira and the British pound sterling. From July 31 to August 1 of 1993, after suffering from the negative impact of large-scale speculation on the French franc, the EMS decided to increase the bilateral exchange rate floating margin from ±2.25% to ±15%, excluding the bilateral exchange rate between the German mark and the Dutch guilder. The crises of September 1992 and July 1993 clearly showed that under a system allowing the free flow of capital between countries, monetary cooperation undertaken between countries with different economic conditions and conflicting monetary policies would face great obstacle.

15.2 Founding of the EMU

In February 1992, leaders of the European Community (EC) signed in Maastricht, Holland, the Treaty of Maastricht, establishing European Union (EU). The Treaty of Maastricht set five economic standards to be satisfied for joining the single currency area: (1) Inflation in the applicant state shall not exceed by 1.5 percentage points the average inflation of the three EMU countries with the lowest inflation rates. (2) Fiscal deficit in the applicant state shall not exceed 3% of its annual GDP. (3) Aggregate national debt of the applicant state shall not exceed 60% of its annual GDP. (4) Its long-term interest rates shall not exceed by 2 percentage points the average interest rates of the three EU nations with the most stable consumer prices. (5) The exchange rates of the member states may float only within the specified range.

According to the Treaty of Maastricht, the EU established the EMU in three stages and would introduce a single currency, the euro.

During the first stage, from July 1990 to the end of 1993, the main task was to achieve free flow of capital among member countries and implement a unified fiscal and monetary policy. On July 1, 1990, the EEC lifted internal control, allowing capital to flow freely. The Treaty of Maastricht officially came into effect on November 1, 1993. Progress made at this point included launching a common European market, elimination of barriers to free capital flow, enhanced coordination of economic policy between member countries, and cooperation between member countries' central banks.

The second stage of this process lasted from 1994 to the end of 1998. The main targets during this stage included promoting economic integration of member states towards a common standard, establishing the European Central Bank (ECB), and laying the groundwork for currency unification. The EEC established the European Monetary Institute (EMI) as the predecessor to the ECB, to further coordinate the monetary policies of its member countries, strengthen independence of member nation central banks and to monitor and control the economic and fiscal policies of the member countries. The EMI set annual upper and lower limits for the growth of the money supply (M3) of EU countries. In this way, the EMI monitored, controlled, and coordinated the monetary policies of member countries. The already narrow range in which EMS currency exchange rates were allowed to float shrank for a second time. On December 16, 1995, the duration of the transitional period to the new currency and its name, the euro, were made official. On June 16 and 17 of 1997, the European Parliament adopted in Amsterdam the Stability and Growth Pact which aimed to ensure financial discipline after the full introduction of the euro and establish a new exchange rate mechanism (ERM II) to achieve stable exchange rates between the euro and other EEC currencies which had not joined the euro area. On May 3 in Brussels, 1998, the European Parliament decided on the first group of 11 countries that would enter the third stage, described in the following paragraph, on January 1, 1999. The ECB was established on June 1, 1998, and on December 31, 1998, the exchange rates for the currencies of these 11 economies vs. the euro were decided.

The third stage began in 1999, and its primary goals were to introduce the euro as the single regional currency and to admit more countries into the euro area. On January 1, 1999, the euro became an official currency and the euro zone was established under the supervision of the ECB. The euro began to be officially used in banking, foreign exchange transactions, and public bond markets. Within the euro zone, permanent fixed exchange rate was set and the currencies, monetary policies, and central banking of the member states were all unified. The ECB has the power of issuing currency and setting monetary policy. The central banks of member countries participate in ECB decision-making and implementing monetary policy set by the ECB. They are responsible for their own operation and manage their foreign exchange reserves according to instructions of the ECB. Greece joined the euro area on January 1, 2001. Euro banknotes and coinage began circulation on January 1, 2002. During the transitional period, member countries' individual currencies remained in circulation. After March 1, 2002, the euro completely replaced the individual currencies of member nations which were withdrawn from circulation. Slovenia joined the euro zone on January 1, 2007, followed by Cyprus and Malta on January 1, 2008, and Slovakia on January 1, 2009. Up to this point, the euro zone has 16 member countries: Austria, Belgium, Finland, France, Germany, Greece, Ireland, Italy, Luxembourg, Holland, Portugal, Spain, Slovenia, Cyprus, Malta, and Slovakia.

It is predicted that in the coming 10 years, the euro zone may cover closely to 30 countries. The franc area countries of Central and West Africa whose currencies were previously pegged to the French franc now peg their currencies to the euro. If some countries in North Africa and the Middle East also peg their currencies to the euro, the euro zone may extend to 50 countries with a total population of over 500 million and a total GDP exceeding that of the United States. In terms of both the scale of the real economy and level of development of the financial markets, the euro will pose the biggest challenge to the international dominance of the dollar.

15.3 Experiences and Lessons of European Currency Cooperation

The great success made in European currency cooperation has provided an example for countries in other regions looking to advance their own currency cooperation. Such success first manifests itself in the orderly establishment and growth of the EMU. From the establishment of the EEC, the process leading up to the official circulation of the euro took about 45 years. The EMS operated for about two decades as a transitional mechanism before the establishment of the euro zone. During this period, the EMS overcame various difficulties and built confidence and laid a firm foundation for the ultimate formation of the single-currency euro zone. Second, the euro's value as a currency is solidly based on the Treaty of Maastricht and the Stability and Growth Pact. These treaties strictly control the size of the fiscal deficits and external debt scales of member countries and impose tight fiscal disciplines on the euro zone member countries. All of this created confidence in the euro's reputation as a stable currency. Under the influence of the German Central Bank, the ECB makes preventing inflation a top priority and is ready to sacrifice economic growth to control inflation. The prudence of the ECB laid a solid foundation for the euro to become an international hard currency. Third, the success of the euro zone is a good example of the endogeneity theory of optimum currency area. Since the establishment of the euro zone, great progress has been made towards integrating the economies and financial markets of member countries. Their economic cycles have become more synchronized, the gap in their economic structures has narrowed, and the frequency and scope of asymmetric economic shocks have been reduced.

However, the euro zone has been slow in responding to the global financial crisis triggered by the American subprime mortgage crisis. The steps it has taken in response to the crisis have been weak. This has led to a deep decline in the euro zone's real economy, which started even earlier than that in the United States. The viability of regional currency union is even called into question. Major lessons for the euro zone in this regard are as follows: the economic cycles of the euro zone member countries do not take place at the same pace, and their economic structures are not the same. For smaller countries, joining the euro zone means yielding the right to adopt their own monetary policies. This also means that they lose the ability to pursue loose fiscal policies in the face of financial crisis. ECB monetary policies are largely controlled by the euro zone's core countries, Germany and France. Smaller member countries then found themselves suffering from asymmetric shocks because ECB policies often favor larger economies. The implication is that a country which joins a currency union before its economic cycles and structures become the same with other member countries will land itself in an unfavorable position in the event of economic crisis. The second lesson is that, since its eastwards expansion led to widening gap between the economic cycles and structures of its member countries, the euro zone has become more vulnerable to asymmetric shocks. Third, unlike the United States, it is difficult for the euro zone to adopt fiscal measures to stimulate its economy. The euro zone is a loose entity. With the exception of monetary policy which is vested in the ECB, the euro zone member countries have final say over their own affairs. Due to different positions taken by different countries, no large-scale, cross-border collective action can be undertaken to rescue the euro zone's financial markets in a timely fashion. Unlike the dollar whose value is supported by a single sovereign country, the United States, the euro has no one single owner or primary supporter. This major defect has made it hard for the euro to replace the dollar any time soon.

Chapter 16

East Asian Currency Cooperation

The 1997–1998 Southeast Asian financial crisis exposed weaknesses in the financial sectors of East Asian countries and spurred progress in East Asian currency cooperation. At present, since East Asian monetary cooperation is still at an initial stage, it cannot yet play the role of stabilizing the regional monetary and financial environment or promoting rapid and healthy growth of the regional economy. To respond to a new round of financial crisis, East Asia should accelerate regional monetary and financial cooperation and establish an independent East Asian mutual emergency aid system closely connected with the regional economy.

16.1 Current East Asian Currency Cooperation

On May 6, 2000, at the Finance Ministers' Meeting held by the Association of Southeastern Asian Nations (ASEAN)+3 (China, Japan, and the Republic of Korea) in Chiang Mai, the Chiang Mai Initiative (CMI) was adopted, marking the official launching of East Asian currency cooperation. Over the last decade, progress has been made in East Asian currency cooperation, as shown in both carrying out the Chiang Mai Initiative and building the East Asian regional bond market.

16.1.1 *The Chiang Mai Initiative (CMI)*

On May 6, 2000, finance ministers and vice governors of central banks of ASEAN+3 held a meeting in Chiang Mai, Thailand. Participants agreed to strengthen fiscal and financial cooperation in East Asia, particularly regarding the establishment of bilateral currency swap system under the current ASEAN+3 framework and expanding the scale of multilateral currency swap signed by the organization's original five countries (member countries of the currency swap arrangement were expanded to all 10 countries at that meeting, increasing the total amount from US$ 200 million to US$ 1 billion). The CMI was thus concluded. It is a milestone in the course of East Asian monetary and financial cooperation which shows that East Asian monetary and financial cooperation entered a new and substantive stage of growth.

(a) Main points of the CMI

The CMI grew out of the ASEAN Swap Agreement (ASA). In July 1997 when financial crisis struck Thailand, central bank governors of five ASEAN countries (Thailand, the Philippines, Malaysia, Indonesia, and Singapore) signed a memorandum of understanding on currency swap arrangement to provide short-term currency swap support to member countries in which encounter balance of payments problems and temporary liquidity shortage. The amount of the initial ASEAN Swap Agreement was US$ 100 million of which each member contributed US$ 20 million. In 1998, the amount was raised to US$ 200 million, with the contribution proportion remaining unchanged.

The CMI signed in May 2000 includes the following elements: (a) expanding the number of member countries from 5 to 10 and increasing the total amount from US$ 200 million to US$ 1 billion. The five original ASA sponsors and Brunei each contributed US$ 150 million, and other member countries each contributed from US$ 5 million to US$ 60 million. In currency swapping, home currency is taken as mortgage. The counter party provides dollars, euros, or Japanese yen with interest rate equal to the London Interbank Offered Rate. Maximum swap permitted is twice the contribution made, with a term of 6 months and extension no longer than 1 year. The purpose is to provide short-term liquidity to support balance of payments; (b) an ASEAN+3 bilateral currency swap network is set up. This is the core mechanism of the CMI. The maximum swap quota of the bilateral swap network will be negotiated by the two parties one by one and be made up by joint contribution. A total of 10% of the swap quota can be automatically appropriated, while appropriation of the remaining 90% must be approved by the International Monetary Fund. (IMF) The loan period is 90 days with a maximum of seven extensions and an interest rate based on the London Interbank Offered Rate plus 150 basis points. A 50 basis points will be added after every two extensions, but will not exceed 300 basis points; (c) a bilateral national bond buyback agreement network was established. To increase short-term liquidity, one party can use either U.S. treasury bonds or its own government bonds as mortgage to apply for loans from a counter party.

In June 2001, the ASEAN 10+3 meeting of financial ministers and central bank vice governors held in Beijing reached agreement on the implementing rules of the CMI. Subsequently, bilateral negotiations on the ASA were conducted. As of February 2006, 27 currency swap agreements had been concluded by and between China, Japan, the Republic of Korea, and the ASEAN 5, with a total amount of US$ 88 billion (see Table 16-1).

In May 2004, the CMI member countries started to review related issues such as the scale of the fund, linkage between providing loans, and IMF loan conditions and decision-making mechanism, etc. An important outcome of the review was that on May 4, 2005, an ASEAN 10+3 meeting of finance ministers adopted three major measures for enhancing the CMI: (a) increase the initial swap scale from US$ 39.5 billion to US$ 79 billion; (b) reduce the proportion of fund linked with IMF loan conditions from 90% to 80%; and (c) decisions on providing assistance will be made by all member countries instead of by individual member countries.

(2) Drawbacks of the CMI
As of February 2006, 27 currency swap agreements had been concluded between China, Japan, the Republic of Korea, and the ASEAN 5 countries, with a total amount of US$ 88 billion. The size of the CMI far exceeded previous regional currency swap agreements including the G10 Swap Agreement (US$ 38.4 billion), European short-term financing facilities (ECU 7.9 billion) mid-term financing facilities (ECU 16 billion), and the North American Framework Agreement (US$ 8.6 billion).

Table 16-1   Bilateral Swap Agreements under the CMI as of February 2006

Signatories	Currencies	Date	Scale
Japan–South Korea	U.S. dollar–won	July 4, 2001	US$ 7 billion (a) one way
Japan–Thailand	U.S. dollar–baht	July 30, 2001	US$ 3 billion one way
Japan–Philippines	U.S. dollar–peso	August 27, 2001	US$ 3 billion one way
Japan–Malaysia	U.S. dollar–ringgit	October 5, 2001	US$ 3.5 billion (b) one way
China–Thailand	U.S. dollar–baht	December 6, 2001	US$ 2 billion one way
Japan–China	yen–yuan	March 28, 2002	US$ 3 billion two ways
China–South Korea	yuan–won	June 24, 2002	US$ 2 billion two ways
South Korea–Thailand	U.S. dollar–won or U.S. dollar–baht	June 25, 2002	US$ 1 billion two ways
South Korea–Malaysia	U.S. dollar–won or U.S. dollar–ringgit	July 26, 2002	US$ 1 billion two ways
South Korea–Philippines	U.S. dollar–won or U.S. dollar–peso	August 9, 2002	US$ 1 billion two ways
China–Malaysia	U.S. dollar–ringgit	October 9, 2002	US$ 1.5 billion one way
Japan–Indonesia	U.S. dollar–rupiah	February 17, 2003	US$ 3 billion one way
China–Philippines	yuan–peso	August 29, 2003	US$ 1 billion one way
Japan–Singapore	U.S. dollar– Singapore dollar	November 10, 2003	US$ 1 billion one way
South Korea–Indonesia	U.S. dollar–won or U.S. dollar–rupiah	December 24, 2003	US$ 1 billion two ways
China–Indonesia	U.S. dollar–rupiah	December 30, 2003	US$ 1 billion one way

(*Continued*)

Table 16-1 *(Continued)*

Signatories	Currencies	Date	Scale
Japan–South Korea	U.S. dollar–won	July 2004	US$ 2 billion one way
Japan–Philippines	U.S. dollar–peso	August 2004	US$ 3 billion one way
Japan–Thailand	U.S. dollar–baht	January 2005	US$ 3 billion two ways
Japan–Indonesia	U.S. dollar–rupiah	August 2005	US$ 6 billion one way
South Korea–Malaysia	U.S. dollar–ringgit	October 2005	US$ 1.5 billion two ways
South Korea–Philippines	U.S. dollar–peso	October 2005	US$ 1.5 billion two ways
China–Indonesia	U.S. dollar–rupiah	October 2005	US$ 2 billion one way
Japan–Singapore	U.S. dollar– Singapore dollar	November 2005	US$ 3 billion one way
Singapore–Japan	U.S. dollar–yen	November 2005	US$ 1 billion one way
Japan–South Korea	U.S. dollar–won	February 2006	US$ 10 billion (c) one way
South Korea–Japan	U.S. dollar–yen	February 2006	US$ 5 billion (c) one way

Notes: (a) Including US$ 5 billion in the New Miyazawa Initiative (June 17, 1999); (b) including US$ 2.5 billion in the New Miyazawa Initiative (August 18, 1999); (c) replacing US$ 5 billion in the New Miyazawa Initiative.
Source: ASEAN Secretariat and Johnson Stock & Master, Hong Kong.

However, funds available for use in an emergency was limited because of the following two reasons: (1) As the currency swap under the CMI is bilateral rather than multilateral, the bulk of funds cannot be effectively utilized. (2) About 80% of the fund payment under the CMI is linked with the lending conditions of the IMF and thus lacks independence.

In terms of organizational structure, the CMI comprises a series of bilateral swap agreements and does not have an independent coordination or management institution. The advantage of such an organizational structure is that every member country can maintain a relatively high degree of control over its currency swap fund. Its major drawbacks are as follows: (1) Due to lack of an intermediary coordination mechanism, it is hard for the CMI to take timely and joint action in a crisis, which weakens its effectiveness in fending off speculative capital. (2) As currency swaps under the CMI are bilateral rather than multilateral, the assistance a country in crisis can acquire is limited, and deterrence against speculative capital is not strong.

Regarding the use of funds, the CMI only allows member countries in need to acquire 20% of the funds, while the remaining 80% of the funds are linked with IMF lending conditions. Such a linkage mechanism has two major advantages: (1) for assistance providing countries, the security of assistance funds is ensured. Because IMF lending conditions are designed not only to improve short-term balance of payments of the assistance receiving country, but also enhance the stability of its economy and its sustainable growth as well as its future solvency. (2) as for countries receiving assistance, the strict conditions reduce the moral hazard involved in using loans. However, such a system also has the following drawbacks: (1) Such a linkage system greatly restricts the immediate assistance that countries can receive and reduces the capacity of the CMI to cope with the impact of speculative capital in the short term. (2) IMF lending conditions are inflexible, featuring the use of tight fiscal policy to improve balance of payments and increase solvency. Such conditions are not suitable to all countries. As the lessons of the Southeast Asian financial crisis showed, IMF lending conditions could even exacerbate financial crisis in the short term. Indonesia, the Republic of Korea, and Thailand which accepted the IMF lending conditions during the crisis did not do better than Malaysia which refused to do so in terms of stabilizing the market and improving economic performance (He Fan, Zhang Bin and Zhang Ming, 2005).

In summary, the two main drawbacks of the CMI lie in the nature of bilateral swap and the linkage with IMF lending conditions. To improve the CMI, it is necessary to switch the arrangement from bilateral to multilateral currency swap, and decouple fund use with IMF lending conditions. This means that East Asian countries should establish an independent regional institution to monitor the macro economy and financial markets of member countries to ensure the security and efficiency of loans provided. Actually, since the CMI was established in 2000, no member country has tried to use the swap system. This is mainly because the economy of East Asian countries was relatively stable from 2000 to the emergence of the global financial crisis. It is also partly due to the drawbacks of the CMI. When the current global financial crisis erupted, the Republic of Korea did not invoke the CMI when it suffered a severe blow, but instead signed new bilateral currency swap arrangements with the United States, Japan, and China. This shows that the CMI is mostly of symbolic significance and is actually quite difficult to put into practice and would be ineffective after being launched (Gao Haihong, 2009a).

(3) Improvement to the CMI and the latest progress in its growth

At the ASEAN+3 meeting of finance ministers in Kyoto in May 2007, member countries agreed to establish a self-managed regional foreign exchange reserve pool (hereafter referred to as the "East Asian reserve pool") in accordance with a proposal made by the CMI multilateralization work group. This represents a breakthrough made by ASEAN+3 in promoting multilateralization of the CMI.

The East Asian reserve pool refers to a certain amount of foreign exchange to be allocated by the central banks of CMI member countries to a regional reserve fund. The member countries manage their respective contributions to the pool during non-crisis periods, but the reserve pool can be used together to provide emergency assistance in crisis. This shows that the East Asian reserve pool has the following features: first, it is not a real fund pool, but a fund commitment made by CMI member countries. Second, the funds are to be managed by member countries' foreign exchange control authorities. Third, no decision has been made as to whether an independent institution should be established to monitor the macro-economy of CMI member countries and manage fund allocation during a crisis.

Preparation for the East Asian reserve pool is being made in three areas: fund contribution arrangement, borrowing conditions, and monitoring schemes. On May 4, 2008, the 11th ASEAN+3 meeting of finance ministers held in Madrid reached the following agreement regarding the contribution plan and borrowing conditions: (1) The East Asian reserve pool is to have a total amount of at least US$ 80 billion, of which China, Japan, and South Korea are to contribute 80% of the total amount and ASEAN is to contribute the remaining 20%. (2) Borrowing conditions will be the same agreed-upon conditions for the bilateral currency swap agreements under the CMI. (3) The parties will establish a system for monitoring their economic and financial sectors, strengthen regular economic evaluation and policy dialogues between the ASEAN+3 financial and vice central bank governors and increase statistical and analytical capacity on regional economic data. (4) Upon its establishment, the East Asian reserve pool will replace the existing system of bilateral currency swap agreements, but the parties can still decide, at their own discretion and according to their own demands, whether to renew bilateral currency swap agreements.

East Asia currency cooperation is steadily advancing to ease the impact of deepening global financial crisis. On February 22, 2009, in Phuket, Thailand, the ASEAN+3 special meeting of finance ministers released Action Plan to Restore Economic and Financial Stability of the Asian Region. This was the most important step taken to enhance the CMI since the introduction of the East Asian reserve pool of US$ 80 billion in May 2008. According to the plan, the size of East Asian reserve pool will be increased from US$ 80 billion to US$ 120 billion. To ensure effective management and use of the reserve fund, it is proposed that an independent surveillance body be established. After these measures are taken, the proportion of the reserve fund linked with IMF loan conditions will be reduced from the current 80%.

The ASEAN+3 meeting of finance ministers held in Bali, Indonesia on May 3, 2009 announced that the regional foreign exchange reserve pool, with a total amount of US$ 120 billion, would be established by the end of 2009. Finance ministers of China, Japan, and the Republic of Korea reached the following agreement on the contribution shares for East Asian reserve pool: China and Japan will each contribute US$ 38.4 billion, and the Republic of Korea will contribute US$ 19.2 billion, representing 32%, 32%, and 16% of the total reserve pool. The 13th ASEAN meeting of finance ministers held in Pattaya, Thailand on April 9, 2009 reached an agreement on the contributions of ASEAN countries to the regional foreign exchange reserve pool. Thailand, Malaysia, Singapore, Indonesia, and the Philippines will each contribute an amount not more than 10% of their foreign exchange reserve, which is about US$ 4.7 billion. The other five ASEAN countries (Brunei, Laos, Vietnam, Cambodia, and Myanmar) will each contribute not more than 5% of their foreign exchange reserve, which is US$ 34 million for Brunei, US$ 120 million for Cambodia, US$ 31 million for Laos, and US$ 1 billion for Vietnam.

Both the East Asian reserve pool and the Action Plan to Restore Economic and Financial Stability of the Asian Region are designed to address the drawbacks of the CMI. Although the Asian Monetary Fund (AMF) proposed by Japan during the Southeast Asian financial crisis failed to materialize due to IMF and U.S. opposition, the proposed East Asian reserve pool and an independent regional surveillance body actually have some of the functions of the AMF. If the new plan to restore economic and financial stability can be adopted soon, with the implementation of new multilateral initiative, an independent surveillance body and the use of fund not linked with IMF lending conditions, it will be a landmark achievement for East Asian currency cooperation.

16.1.2 *The East Asian bond market*

With the signing and expansion of the CMI, the confidence of East Asian countries in regional monetary cooperation has increased, and there is growing call for creating an East Asian bond market. At present, at least four regional organizations, namely, the Executives' Meeting of East Asia Pacific Central Banks (EMEAP), ASEAN+3, Asia-Pacific Economic Cooperation (APEC), and Asian Co-operation Dialogue (ACD), are actively working on creating an East Asian bond market in different ways. EMEAP calls for building an Asian Bond Fund (ABF) to increase the popularity and attractiveness of East Asian bond products. ASEAN+3 and APEC mainly promote the innovation of new bond products, improvement of credit rating systems, and the establishment and improvement of infrastructure and systemic framework. ACD is responsible for providing political support and integrating political resources (Huang Meibo and Lin Yang, 2008). The ABF under the EMEAP framework and the Asian Bond Markets Initiative (ABMI) under the ASEAN+3 will be discussed in the following paragraphs.

(1) The ABF

At the World Economic Forum East Asian Economic Summit held in Kuala Lumpur in October 2002, then Prime Minister of Thailand Thaksin Shinawatra proposed the creation of an ABF to promote the development of a regional bond market using East Asia's abundant foreign exchange reserves. Thaksin proposed that through voluntary participation, each member country could contribute 1% of its foreign exchange reserve towards creating a fund for East Asian bond markets. The fund would be invested in sovereign bonds denominated in non-regional currencies such as the dollar or the euro issued by East Asian countries to promote stability and development of the region's financial markets.

On June 2, 2003, EMEAP announced that the first ABF1 would be launched, with the central banks of EMEAP member countries jointly contributing US$ 1 billion for investment in the sovereign and quasi-sovereign dollar bonds issued by eight members (China, Hong Kong, Indonesia, South Korea, Malaysia, Philippines, Singapore, and Thailand). In terms of operation, the ABF would be equivalent to an open fund, and the Bank for International Settlements would act as its manager. The minimum subscription was US$ 25 million, which could be redeemed by the fund holder by giving advance notice to the Bank for International Settlement. In terms of capital contribution, Thailand would contribute US$ 120 million, China at least US$ 100 million, the Republic of Korea, Japan, Singapore, and the Philippines would each contribute US$ 100 million, Indonesia and Australia each US$ 50 million, and New Zealand would contribute US$ 25 million.

On December 16, 2004, EMEAP announced that the second ABF2 would be officially established in early 2005 with a total contribution of US$ 2 billion from its members. The ABF2 includes a Pan Asia Bond Index Fund (PAIF) and eight single market funds (SMF). The PAIF consists of US$ 1 billion for investment in the bond markets of the eight member countries (the same as in the first Asian Bond Fund). The investment targets are sovereign and quasi-sovereign bonds denominated in the legal tender of member countries but quoted in the dollar. The total size of the other eight single market funds is also US$ 1 billion, which is for investment in the bond markets of corresponding currencies. On May 12,

2005, the ABF2 was officially launched in two stages. In the first stage, both the PAIF and single market funds accepted only subscriptions from the central banks of the 11 EMEAP members (the above eight members plus Japan, Australia, and New Zealand). In the second stage, the ABF2 would be open to other institutional and private investors, and PAIF was listed in Hong Kong in July 2005.

(2) The Asian Bond Market Initiative (ABMI)
At the sixth ASEAN+3 meeting of finance ministers held in Manila on August 7, 2003, ABMI was adopted, which is supported by the Asian Development Bank (ADB) and funded by the Japanese government. ABMI is implemented in two ways: (1) To create an environment in each country favorable for bond market development; and (2) To hold policy dialogues and discussions on a regular basis. Six working groups were set up at the meeting to implement ABMI. Working group one, led by Thailand, is responsible for innovation in credit securitization instruments. Working group two, jointly led by the Republic of Korea and China, is responsible for credit guarantee and investment systems. Working group three, led by Malaysia, is responsible for foreign exchange transactions and clearance. Working group four, led by China, is responsible for multilateral development banks, foreign government agencies, and Asian transnational companies that issue local currency bonds. Working group five, jointly led by Singapore and Japan, is responsible for regional credit rating system and information disclosure. Working group six, jointly led by the Philippines, Malaysia, and Indonesia, is responsible for coordination of technical assistance. To ensure coordination between working groups, it was decided at the AFMM+3 held in Cheju Island of South Korea on May 15, 2004, to establish a focal group which will hold a meeting every six months.

Thanks to work in the past several years, some of the working groups have met their targets. In East Asia, cross-border issue of local-currency bonds by foreign institutions has been realized. For instance, the ADB, the International Financial Corporation (IFC), which are high rating financial institutions, have issued local-currency denominated bonds in Malaysia, Thailand, and China.

16.2 Limitations of Current East Asian Currency Cooperation

East Asian currency cooperation, triggered by the 1997 East Asian financial crisis, is designed to overcome drawbacks in East Asian economies that were exposed during the crisis. These drawbacks include the following: first, the balance sheets of East Asian financial institutions generally have "double mismatches",[1] namely, currency mismatch and maturity mismatch. This shows that East Asian financial institutions have a common vulnerability; second, East Asian countries often pursue exchange rates that are either officially or in reality pegged to the dollar. Third, there is a lack of monetary cooperation system in East Asia which can manage and prevent monetary crisis. A painful lesson of the Asian financial crisis is that the IMF's role as a last resort international lender is very limited — it cannot provide liquidity support in a timely manner or with an adequate amount, and the conditions attached to loans it provides are not reasonable.

East Asian currency cooperation has been pursued for about a decade. As stated above, East Asian currency cooperation has been carried out at bilateral or multilateral levels, namely, currency swap agreements (such as the CMI) and in regional bond markets. It should be admitted that progress made in East Asian currency cooperation has been limited. At present, under the CMI, the total size of bilateral currency swaps is less than US$ 100 billion. The size of the East Asian reserve pool, even upon expansion, is only US$ 120 billion, and the total size of the ABF and ABF2 is less than US$ 3 billion. As the total foreign exchange reserves of East Asian countries are between US$ 4 to 5 trillions, the CMI and the ABF are insignificant. As a whole, current East Asian currency cooperation is loose in structure and not able to resolve the aforementioned

---

[1] Currency mismatch refers to the fact that since the local currencies of East Asian countries cannot be used for international borrowing and lending, and the regional bond markets are limited in size, East Asian countries have to borrow a huge amount of foreign-currency (US$ or JPY) loans and thus East Asian financial institutions generally have mismatch between local currency assets and foreign currency liabilities. Maturity mismatch means that East Asian countries usually borrow short-term dollar loans to finance longer-term domestic investment.

drawbacks in the East Asian economy. In 2000, while working at the People's Bank of China and leading a research project on Asian financial cooperation and the regionalization of the renminbi, this author pointed out that loose monetary cooperation is quite limited in nature. There are two major goals in pursuing regional currency cooperation: (1) To develop and stabilize the regional financial markets to promote trade, investment, employment, and economic growth; and (2) To improve the region's role and shares in global resource allocation, especially in global reserve allocation. The major means of conducting regional currency cooperation are to stabilize exchange rates, open markets to each others, conduct policy dialogue, and establish a regional mechanism governing balance of payments. However, if the cooperation mechanism is not tightly structured, the role played by these means would be quite limited.

East Asian currency cooperation has not involved exchange rate cooperation, and its progress is slow. The lacking of a solid foundation in business cooperation is the main cause. Business cooperation and monetary cooperation are mutually reinforcing, with the former being the foundation. Unified currency is the highest form of business cooperation, which usually takes a long and tedious process, from forming tariff alliances, to economic union, and finally to currency union. Close business cooperation should have the following features: Regional trade and investment barriers are basically eliminated; goods, services and capitals can flow relatively freely; and trade between member countries in the region constitutes a fairly high proportion of their respective total trade. The success of European monetary cooperation is due to the fact that it gradually achieved integration in trade and investment. Without the momentum created by business cooperation, Europe could not unify its currencies. Britain's failure to set up the Sterling Group shows that without a foundation for close business cooperation, monetary cooperation would often be loose, unstable, and unlikely to succeed. In summary, loose business cooperation restricts the coordination capacity of exchange rate policies and the potential of open markets in the region. Policy dialogue and coordination systems are limited in operation and lack binding power. Loose business cooperation also limits the effectiveness of balance of payments adjustment mechanism in the region.

16.3 Evaluation of East Asian Currency Cooperation

Strictly speaking, business cooperation is not the same as monetary cooperation. The former refers to cooperation in real economy such as trade and investment, while the latter refers to cooperation in virtual economy such as in monetary and financial sectors. Factors affecting monetary cooperation are naturally unique. But as discussed earlier, close business cooperation is the foundation of monetary cooperation. Therefore, factors affecting business cooperation have also become, to some extent, factors affecting monetary cooperation. At present, three main factors hinder East Asian currency cooperation.

16.3.1 *Problems with optimum currency areas*

In terms of economics, the current East Asian region is not yet an optimum currency area because East Asian countries have rather high heterogeneity in terms of their economic cycles and structures. In addition, economies in East Asia are at different levels of development, including developed economies with high per capita income such as Japan, Hong Kong, and Singapore and developing economies with relatively low per capita income such as China, Vietnam, and Thailand. Such a huge gap in level of development has made monetary cooperation difficult.

Nevertheless, according to the latest theories of optimum currency area, if an optimum currency area is endogenous, by carrying out regional currency cooperation, gap between economic cycles and structures of East Asian countries could be narrowed. Additionally, large number of empirical studies on market integration, economic openness, frequency and intensity of impact of non-hedged shocks and actual exchange rate linkage in East Asia show that East Asian countries have met some conditions for building a currency union.

16.3.1.1 *Non-economic factors*

East Asian countries are diversified in religion and culture, and their historical relations are riddled with conflicts. Deep-seated problems such as Japan's attitude towards its war past and historical conflicts between other countries cannot be solved overnight, which makes it difficult for East Asian countries to establish mutual trust in many areas. It is therefore hard to make substantial progress in East Asian currency cooperation in a short period of time. Additionally, East Asian countries have different political and economic systems, which is also an important factor hindering East Asian currency cooperation. Current monetary cooperation in East Asia is crisis driven, as financial crisis has made East Asian countries seek common ground while setting aside their differences and take collective action based on common interests. Just as the Southeast Asian financial crisis served as a catalyst for creating the Chiang Mai Initiative, we have reason to believe that the current global financial crisis will further advance East Asian currency cooperation.

16.3.1.2 *Who will be the leading country*

This is by far the biggest problem facing East Asian currency cooperation. Japan is the biggest and most developed economy in East Asia, but it is unable to play the role of a leading country in East Asian Region for the following reasons:

First, Japan does not represent the interests of many East Asian countries. Monetary cooperation is generally based on a close free trade area. In addition to conditions such as complementary economies, compatible wwweconomic systems, and geographic proximity, a free trade area must have a leading country that can represent its interests in global economic policy coordination. Otherwise, this will affect the mutual interests of the free trade area and make it leaderless, and its role in international economic policy coordination will thus be weakened. Currently, tension between developed countries and developing countries remains a major issue. Despite the fact that Japan is the leading East Asian economy, its trade, however, is mainly conducted with the United States and Europe, and capital flow takes place mainly between Japan, Europe, and the United States. There is tension between Japan and developing East Asian countries, just as there is tension between the United States and Europe on the one hand and the developing East Asian countries on the other. Thus, Japan is unlikely to represent the East Asian developing countries.

Second, in order to play an important role in a free trade zone and in the world, a leading country should maintain close interaction with its neighbors. But Japan has not yet established a free trade area or maintain close business cooperation with any of the East Asian countries. Germany has played a leading role in promoting European currency cooperation. Before signing the "Treaty for the Establishment of a European Economic Community" in 1957, Germany, France, Holland, Italy, Belgium, and Luxembourg invited Britain to join it, but was turned down. From the 1950s to the early 1960s, in terms of military, political, and economic strength, Germany could not match Britain. Yet Germany defeated Britain in the competition to become a European leader. By isolating itself from other European countries and failing to represent their interests, Britain gave away its chance to be a regional leader to Germany and France.

Third, Japan is not qualified to act as a leading country. To be a leading country, the following conditions should be met: a country should have a large and developed economy, a large export sector, a large capital market, fairly large landmass, fairly high international political status, and strong cultural compatibility. Japan is the second largest economy in the world, but its economy is vulnerable because of its heavy reliance on export. While Japan has a big domestic market, its lack of openness and particularly its closed agricultural market have always been the subject of international criticism. Yet agriculture is strong for many East Asian economies. More importantly, the Japanese yen has failed to acquire international position commensurate with its economic strength due to various causes that cannot be resolved any time soon.

In discussing who should be the leading country in East Asian currency cooperation, it is necessary to look at China. China is the second largest economy in East Asia and is expected to surpass Japan this year. As China is a developing country, its economy and the financial market are not developed enough for it to take up the role as the leading country in the short term. However, from the mid-term and long-term view, the rapid growth of China's economy, the improvement of its financial market and the international position of the renminbi will enable China to play a bigger role in Asian currency cooperation.

Chapter 17

China and East Asian Currency Cooperation

China is the second biggest economy in East Asia, and its growth over the last two to three decades has been unparalleled in the region. This has laid the economic foundation for China to participate in East Asian currency cooperation. With its rapid economic growth and deepening business cooperation with neighbors in East Asia, China will undoubtedly play a key role in promoting East Asian currency cooperation.

17.1 The Economic Foundation for China's Participation in East Asian Currency Cooperation

As the biggest emerging economy in East Asia, China has formed increasingly close trade and investment ties with other East Asian countries. East Asian countries generally have high savings rates and export-oriented growth models. These similarities mean that these countries tend to have fairly synchronized economic cycles. As shown in Figure 17-1, China had the highest growth rate among East Asian countries in the first decade of the 21st century, but its growth model is similar to those of other East Asian countries. For instance, between 2000 and 2007, all the East Asian countries registered continued economic growth. But such growth declined in 2008, hit a bottom in 2009 and rebounded in 2010. The cyclical economic

(*Percent*)

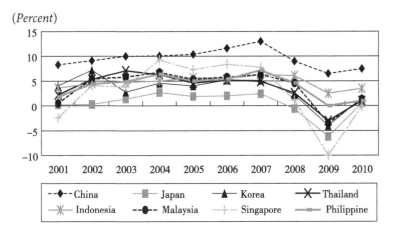

Figure 17-1   Cyclical Synchronisms in East Asia

Note: The index is the year-on-year growth rate of real GDP.
Source: IMF, *World Economic Outlook* (April 2009).

synchronism between China and other East Asian countries shows that their growth to a large extent hinges on demands outside of East Asia.

As the trade structures indicated in Figure 17-2 and Table 17-1 show, China and its East Asian neighbors have established close international division of labor and trade ties. From 1984 to 2008, the share of Chinese export to other East Asian countries declined from 68% to 46%, an indication of the increasing diversification of China's export markets. The proportion of China's imports from these countries increased from 49% to 62%, which shows the growing importance of processing trade in China's foreign trade. In 2004, 40% of China's total imports were imports for processing. Of this, 70% were from other East Asian economies, and only 5% and 10%, were respectively from the United States and 15 European Union (EU) countries. As to China's export structure, in 2004, processing export made up 55% of China's export, 25% of which went to the United States, 18% of which went to the EU, and 25% of which went to East Asia (excluding Hong Kong). This model of processing trade reflects a highly asymmetrical balance of trade between China, East Asia, and other regions. In 2004, China's trade surplus with the United States and 15 EU countries stood at US$ 111.9 billion US$ 110.2 billion of which came from China's processing trade. During the same period, China ran a trade

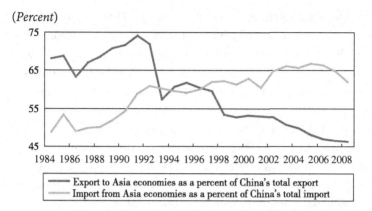

(Percent)

Export to Asia economies as a percent of China's total export
Import from Asia economies as a percent of China's total import

Figure 17-2   Proportions of China's Intra-Regional Trade to Total Trade (1984–2008)

Source: CEIC.

Table 17-1   China's Trade and Payment Structure (2004)

	World	South Korea and Taiwan	Japan	ASEAN 5	Hong Kong	USA	EU 15	Other regions
Import (%)								
Total imports	100	23	17	11	2	8	12	28
General imports	44	6	6	4	1	4	8	15
Processing imports	40	14	7	5	1	2	4	7
Others	16	3	4	2	0	2	1	5
Export (%)								
Total exports	100	7	12	6	17	21	17	19
General exports	41	3	5	3	4	6	7	13
Processing exports	55	4	7	3	12	14	10	5
Others	4	0	0	0	1	1	0	2
Balance of trade (US$ 1 billion)								
Net balance of trade	32	–85.6	–20.8	–22.9	89.1	80.3	31.8	–39.9
General trade	45.9	–14.7	–5.7	–2.9	19.9	13.7	–2	37.6
Processing trade	106.3	–54.9	3.3	–11.7	64.3	72.7	37.5	–5
Other	–69.7	–16	–18.4	–8.3	4.9	–6.2	–3.7	–21.9

Note: "Processing imports" refer to commodities imported to then be processed for export. "Processing exports" refer to processing imports that are exported upon completion. "General imports" refer to products and commodities imported for domestic consumption. "General exports" refer to the export of commodities produced using domestic inputs.

Source: Chinese customs statistical data cited from Willem Thorbecke (2006).

deficit with East Asian economies (excluding Hong Kong) of US$ 106.4 billion US$ 63.3 billion of which was from processing trade. Seen in this light, China's trade surplus with the United States and the EU was actually the trade surplus of all East Asia with the United States and the EU. Such international division of labor and trade model in East Asia have come about owing to the emergence of Wintelism in the early 1990s. Winterlism became a fairly developed system of international division of labor in production in the late 1990s, which has become an important model of production in traditional industries such as the automobile sector (Huang Weiping and Zhu Wenhui, 2004). The increasing use of this production model will make international division of labor and trade ties between China and other East Asian economies ever closer.

Foreign direct investment (FDI) made in China by investors from elsewhere in Asia far exceeded that from Europe and North America (Figure 17-3). The proportion of FDI made in China by investors from Asia, Europe, and North America in 1995 was respectively 81%, 6%, and 9% of total FDI in China. In 2008, these figures were 51%, 5%, and 3%. The proportion of FDI coming from the British Virgin Islands in 2008 was 15%, most of which also came from Asian sources.

China's direct overseas investments are mainly made in Asia and Latin America (Figure 17-4). In 2005 and 2006, China's investment in Asia was lower than that of Latin America, but such investment in East Asia far exceeded than in Latin America in 2007.

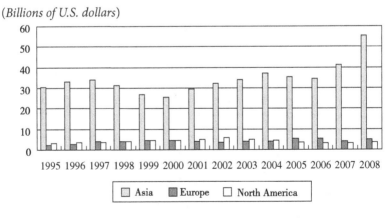

Figure 17-3   Major Sources of FDI Entering China (1995–2008)

Source: CEIC.

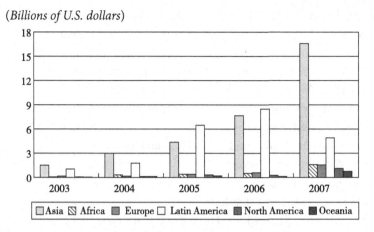

Figure 17-4 Major Destinations of Chinese Outward FDI (2003–2007)
Source: CEIC.

As mentioned earlier in this chapter, similarities between the growth models and economic structures of China and other East Asian economies has led to a certain degree of synchronism in the growth rates of these countries. In terms of foreign trade and direct overseas investment, China is much more closely linked with its East Asian neighbors than with countries in other regions. This shows that China has a solid foundation for participating in East Asian regional currency cooperation.

17.2 The Foundation of Business Cooperation for China's Participation in East Asian Currency Cooperation

The successful establishment of the China–ASEAN (Association of Southeast Asian Nations) Free Trade Zone has created a solid foundation for China to participate in East Asian currency cooperation. At the Fourth Annual ASEAN–China (10+1) Summit held in Singapore in September 2000, China's then Premier, Zhu Rongji, proposed the establishment of the China–ASEAN Free Trade Zone, which was endorsed by the ASEAN countries. At the following ASEAN–China Summit held in Brunei in November 2001, China and the 10 ASEAN member countries announced the goal to establish the China–ASEAN Free Trade Zone within the following 10 years. On November 4, 2002, the Sixth Annual China–ASEAN Summit was held in Phnom Penh, the capital of Cambodia. During this summit, leaders from China and the 10 ASEAN countries signed the China–ASEAN Framework Agreement on Comprehensive Economic Cooperation, committing themselves to establish the China–ASEAN Free Trade Zone in 2010. This inaugurated the process of establishing the China–ASEAN Free Trade Zone. It was pointed out in the statements of participating governments that the establishment of the China–ASEAN Free Trade Zone was designed not only to remove tariff and non-tariff barriers between China and ASEAN countries, but also to establish an integrated framework among the participant countries to accelerate market integration through investment promotion, facilitating trade, and adopting new rules and standards.

The China–ASEAN Free Trade Zone is the first free trade zone established by China, which has made fast progress and has been highly successful. It has further grown with the implementation of the Goods Trade Agreement and the Service Trade Agreement. Tariff reduction has greatly promoted trade of goods between China and ASEAN. The rapid growth of trade between China and the ASEAN countries is due to the complementary nature of both economies and geographical proximity. This means that the China–ASEAN Free Trade Zone is quite resistant to external shocks. For example, despite the global financial crisis, trade between China and ASEAN has expanded continuously. Total trade between China and ASEAN in 2008 reached US$ 231.1 billion, 9% of China's annual foreign trade. This figure represented a year-on-year growth rate of 13.9%, making the ASEAN countries collectively China's fourth largest trading partner and third largest source of import. The growth of China–ASEAN Free Trade Zone went through a critical period in 2009–2010. In accordance with the Free Trade Zone's tariff reduction target, the average import tariff placed by China on goods from ASEAN countries was reduced to 5.8% by the end of 2008, and it was further reduced to 2.4% on January 1, 2009. By 2010, 93% of ASEAN's exports to China received zero tariff treatment. ASEAN countries also reduced tariffs on imports from China. China and ASEAN countries agreed to open over 60 service sectors among each other, with the level of openness in services higher than that required by the World Trade Organisation (WTO). Bilateral investment between China and ASEAN is also growing rapidly. According to statistics released by the Chinese Ministry of Commerce, despite the negative impact of the global financial crisis, bilateral investment between China and ASEAN approached US$ 60 billion in 2008. The signing of the China–ASEAN Investment Agreement at the China–ASEAN Summit in Thailand in April 2009 marked the successful conclusion China–ASEAN Free Trade Zone negotiations.

The establishment of the China–ASEAN Free Trade Zone is a landmark event in China–ASEAN business cooperation. It will create an economic area with 1.9 billion consumers, nearly US$ 6 trillion of GDP and US$ 1.2 trillion of trade. It will be the largest free trade zone in the world in terms of population and the third largest one in terms of size, next only to the EU and North American Free Trade Agreement. Like the EU, the China–ASEAN Free Trade Zone will greatly boost bilateral economic exchange and trade, enhance currency cooperation, and promote mutual trust and interaction. The establishment of the China–ASEAN Free Trade Zone has provided a good foundation for China's participation in East Asian currency cooperation.

17.3 Current State of China's Participation in East Asian Currency Cooperation

At present, China's participation in East Asian currency cooperation mainly involves the East Asian liquidity mutual-assistance mechanism and the building of East Asian bond market. As shown in Table 17-2, the Chinese government is helping build the supply network for East Asian liquidity mutual-assistance mechanisms on two levels. At the first level, China is participating in East Asian currency cooperation within the framework of the Chiang Mai Initiative (CMI). Since 2001, China has participated in bilateral currency swap arrangements totaling US$ 23.5 billion with Thailand, Japan, South Korea, Malaysia, the Philippines, and Indonesia. Agreements between China and Japan and the Republic of Korea involve two-ways currency swaps, while agreements with the other four nations listed involve one-way currency swaps (China provides liquidity to its counter parties). China has also actively participated in the building of the East Asian reserve pool, a part of the multilateral framework of the CMI agreement. The size of this reserve pool has increased from US$ 80 billion to US$ 120 billion. About 80% of this sum is

Table 17-2   China's Participation in the East Asian Liquidity Mutual-Assistance Mechanism

Participants	Scale	Execution date
CMI		
Bilateral Currency Swap Agreement		
China–Thailand (unilateral)	US$ 2 billion	December 2001 through December 2004
China–Japan (bilateral)	US$ 6 billion	March 2002
China–South Korea (bilateral)	US$ 8 billion	June 2002
China–Malaysia (unilateral)	US$ 1.5 billion	October 2002
China–Philippines (unilateral)	US$ 2 billion	August 2003; revised in April 2007
China–Indonesia (unilateral)	US$ 4 billion	December 2003; revised in October 2006
Multilateral Reserve Currency Fund		
China, Japan, South Korea, and ASEAN	US$ 80 billion	May 2008
China, Japan, South Korea, and ASEAN	US$ 120 billion	February 2009
Bilateral Local Currency Swap Between Central Banks		
China–South Korea	RMB 180 billion	December 2008
China–Hong Kong	RMB 200 billion	January 2009
China–Malaysia	RMB 80 billion	February 2009
China–Belarus	RMB 20 billion	March 2009
China–Indonesia	RMB 100 billion	March 2009
China–Argentina	RMB 70 billion	March 2009

Source: Gao Haihong (2009b).

collectively contributed by China, Japan, and the Republic of Korea. China's share of contribution is 32% of the total sum, or US$ 38.4 billion, a figure equal to that provided by Japan.

On the second level, against the backdrop of the subprime mortgage crisis escalating into the global financial crisis, China began in late 2008 to sign a series of local currency swap agreements with the Republic of Korea, Hong Kong, Malaysia, Belarus, Indonesia, and Argentina with a total amount of RMB 650 billion Yuan. While signing these agreements, the People's Bank of China (PBC) did not enter into additional agreements with the central banks of other countries allowing for the purchase of dollars with renminbi from the PBC. This shows that China's participation in monetary cooperation with other countries not only helped those countries resist the impact of financial shocks but also promoted the internationalization of the renminbi. China has, thus, contributed to the stabilization of the international monetary system and promoted monetary cooperation between China and the rest of East Asia.

The Chinese government has also actively participated in the development of the East Asian bond market. The PBC is a major contributor to Asian Bond Fund (ABF1) and (ABF2). China is responsible for the operation of two working groups within the Asian Bond Market Initiative (ABMI). One is on credit guarantee and credit investment mechanisms, and the other is on the issuance of local currency-denominated bonds by multilateral development banks, foreign government organizations, and Asian transnational companies. There is also progress on the issuance of renminbi-denominated bonds by foreign financial institutions within China and the issuance of renminbi-denominated bonds by Chinese financial institutions in offshore financial markets. In October 2005, the International Finance Corporation (IFC) and the Asian Development Bank (ADB) issued two groups of "Panda Bonds" worth RMB 1.13 billion Yuan and RMB 1 billion Yuan respectively in China's intra-bank bond market. Table 17-3 shows that since June 2007, five Chinese financial institutions have issued seven batches of renminbi-denominated bonds in the Hong Kong market. The average bond maturity is between 2 and 3 years with a bond interest rate of between 3% and 3.4%. All the bonds were oversubscribed, raising RMB 22 billion Yuan.

17.4 Prospects of China's Participation in East Asian Currency Cooperation

With the growth of its overall national strength and its further integration into the global economy and finance, China will play an increasingly important role in East Asian and global affairs. China has not yet fully opened its capital accounts and the renminbi is not yet freely convertible.

Table 17-3   RMB Bonds Issued by Chinese Financial Institutions in Hong Kong

Issuers	Date of issue	Amount (RMB 100 million)	Maturity (years)	Interest rate	Subscription ratio
China Development Bank	June 2007	50	2	3.00	1.91
China Export–Import Bank	August 2007	20	2	3.05	1.68
			3	3.20	
Bank of China	September 2007	30	2	3.15	1.78
			3	3.35	
Bank of Communications	July 2008	30	2	3.25	6.80
China Export–Import Bank	September 2008	30	3	3.40	2.75
China Construction Bank	September 2008	30	2	3.24	1.81
Bank of China	September 2008	30	2	3.25	4.16
			3	3.40	

Source: Hong Kong Monetary Authority.

But this should not be an obstacle to the internationalization of the renminbi. China can participate in East Asian currency cooperation while maintaining control over part of its capital accounts.

Regional currency cooperation can promote international currency cooperation. To reach agreement on international currency cooperation is very difficult, while it is much easier to pursue such cooperation among economies within a smaller geographical area and with a similar level of development. The integration of Europe's monetary system has broken the dollar's monopoly and provided a good example of regional monetary cooperation. The development of currency cooperation in other regions will challenge the dollar's dominance and make international currency cooperation possible.

Since the outbreak of the global financial crisis, the U.S. government has resorted to extremely loose fiscal and monetary policies to save both its financial market and its real economy. By doing so, it has created the risks of the decline of U.S. debt's market value and the devaluation of the dollar. As the United States' largest international creditor, China could suffer tremendous losses in its dollar denominated reserves assets. In view of this, China began in the second half of 2008 to adjust its international financial strategy to reduce its dependence on the dollar. The new strategy has three goals: to internationalize the renminbi, participate in regional currency cooperation, and work to rebuild the international monetary system. This is aimed to create a more stable and equitable environment for the development of China and other developing countries as well as the growth of the global economy.

Some people see a potential conflict between the internationalization of the renminbi and regional currency cooperation. In their view, the renminbi's internationalization is to be pursued by China unilaterally, whereas joining regional currency cooperation requires working with developed countries such as Japan; and China can only choose between the two options. But this should not be the case. Internationalizing (or regionalizing) the renminbi will not prevent China from participating in regional currency cooperation. On the contrary, China's participation in regional currency cooperation and the renminbi's internationalization are a mutually reinforcing process. Using the renminbi as a clearing currency for trade in East Asia will enhance the renminbi's position in East Asian financial cooperation, and China's participation in regional monetary and financial cooperation will strengthen the renminbi's position as a reserve currency in East Asia.

In internationalizing the renminbi, China can choose three paths: the path of the dollar (unilateral internationalization), the path of the German mark (participating in regional monetary and financial cooperation and eventually disappearing altogether), and the path of the British pound sterling (participating in European monetary cooperation and then withdrawing from the euro exchange rate linkage mechanism). There is no need for China to commit itself to any one path earlier than necessary (Zhang Ming, 2009).

Which country should play the leading role is an unavoidable question for China when participating in East Asian currency cooperation. In terms of the size of the economy, level of development and maturity of the financial market, Japan is in a position to play such a role. But it has failed to do so. China has no intention to compete with Japan for leadership over East Asian currency cooperation. Which country can play a leading role in East Asian economic, trade, and currency cooperation does not hinge on anyone's will. In essence, it is a question about economic strength and about whether a country is willing to make sacrifice. There is always a trade-off involved here. Being the leading country means having to make both sacrifices and contributions. For example, the leading country needs to adjust the export-oriented growth model, increase import, and provide more assistance to others. It needs to undertake more responsibilities and obligations in cooperation. For East Asian currency cooperation to move forward, a currency needs to play the leading role. Which currency can assume this responsibility? It depends on economic strength and a willingness to make sacrifice. At present, no currency in East Asia can meet these criteria. Such a currency, or possibly a basket of currencies, may eventually emerge as a result of natural choice in East Asian cooperation.

Part Six

Internationalization
of the Renminbi

Over the years, the dollar-based international monetary system has been an effective means used by the United States to maintain its position as the world leader. However, the global financial crisis has not only hit the U.S. economy hard, but also dealt a fatal blow to the dollar's international status, reforming the current international monetary system has become the consensus of the international community, which will provide a rare opportunity to accelerate the internationalization of the renminbi. This section will, on the basis of discussing the connotation of currency internationalization and reviewing the experiences and lessons of the internationalization of major currencies, analyze the advantages and disadvantages of the internationalization of the renminbi and propose a pathway for achieving this goal.

Chapter 18

Currency Internationalization

While the international circulation of a currency is not new, study on the internationalization of currencies was fairly recent. After the 1960s, with the beginning of the internationalization of the Japanese yen and the success of European currency integration, more scholars started to study the internationalization of currencies. This chapter briefly discusses what the internationalization of currencies is about.

18.1 Defining Currency Internationalization

Before giving a definition of "currency internationalization", it is necessary to have a clear idea about the concept of an international currency.

Cohen (1971) proposed two generally accepted standards for defining an international currency. First, with regards to its monetary function, an international currency is a currency commonly accepted and used in the global market. It generally has part of or all the monetary functions, such as being the standard in determining price for international settlement, a means for circulation, a means of payment, and a store of value. Second, an international currency can be invested not only in one country, but also in other parts of the world.[1]

---

[1] Benjamin Cohen (1971), pp. 494–507.

Cohen's analysis is consistent with Karl Marx's concept of "world currency". In Karl Marx's view, a currency generally has four functions — as a measure of value, a means of circulation, a means of payment, and a store of value. When a country's currency performs these functions in the world, it becomes a world currency.[2] Generally, international currencies refer to the dollar, the Japanese yen, euro, British pound sterling, the Hong Kong dollar, the Canadian dollar, the Australian dollar, the South African rand, etc., while a world currency refers exclusively to an international currency which can most effectively and fully exercise monetary functions. Currently, only the dollar can be called a world currency.

Hartmann (1998) outlined the three main functions of an international currency. First, it functions as a medium of exchange and as an intervention currency. Here, exchange includes trade of goods and capital transaction. In the private sector, an international currency is used as a medium of exchange, whereas for the government, an international currency is the means for market intervention with which to ensure balance of payments. Second, an international currency serves as a unit of account and as an anchor currency. It acts as a unit of account for trade of goods or financial transactions in the private sector. When it is used by a country as the standard in determining the official exchange rate (e.g., when another country pegs the exchange rate of its currency to this currency), it functions as an anchor currency. Finally, an international currency can also function as a store of value and a reserve currency. If an international currency is used as the investment currency for financial assets in the private sector, then it is used as a private store of value. If the government holds an international currency or financial assets priced in it, the international currency functions as a reserve currency.[3]

Hartmann's view on the function of an international currency can be summarized as follows: first, he outlined three separate functions of an international currency for the private sector and the government, which take six forms. Second, all the three major functions of an international currency, namely, as a medium of exchange, an intervention currency, and as a store of value and reserve currency, require the involvement of

---

[2] Guo Dali and Wang Yanan (1963), pp. 72–132.
[3] Phillip Hartmann (1998), pp. 35–39.

corresponding currencies or assets. When functioning as a unit of account and an anchor currency, an international currency's value does not necessarily correspond with real currencies or assets, as its role is just to provide a virtual standard or scale. Finally, an international currency does not require having all the three functions or taking all the six forms, because some currencies can only have some of these functions. For instance, the Japanese yen, while an important international currency, functions mainly as store of value and a reserve currency.

Based on the above mentioned analysis of an international currency, we can define currency internationalization as the process of partially or fully expanding the functions of a domestic currency to other countries or even the whole world.

18.2 Levels of Currency Internationalization

Different levels of currency internationalization reflect the international status of international currencies. For one currency, different levels of its internationalization reflect changes it has gone through in different stages of this process. Generally speaking, a currency's internationalization starts from one region and expands to the whole world. In terms of monetary functions, a currency starts with the most basic function of a medium of exchange and then acquires other functions. Demand for such currency always originates in the private sector of other countries. Only when the currency has obtained a large share of market trade and gained enough influence will there be a demand for it from foreign governments to be used as a means for making market intervention and as a reserve currency.

18.2.1 *Degree and scale of currency internationalization*

The degree of currency internationalization depends on the scale of its use. For instance, thanks to the economic size of South Africa and its influence in Southern Africa, its currency, the rand (ZAR), is widely circulated both at home and in its three neighboring countries. In 1986, Southern African countries reached the Common Monetary Area Agreement whereby the rand became the official currency in Lesotho and

Swaziland. In 1992, following its independence, Namibia also joined this agreement. Yet, the level of the rand's internationalization is not high, because it is used only in these four southern African countries. By contrast, the Japanese yen is widely used in East Asia and Southeastern Asia, with many functions of an international currency, although not all its functions. The yen is mainly used for settlement in international trade, but its percentage for such settlement is not high. Other countries rarely use yen as their anchor currency. Among international currencies, the dollar is used most extensively. This is particularly the case in Latin America where the dollar is used as an anchor currency. In East Asia which has the largest number of emerging economies, most countries peg their currencies to the dollar. In international trade, many products such as oil, soy beans, corn, etc., are quoted in dollar.

18.2.2 *Functions of an international currency*

The most basic function of an international currency is to act as a medium of exchange. Here, exchange mainly includes trade of goods and services and capital transactions. In trade of goods, the degree of currency internationalization is mainly reflected by the rate at which a currency is used for settling accounts in import and export of goods. In capital transactions, the degree of currency internationalization is reflected mainly by the rate at which the currency is used for foreign exchange transactions.

In international trade payment and settlement, the dollar is used by many countries for 50% or more of their imports and exports accounts. Only in France, Britain, and Germany, the use of the dollar makes up 30% of their total exports. But its percentage is higher for imports of these countries (Tables 18-1 and 18-2). So it is evident that in world imports and exports, the dollar is the most important payment and settlement currency. The euro mainly functions as a medium of exchange within the euro zone and is less used outside the zone. The dollar and the euro are the main settlement and pricing currencies in international trade. By comparison, the yen is less used as a medium of exchange, and it is even not as commonly used for imports as the British pound sterling and the Australian dollar.

Table 18-1 Major Currencies Invoicing in the Export
(Percent)

	German	France	Great Britain	Japan	Australia	South Africa	Canada	South Korea	Pakistan
EUR	57.7	49.5	21.0	8.5	0.9	17.0	—	4.9	4.0
U.S. dollars	26.6	37.9	27.8	51.2	67.4	52.0	70.0	85.9	91.4
Local Currency	57.7	49.5	49.0	36.3	28.8	25.0	23.0	<9.2	<4.6

Note: Data for Germany is an average for the years 2002 to 2004; France, Japan, Australia, and South Korea are averages for 1999 to 2003; Britain is an average for 1999 to 2002; South Africa from 2003; Canada from 2001; and Pakistan from 2001 to 2003.
Source: Annette Kamps (2006), pp. 43–50.

Table 18-2 Major Currencies Invoicing in the Import
(Percent)

	U.S.	Germany	France	Great Britain	Australia	Japan	South Korea	Pakistan
EUR	2.0	52.0	42.0	22.0	8.5	3.6	4.4	6.5
U.S. dollars	90.3	34.8	48.7	34.8	49.7	69.4	80.4	83.9
Local Currency	90.3	52.0	42.0	38.8	30.2	24.1	15.3	9.6

Note: U.S. data is for 2003; Germany is an average from 2002 to 2004; France, Japan, Australia, and South Korea are averages from 1999 to 2003; Britain is the average from 1999 to 2002; Pakistan is the average from 2001 to 2003.
Source: Annette Kamps (2006), pp. 43–50.

In terms of capital transactions, currencies differ in their function as a medium of exchange. Table 18-3 shows that the dollar holds the dominant position in global foreign exchange transactions. The euro takes the second place, but there is a significant gap between the two, which is consistent with the role of the euro in international trade settlement. Finally, the yen follows the dollar and the euro in terms of use in foreign exchange transactions, which is also consistent with its position in international trade settlement. But its share in total foreign exchange transactions is far

Table 18-3   Currency Distribution of Reported Foreign Exchange Market Turnover
(*Percentage shares of average daily turnover in April 2007*)

	2001	2004	2007
U.S. dollar	90.3	88.7	86.3
Euro	37.6	36.9	37.0
Yen	22.7	20.2	16.5
Pound sterling	13.2	16.9	15.0
Swiss franc	6.1	6.0	6.8
Australian dollar	4.2	5.9	6.7
Canadian dollar	4.5	4.2	4.2
Swedish krona	2.6	2.3	2.8
Hong Kong dollar	2.3	1.9	2.8
Norwegian krone	1.5	1.4	2.2
New Zealand dollar	0.6	1.0	1.9
Mexican peso	0.9	1.1	1.3
Singapore dollar	1.1	1.0	1.2
Won	0.7	1.2	1.1
Rand	1.0	0.8	0.9
Danish krone	1.2	0.9	0.9
Ruble	0.4	0.7	0.8
Zloty	0.5	0.4	0.8
Indian rupee	0.2	0.3	0.7
Renminbi	0.0	0.1	0.5
New Taiwan dollar	0.3	0.4	0.4
Brazilian real	0.4	0.2	0.4
All currencies	200.0	200.0	200.0
Emerging market currencies	16.9	15.4	19.8

Note: Because two currencies are involved in each transaction, the sum of percentage shares of individual currencies totals 200% instead of 100%, adjusted for local and cross-border double counting. Data for 2004 have been revised. Emerging market currencies is defined as the residual after accounting for the top eight currencies, the Norwegian krone, the New Zealand dollar, and the Danish krone. *Source*: BIS (2007).

higher than its share in trade settlement. Despite the rapid growth of the use of the currencies of some emerging economies such as the Russian ruble (RUB), the Indian rupee (INR), and the renminbi (RMB) in global foreign exchange transactions, their share in such transactions is still insignificant. This shows that the degree of internationalization of these currencies is still low.

In terms of functioning as a store of value, both the euro and the dollar are important. As Table 18-4 shows, between 1998 and 2007, bonds or bills issued in the dollar or the euro made up about 90% of the world total. Following the creation of the euro, the monopoly of the dollar in bond and bill issuing market was weakened. The proportion of euro-issued bills and bonds increased rapidly, whose amount even slightly surpassed that of the dollar. Bonds or bills issued in other currencies made up a small percentage of the total issuance.

The official foreign exchange reserves of countries are mainly made up of the dollar, followed by the euro. The pound sterling and the yen only play an auxiliary role. Figure 18-1 shows changes in the percentage of

Table 18-4 Dollar, Euro, Yen, and Swiss Franc Pricing International Bonds and Bills
(*Percent*)

	U.S. dollar	Euro	Yen	Swiss franc
1998	60.3	—	3.8	1.1
1994	7.6	46.0	2.1	0.4
2000	50.9	38.9	1.0	0.0
2001	49.3	43.8	1.3	0.4
2002	43.3	49.0	1.8	0.8
2003	30.8	57.5	0.3	1.2
2004	24.1	59.4	1.8	0.9
2005	26.4	54.8	0.2	0.7
2006	39.1	46.0	0.7	1.1
2007	41.8	41.5	3.3	1.2

Source: BIS Global Derivatives Statistics.

(Percent)

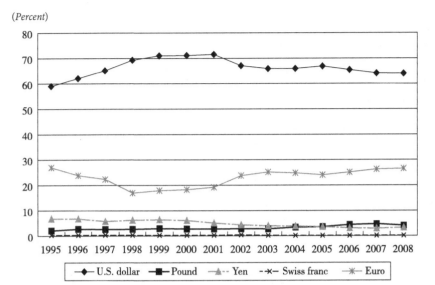

Figure 18-1   Major International Currencies in World Foreign Exchange Reserve (1995–2008)

Note: For 1995 to 1998, since the euro did not yet exist, data is a sum of the percentages of these four currencies: Deutsch mark, French franc, the Dutch guilder, and European Currency Unit (ECU).
Source: IMF (2009).

various currencies used in international foreign exchange reserve between 1995 and 2008. The percentage of the dollar reserves were at 60–70%, while the euro reserves were around 20%. Together, they constituted more than 90% of the global foreign exchange reserves. In 2008, the percentage of British pound sterling, the yen, and the Swiss franc, was 4.08%, 3.27%, and 0.13% respectively. Other currencies together made up less than 2% of the total global foreign exchange reserves.

Chapter 19

Internationalization
of Major Currencies

The history of the evolution of international monetary systems is also a history of the internationalization of major currencies. This chapter reviews the internationalization of the British pound sterling, the dollar, the Deutsch mark, and the Japanese yen to provide reference for the internationalization of the renminbi.

19.1 Internationalization of the British Pound Sterling

During the gold standard period, Britain ushered in the era of the pound sterling in the world by utilizing its maritime dominance and pursuing a free trade policy. Until the outbreak of World War I, the pound sterling was the most important international instrument of payment and reserve currency in the world. However, World War I devastated the foundation of the gold standard, and the international status of the pound sterling declined and was ultimately replaced by the dollar.

19.1.1 *Rise and glory of the British pound sterling*

From the mid to late 16th century, Britain became the dominant maritime power. The first Industrial Revolution in the 1760s pushed Britain into the central stage of the world. The Industrial Revolution greatly boosted Britain's productivity. From 1800 to 1850, British industrial output shot up by 324%, which was unprecedented in world history. But workers' income in Britain declined by 9.1% during the same period.[1]

As huge quantities of goods produced exceeded domestic market demand, Britain used gunboats to develop overseas markets and built an empire where the sun never set, and this led to the creation of a unified world market. From 1850 to 1899, Britain's international trade increased from £174 million to £749 million, representing a 330% growth.[2] These figures were based on the current-year prices. Under the gold standard, prices in Britain were stable, and there was even some deflation during the second-half of the 19th century. Therefore, the 330% growth rate could be underestimated.

During this period, international production and trade expanded rapidly, which generated a large demand for a single, unified medium of exchange. Due to its natural advantages and value, gold was accepted by many countries and was circulated all over the world. In 1821, Britain became the first country to legally establish the gold standard. In the second-half of the 19th century, with the adoption of the gold standard by other major industrial countries, the gold standard era began. Since Britain was the global trade and financial center and a leading colonial power, the pound sterling gained international acceptance. It became a world currency with the same status as gold. This created the "gold-pound standard".

19.1.2 *Decline of the British pound sterling*

Britain's domination of the international economy was challenged by the rapid development of other countries, especially the United States and Germany. The status of the pound sterling as the world currency was also weakened after two world wars. The outbreak of World War I in 1914 led to the suspension of the gold standard. Britain restored the gold standard

---

[1] Miqieer (2002b). The data has been calculated using the Industrial Output Index and Salary Index therein.

[2] *Ibid.*

in 1925, but the pound sterling was overvalued. From 1925 to 1926, the British trade deficit grew at an annual rate of over 17%,[3] leading to severe disequilibrium in the balance of payments and massive gold outflow. This dealt a heavy blow to the British economy. In 1931, Britain ended free conversion between the pound sterling and gold, abandoning the gold standard. The pound sterling thus lost its status as the sole world currency, and its influence was limited to the British Commonwealth.

19.2 Internationalization of the Dollar

The economic strength of the United States was the foundation for the dollar to become an international currency. The two world wars provided an opportunity for the internationalization of the dollar. The Bretton Woods system strengthened the international position of the dollar. Despite of the rise of the Deutsch mark and the Japanese yen, the dollar has remained the leading international currency.

19.2.1 *The quiet rise of the U.S. economy*

In the mid-1800s, the United States was behind Britain, France, and Germany in economic and industrial development. After the Civil War, U.S. economic development greatly accelerated (Figure 19-1), which was mainly caused by the following three factors. First, the Civil War led to the reunification of the country and created a vast domestic market for the development of capitalism in the United States. Before the war, capitalist industry and agriculture grew fast in the northern states, while plantation farming dominated the economy in the South. After the Civil War, the U.S. government created a closely integrated domestic market. Second, the Civil War abolished slavery and provided additional free labor for the development of capitalism. Before the war, the South had 15 slave-holding states with over 4 million black slaves. The system of slavery collapsed after the war. This not only helped meet the demand for new sources of labor, but also created more consumers. Finally, the advent of the second industrial revolution powered U.S. economic development.

---

[3] *Ibid.*

(*Billions of U.S. dollars*)

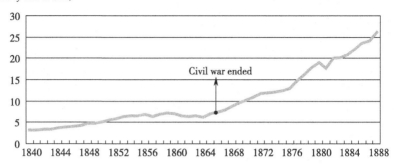

Figure 19-1   Changes of U.S. GNP (1840–1888)

Note: Based on 1929 prices.
Source: Miqieer (2002a).

The use of electricity marked the start of the second scientific and technological revolution. New technologies like the internal combustion engine, thermodynamics, and the petrochemical industry greatly boosted productivity in the United States. Between 1870 and 1913, U.S. industrial production grew over eight times, while that of Britain and France just more than doubled and tripled respectively. The U.S. heavy industry registered remarkable growth. From 1880 to 1920, U.S. steel output increased from 1.26 million tons to 42.8 million tons, making up 59% of the world's steel output. Pig iron output grew from 3.89 million tons to 37.51 million tons, accounting for 58.6% of the world's total. Electricity generation increased from 5.9 billion kilowatts to 116.7 billion kilowatts between 1902 and 1929. From 1880 to 1929, U.S. oil output increased from 26.28 million barrels to 1 billion barrels. Electricity and oil became the main sources of energy in the United States.[4]

Around the 1870s, U.S. real national income and productivity exceeded that of Western Europe. In 1929, U.S. economy was far ahead of the rest of the world, with its gross industrial output reaching 50% of the total world output and surpassing the combined industrial output of Britain, France, Germany, and Japan. Although the pound sterling was in decline, it maintained its status as the world currency because of the

---

[4] Xu Wei (1989).

"inertia"[5] of the international monetary system, which is why the dollar did not surpass major European currencies in terms of international influence before World War II.

19.2.2 *The dollar's rise to supremacy*

The outbreak of World War I provided an opportunity to internationalize the dollar. As the European countries were drawn into the war, most of their currencies dropped in value, and they had to maintain inflated exchange rates and impose foreign exchange control. But the dollar maintained fixed parity with gold. Individual investors reduced transaction risk by holding more dollars, and the dollar holdings by European governments as liquid assets also increased sharply.

World War II boosted the U.S. economy, and the dollar's international influence grew accordingly. While the war ravaged European countries were struggling to survive, the United States was growing richer because of the war and became the leading global power. During World War II, the U.S. provided military supplies to Europe. To raise dollars to pay for these supplies, European countries sold their large U.S. investments. In addition to selling US$ 3 billion worth of securities to the United States, European governments also sold large quantities of gold to the United States. As World War II intensified, the U.S. economy grew even stronger. Between 1935 and 1940, U.S. GNP grew by 33%; in the following 5 years, the U.S. economy grew by 75% (Figure 19-2). The United States amassed a huge fortune during the two world wars without bearing the brunt of the war, and its economic power continuously increased. During the same period of time, the dollar's status soared. When World War II ended, Europe was devastated, the role of British pound sterling as an international reserve currency sharply declined, but the dollar became a safe reserve currency comparable to gold.

Another effective way used by the United States to consolidate the dollar's power was through increasing foreign investment due to trade surplus. Figure 19-3 shows the huge changes in yields from trade surplus and investment in 10 years before World War II. In the mid-1930s, U.S.

---

[5] He Fan and Li Jing (2002).

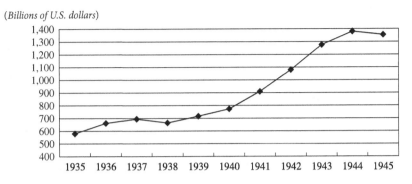

Figure 19-2   Changes in U.S. GNP (1935–1945)

Source: Miqieer (2002a).

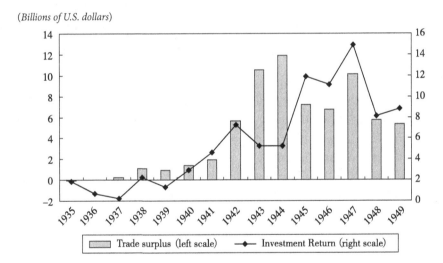

Figure 19-3   U.S. Trade Surplus and Investment Return (1935–1949)

Note: Based on annual current prices.
Source: Miqieer (2002a).

international trade was still essentially balanced and had a small trade surplus. But the United States' trade surplus rose sharply during World War II, and it needed to seek more investment channels for its ever-growing trade surplus. Thanks to direct overseas investment by American transnational companies and foreign loans and securities issued by the American financial sector and increasing dollar liquidity overseas, huge investment returns flowed back to the United States. In the 1930s, the United States still had net investment return outflow, but a decade later, its annual net investment return exceeded US$ 10 billion for many years.

In 1944, the dollar based Bretton Woods system was officially established, inaugurating the dollar's supremacy. After World War II devastated the world economy, countries all needed huge capital and supplies to rebuild their economy, and the United States met this demand by exporting on a massive scale both goods and the capital. The demand for dollars around the world resulted in a dollar shortage and made the dollar strong. By carrying out the Marshall and Dodge Plans, the United States provided investment and loans to Europe and Japan. This ended the pound sterling's position as the leading international currency in capital export.

From the end of World War II to 1971, thanks to the support of the Bretton Woods system and the United States' huge advantage in international division of labor, the dollar was widely circulated around the world, becoming the most important international currency.

19.2.3 *Power of the dollar challenged*

While the dollar was enjoying the prestige and benefits of being the world currency, challenges to it also arose. In his 1960 book, *Gold and Dollar Crisis*, Yale University Professor Robert Triffin (1960) introduced the concept of the "Triffin Dilemma". He concluded that as the dollar was linked with gold and other currencies were linked with the dollar, the dollar acquired the position as the international core currency. To develop international trade, countries have to use the dollar as a clearing and reserve currency. Thus, it will result in overseas accumulation of the dollar and cause long-term trade deficit for the United States. However, the core prerequisite for the dollar to be an international currency is to maintain its stable and strong value, which requires the United States to be long-term trade surplus country. Since these two requirements contradict each other, it is a paradox.

As time passed, Professor Triffin's concern became true. From 1950 to the mid and late 1960s, the United States competed with the Soviet Union for military and technological superiority. During the Vietnam War, it expanded military spending and introduced domestic welfare programs at the same time. This led to a dramatic increase of the fiscal deficit and current account deficit, and the U.S. gold reserve started to dwindle due to increasing outflow of gold. Facing Triffin's dilemma, the U.S. government adopted the policy of "drinking poison to quench its thirst" by pursuing expansionist monetary policy which triggered serious inflation. During the 1950s, the U.S. money supply was stable. Money supply rose from US$ 30 billion to US$ 32 billion from 1953 to 1961, increasing only by 6.7%. In the 1960s, the dollar supply started to increase sharply. From 1961 to 1968, money supply increased from US$ 32 billion to US$ 48 billion, an increase of 50%. From 1968 to 1974, the dollar supply increased nearly 70%.[6] Increasing dollar supply caused the U.S. price level to shift from sustained low inflation to high inflation for several years. In the 1950s, the United States only experienced inflation in 1 or 2 years, and its growth did not exceed 5%. However, from 1962 to 1974, the annual inflation rate was frequently above 5% and even exceeded 15% in 1972 (Figure 19-4). It was generally believed that the oil crisis in the early

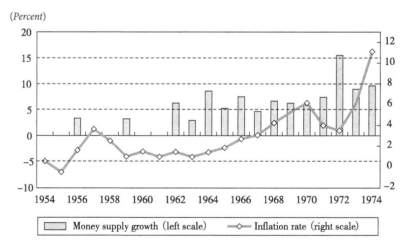

Figure 19-4   U.S. Expansionary Monetary Policy (1954–1974)

Note: Calculated from the money supply and Consumer Price Index (CPI).
Source: Miqieer (2002a).

---

[6] Miqieer (2002a).

1970s caused by rising price of oil was the cause of high inflation experienced by the United States and other countries. However, Milton Friedman, a professor of monetary economics, did not agree with this theory. In his view, the rise of oil prices could only explain a onetime rise in prices, instead of sustained inflation. It is the expansionist monetary policy which changes money supply that is the true culprit for inflation.

The increase of the dollar supply was so out of proportion with the gold reserve. Dollar's actual gold content declined sharply, and its fixed parity with gold (US$ 35 to one ounce of gold) resulted in overvaluing of the dollar. The dollar seemed to face the same dilemma that resulted in the overvalued pound sterling in 1925. The U.S. trade surplus declined and its balance of payments fell into deficit. This turned the United States from the biggest creditor country into the biggest debtor country in the world. Its continuous expansionist monetary policy made it difficult to sustain the Bretton Woods system. As a result, the dollar's dominance was broken, and the international monetary system entered a new phase of multiple currencies led by the dollar.

19.3 Internationalization of the Deutsch Mark

The rise of the mark benefited to a great extent from the increased economic strength of the Federal Republic of Germany after World War II and its pursuit of a sound and prudent monetary policy.

19.3.1 *The Federal Republic of Germany's economy strengthened after World War II*

The Federal Republic of Germany, assisted by the Marshall plan, endeavored to promote economic development after World War II. Figure 19-5 shows the growth paths of Federal Republic of Germany and Britain had similar level of development, from 1950 to 1970. In 1950, the two countries had roughly the same size of population, about 50 million each, but Britain's GDP was more than 1.5 times that of the Federal Republic of Germany. Afterwards, the Federal Republic of Germany surpassed Britain in about 10 years. By 1970, the economy of the Federal Republic of Germany was 1.5 times that of Britain.

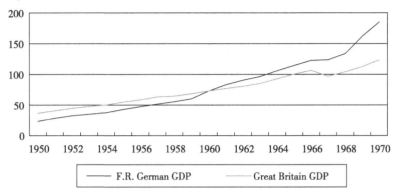

Figure 19-5   Economic Development of Great Britain and the Federal Republic of Germany after World War II

Source: Data and Statistics, IMF, IFS (2009).

19.3.2 *Development of economic and trade ties between the Federal Republic of Germany and other European countries*

After World War II, the Federal Republic of Germany became the largest trade partner of many European countries due to the rapid expansion of its economy, and this made the mark the core currency in the region. In the European Monetary System (EMS) established in 1979, the mark soon became a key currency, and it was widely used as an unofficial parallel currency in Eastern Europe.

19.3.3 *Prudent monetary policy of the Federal Republic of Germany*

The prudent monetary policy pursued by the German Central Bank maintained the purchasing power of the mark and won market confidence. According to the 1957 Deutsche Bundesbank Law, the Central Bank adopts policy independently from the government. This ensures that the German Central Bank maintains independent policy for regulating the circulation and supply of currency in achieving the intended money supply growth. In setting a monetary policy target, the German Central Bank mainly considers such factors such as expected growth of output, changes in the utilization of economic productivity, short-term inflation, and expected changes in the velocity of money supply.[7] This enables it to conduct close fine-tuning of and monitoring on money supply and maintain both the internal and external values of the mark. For this reason, Germany had a low inflation rate than other countries. The mark dollar exchange rate was US$ 0.238/DM in 1950 and about US$ 0.62/DM in 1990.

19.3.4 *Stable value and steadily appreciated exchange rate of the mark*

The low inflation rate and low exchange rate fluctuation were responsible for mark's rise to a major international reserve currency. In nearly two decades from 1960 to 1980, the average annual inflation rate of Germany was 4%, while that of Japan and the United States was over 6% (Figure 19-6).

The internationalization of the mark not only benefited from stable domestic prices, but also from its steadily appreciating exchange rate. With the country's rising economic power, the mark also appreciated steadily. From 1970 to 1986, it appreciated around 100% (Figure 19-7).

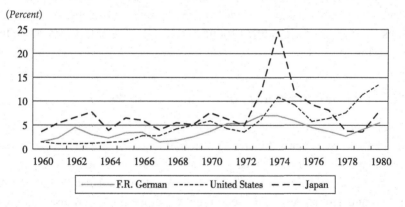

Figure 19-6   A Comparison of Inflation Rates: The Federal Republic of Germany, United States, and Japan (1960–1980)

Source: Data and Statistics, IMF, IFS (2009).

---

[7] H-J Dulder (1984).

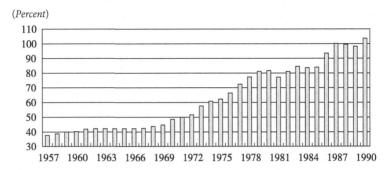

Figure 19-7 Appreciation of the Mark (1957–1990)

Note: The above figure shows the annual nominal effective exchange rate.
Source: Data and Statistics, IMF, IFS (2009).

It should be noted that the internationalization of the mark took place when the Federal Republic of Germany's capital account was still not completely open. Between 1971 and 1989, German government's remaining control over capital introduction, namely, restrictions imposed on mark bond issuing banks and on types of bond, were phased out. The internationalization of the mark gained momentum during the same period. With progress made in European integration, the Deutsch mark was increasingly used for trade and investment among European countries. It was also an important foundation for the European Currency Unit (ECU) in the EMS.

19.4 Internationalization of the Japanese Yen

After World War II, Japan became a foothold for the United States in Asia. The United States gave Japan huge economic, technical, and military aids. U.S.–Japan cooperation made it possible for Japan to achieve rapid economic recovery and join the ranks of the Western industrial powers in the 1960s and 1970s. As Japan's economy developed, the yen also started to become internationalized, but at a rather slow pace. While Japan has become the world's second largest economy, the yen has not become an important international currency.

19.4.1 *Recovery of the Japanese economy after World War II*

After its defeat in World War II, Japan achieved miraculous economic recovery. Japan adopted the "priority production system" proposed by Japanese economist Hiromi Arisawa. Japan put its limited resources on developing coal mining and reining in inflation. At the same time, the United States implemented the Dodge Plan[8] in Japan. Thanks to these efforts, Japan succeeded in keeping hyperinflation under control and brought the yen–dollar exchange rates to the stable level of 360JPY/US$ in 1949. Manufacturing recovered and the financial order became stabilized.

In 1950, the Korean War began. Since Japan was close to Korea, the United States secured many of its military supplies from Japan. The increased production enabled the Japanese economy to rapidly recover from the devastation of the world war. The rapid economic growth of Japan continued for about 20 years. In 1955, Japan's GDP reached JPY 42 trillion, which rocketed to JPY 152.5 trillion by 1970, nearly tripling in size.[9]

19.4.2 *Trade surplus — currency appreciation — internationalization*

As its economy grew in strength and it pursued the strategy of trade-based development, Japan had a trade surplus for the first time in 1965. For years afterwards, except for one or two years during the oil crisis, Japan's trade surplus continued and reached JPY 4 trillion in 1978 (Figure 19-8).

In addition to exporting goods, Japan also began to export capital, and its investment in Asia grew particularly very fast. At the same time, the Japanese government also gradually relaxed control of the yen. In 1964, Japan announced its acceptance of Article VIII of the International

---

[8] Dodge Plan was put forward by Joseph Dodge, former President of the Detroit Bank, then economic advisor to MacArthur, to meet U.S. government's goal of stabilizing the Japanese economy. Its main goals included: (1) balancing the budget; (2) eliminating subsidies; (3) ending the issuing of bonds from the Reconstruction Gold Pool and setting up the Dollar Fund; (4) fixing the yen exchange rate at 360 JPY/US$.
[9] IMF, Data and Statistics, IFS, Annual Report (2010).

(Billions of yen)

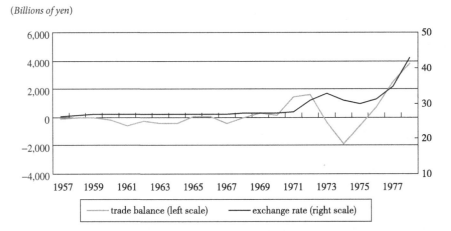

Figure 19-8   Japanese Trade and Exchange Rates in the Post-War Period

Note: The above figure shows the annual trade balance and nominal effective exchange rate of Japan.
Source: Miqieer (2002b).

Monetary Fund Agreement and realized the free conversion of the yen under the current account.[10]

The economic recovery of Japan and Federal Republic of Germany and the relative decline of the U.S. economy created pressure for adjusting the international monetary system. In the 1970s, as the dollar weakened, there was pressure for appreciating the yen. In the 7 years following the dollar crisis in 1971, the nominal exchange rate of the yen grew by a total of 54% (Figure 19-8). During this period, Japan began to adjust its industrial structure by implementing a policy of downsizing and developing tertiary industry. So, the Japanese economy not only withstood the oil crisis, but remained unaffected by the large appreciation of the yen. After a temporary decline, Japan's trade surplus rebounded and was maintained

---

[10]Article VIII of the Agreement of International Monetary Fund stipulates that: (1) no member shall, without the approval of the Fund, impose restrictions on the making of payments and transfers for current international transactions; (2) no member shall engage in any discriminatory currency arrangements or multiple currency practices; (3) as for the local currencies aggregated by other member countries in current accounts, at the request of the opposite party to convert for payment of its current account, the member countries should convert back the currencies using gold or the currency of the opposite party.

at a high level. Japan's overseas investment also registered rapid growth. By the mid-1980s, Japan overtook the United States to become the biggest creditor country in the world. As a result, there was mounting call for yen appreciation. In 1985, at a meeting of finance ministers of five countries led by the United States, the Plaza Accord was signed on the appreciation of the yen. The yen thus started a long-term process of appreciation, and the yen–dollar exchange rate peaked at 79.75 JPY/US$ in 1995.

As the yen appreciated, the Japanese government actively promoted the internationalization of the yen by expanding the use of the yen for transaction and investment, for international trade clearing, in the foreign and domestic financial markets and as a reserve currency. Along with the yen's long-term appreciation, these measures enabled the yen to perform some of the functions of an international currency. But they also prevented the yen from performing other functions of an international currency.

The promotion of using the yen as a reserve currency is a case in point. On the one hand, the Japanese government issued offshore yen-denominated bonds so that international capital could be invested in the Japanese stock market. The long term prospect of a strong yen made yen-denominated bonds attractive to both foreign private investors and governments. So such bond issuance was quite successful. By the mid-1980s, the Japanese bond market was on a par with the European and American bond markets, and its stock market was bullish. In some countries, the Japanese yen served as an important reserve currency, second only to the dollar and Deutsch mark.

On the other hand, yen-denominated mid- and long-term overseas lending and the yen's use in international trade settlement were stalled by the continued appreciation of the yen. For one thing, the long-term appreciation of the yen imposed a heavy debt burden on borrowing countries. Importers were unwilling to pay for imported goods with the yen for the same reason, which made it difficult for yen-based import financing to expand. In spite of the strong measures adopted by Japan, the internationalization of the yen did not achieve its goal.

The rise of the Japanese economy was the general background for the internationalization of the yen. However, Japan's export-led economic development became a barrier to it. Japan's trade-based growth model resulted in a high trade surplus and corresponding appreciation of the yen.

Additionally, Japan was at a disadvantage in its economic and political relations with the United States, so it could not resist the pressure from the United States for yen appreciation. But the yen's appreciation prevented its further internationalization. Ironically, the rapid growth of Japan's foreign trade both stimulated and hindered the internationalization of the yen.

19.5 Major Currencies' Path to Internationalization

The internationalization of the above currencies has some common features, which are the basic conditions for the internationalization of a currency.

First, a strong economy is the most important requirement for the internationalization of a country's currency. Pound sterling became an international currency because Britain's GDP made up 5% of the global total.[11] When the dollar replaced the pound sterling as an international currency, U.S. GDP accounted for 27% of the world's GDP.[12] When the Deutsch mark became an international currency, the GDP of the Federal Republic of Germany made up 15% of the European GDP and 5% of the world's total.[13] When Japan's GDP reached 7% of world total, the Japanese yen started to internationalize.[14] These figures show that a currency can be internationalized only when its economy reaches a significant scale.

Second, a country's import and export should account for a fairly large part of the world trade. Currency internationalization is an important form of economic internationalization, and the size of a country's foreign trade determines international demand for its currency. In the early period of the internationalization of pound sterling, Britain's international trade made up nearly one-fourth of the world's total. After World War II, the

---

[11] The 1820s in which Great Britain established the gold standard is seen as the point when the pound became an international currency. The data for the figures was calculated from *Shijie Jingji Qiannianshi* (2003), pp. 117, 178.

[12] The establishment of the Bretton Woods system was the turning point for the dollar to replace the pound as the international currency. *Data source: Ibid.*, pp. 273, 327.

[13] The 1980s is considered the main period of time for the mark to become an international currency. *Data source: Ibid.*, pp. 270–272, 327.

[14] The late 1900s are considered the period of internationalization for the yen. *Data source: Ibid.*, pp. 296, 327.

international influence of the dollar grew steadily and the U.S. foreign trade made up about 15% of the world trade. Both the Federal Republic of Germany and Japan started the internationalization of their currencies when their foreign trade made up about 10% of world trade.[15]

Third, the value of the currency involved should be fairly stable. The competitiveness of a currency depends on its value. In many cases, the more stable the value of a currency is, the lower the cost of holding it will be; then demand for it will be stronger, and the possibility for it to be internationalized will be higher. The primary goal of the Federal Republic of Germany's monetary policy is to forestall inflation. From 1970 to 1989, the country's annual inflation rate was 3.9% and annual change in the exchange rate was only 1%. This created confidence in the Deutsch mark and laid the foundation for it to become an international currency. Expectation of currency stability and increase in value is a necessary condition for its internationalization. Such expectation is seen as follows: first, international trade calls for a stable payment and settlement currency. Second, the appreciation of the payment and settlement currency should be predictable so to avoid exchange rate risk, as people would not use an unstable and unpredictable currency as settlement currency. The dollar became an indisputable international currency because of the fixed exchange rate provisions made under the Bretton Woods system. Other currencies should meet this condition to become international currencies. The process of internationalization of the Deutsch mark and the Japanese yen illustrates the importance of this. The instability of the Japanese yen and its unpredictable appreciation and devaluation (also known as free floating) are the main causes for its lack of success in becoming an international currency.

In addition to the above three core conditions, there are other conditions, including government promotion, level of development of the domestic financial sector and the capital market, a fully convertible currency as well as goods and services an economy can provide and the quality of such goods and services, etc. Therefore, the internationalization of a currency is bound to be a long process requiring sustained economic and social development. It is not something that can be achieved overnight.

---

[15] Data is from Miqieer (2002a, 2002b).

Chapter 20

Current State of the Internationalization of the Renminbi

At present, the renminbi is already being circulated and used in China's neighboring countries and regions. As its economic strength increases, China will have more say in international trade, investment, and finance, which will create greater momentum for the internationalization of the renminbi (Li Ruogu, 2008).

20.1 Circulation of the Renminbi in China's Neighboring Countries and Regions

This chapter will study the range of circulation and the scope of use of the renminbi.

20.1.1 *Range of the renminbi circulation*

The renminbi has been used in Hong Kong and Macao mainly by tourists or for family visits. The circulation and use of the renminbi in the two economies has reached a substantial scale thanks to the ever increasing economic and trade ties between them and the mainland. Since 2004 when

253

the mainland signed the Closer Economic Partnership Arrangement (hereafter referred to as CEPA) with Hong Kong and Macao Special Administrative Regions (SARs), residents in several dozen mainland cities have been able to visit the two SARs as individual tourists. As a result, the number of Mainland visitors to the two cities soared. With expectation of renminbi appreciation, shops and money changers in Hong Kong and Macao are eager to accept the renminbi, and its circulation in Hong Kong and Macao has increased as a result. To enable the renminbi to flow back to the mainland, with the approval of the State Council and after consulting with the monetary authorities of Hong Kong and Macao, the People's Bank of China started to provide clearing services for individual renminbi transactions for banks in Hong Kong beginning from November 19, 2003, and banks in Macao from November 4, 2004. These initiatives have promoted closer economic ties and facilitated mutual visits and tourist consumption between the mainland and the two SARs.

After the Southeastern Asian Financial Crisis broke out, because of the relative stability of the renminbi and rise in its value and the increasing economic and trade relations across the Taiwan Straits, more people in China's Taiwan region began to use the renminbi. In January of 2001, when direct postal, trade, and shipping links were opened between the mainland and Jinmen and Mazu Islands of Taiwan which are closest to the mainland, the renminbi were used on the two islands along with the New Taiwan Dollar (NT dollar). On October 3, 2005, the Taiwan authorities started a pilot program of renminbi exchange in Jinmen and Mazu. According to figures released by the Taiwan financial authorities, by the end of 2007, over RMB 61,900 exchange transactions were made, involving 4.56 million. In June 2008, exchange of the NT dollars and the renminbi was extended to cover the whole of Taiwan, and all the residents, tourists and foreigners in Taiwan may exchange the renminbi with the amount not exceeding RMB 20,000 per transaction. In December 2008, postal, trade, and shipping links were officially launched between the mainland and Taiwan, which have boosted economic and cultural exchanges between the two sides and further promoted the use of the renminbi in Taiwan.

The renminbi is also used in countries around China in three ways: (1) the renminbi is used to stabilize the local economy; (2) in countries like Vietnam, Russia, Nepal, Mongolia, Pakistan, Kyrgyzstan, etc. which have close border trade ties with China, the renminbi is circulated through trade clearing; (3) in countries like Cambodia, Thailand, Singapore, Philippines, the Republic of Korea, etc. not bordering with China, the renminbi is used mainly by individuals such as tourists.

20.1.2 *The renminbi's functions as an international currency*

The renminbi is now mainly used as a medium of exchange in China's neighboring countries for settling border trade and for use by Chinese tourists. Since some of the goods in cross-border trade and tourist products are priced in the renminbi, it also functions as a pricing currency. However, the renminbi is mainly used in non-government sectors. No foreign government has yet used the renminbi as a currency anchor or an intervention currency. The renminbi does not play the role of either a currency anchor or an intervention currency.

Progress has been made in the use of the renminbi as a reserve currency and a store of value. In December of 2006, the renminbi was first designated by the Philippines as a reserve currency,[1] followed by the central banks of Malaysia, the Republic of Korea, and Cambodia. The renminbi is used as a store of value in two ways: first, it is held by individuals against inflation in Myanmar, Laos, and other countries. Second, in February 2004, banks in Hong Kong opened renminbi deposit services, including demand deposit, savings deposit and time deposits, and the renminbi has thus become a store of value in Hong Kong. In June 2007, the China Development Bank first issued renminbi bonds in Hong Kong, which was followed by the Export–Import Bank of China, Bank of China, Bank of Communications, and China Construction Bank (Table 20-1). This has also made it possible for the renminbi to function as a store of value in Hong Kong. Hong Kong has thus become the springboard for internationalizing the renminbi.

Due to lack of channels for value storage, the renminbi functions mainly as a medium of exchange in China's neighboring countries. The

---

[1] Data is from Miqieer (2002a, 2002b).

bulk of renminbi transactions flows in and out of borders, with relatively little amount being kept abroad. According to a survey conducted by the People's Bank of China in 2005, by the end of 2004, the renminbi cash kept in China's neighboring countries and in Hong Kong and Macao was about RMB 21.6 billion. The total amount of two-way across border cash flow for the whole year was RMB 771.3 billion, with a net outflow of RMB 9.9 billion.[2] Zhong Wei (2009) estimated that the amount of the renminbi circulating in Hong Kong, Macao, Singapore, Vietnam, Thailand, Indonesia, and other neighboring countries was about RMB 30.4 billion. Of the total sum, approximately RMB 28.8 billion was kept in Hong Kong, Macao, and Vietnam. According to a survey on the outflow of the renminbi by the end of 2004 conducted by the Renminbi Outflow Survey Project Team, half of the renminbi outside the mainland of China was held in Hong Kong, Macao, and Vietnam. Assuming that this figure remained relatively stable, by the end of 2008, the amount of the renminbi retained overseas amounted to approximately RMB 57.6 billion, accounting for 1.68% of the total amount of the renminbi in circulation.[3]

20.2 Renminbi Transaction in the International Financial Market

Trading of the renminbi in the international financial market is conducted against the background of strict control over the renminbi capital accounts and the long-held expectation of renminbi appreciation (Figure 20-1). Thus, renminbi-related trading in the international financial market has two features: fast development of offshore non-deliverable forwards (NDFs) business and very limited development in business delivered in the renminbi itself.

20.2.1 *Renminbi NDF market*

Trading in renminbi-NDFs is important for analyzing market expectation of renminbi appreciation. This form of transaction was introduced in the

---

[2] *China Finance* (2005).
[3] Amount of the renminbi in circulation is sourced from the People's Bank of China: "2008 Statistics: Overview of Money", http://www.pbc.gov.cn.

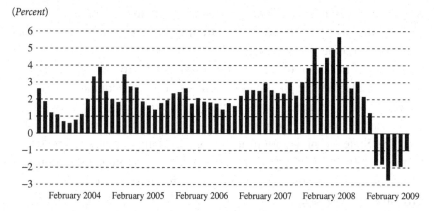

Figure 20-1   Appreciation Expectation of the Renminbi since 2004

Note: The official exchange rate (spot exchange rate) minus the NDF market rate (6-month forward exchange rate), then divided by the official exchange rate, which gives us the appreciation expectation of the Chinese yuan exchange rate.

Source: Bloomberg (2009).

two offshore markets of Singapore and Hong Kong in 1996. After the 1997 Asian Financial Crisis, trading in renminbi-NDF became active. Singapore and Hong Kong are now the biggest renminbi derivatives markets in the world. Traders are major overseas banks and investment institutions who represent transnational companies with huge renminbi revenue made in China, Chinese companies headquartered in Hong Kong, as well as hedge funds and other investors.

Hong Kong has a huge number of small and medium businesses and individual clients who are at short position in their frequent renminbi related transactions. To provide them with derivative instruments to avoid renminbi related foreign exchange risk, the Treasury Markets Association (TMA), under the Hong Kong Monetary Authority officially introduced retail renminbi-NDFs on November 9, 2005. Such NDFs are settled with the dollar, with a minimum of US$ 10,000 required for making a transaction.

Despite the fact that positions in the renminbi-NDF market are squared with the dollar and no renminbi actually changes hands during the transaction, the NDF market is influential in renminbi trading. This is because the NDF market takes the renminbi as the pricing unit while not requiring renminbi capital. The offshore and onshore markets are linked by the same pricing unit. With increasing expectation of renminbi appreciation, the size of renminbi-NDF trading is substantially bigger than onshore renminbi forward trading. The market size of renminbi-NDF is 10 times that of the latter, though the former is still relatively small compared to trading of other major Asian currencies. The expectation of renminbi appreciation as reflected in the exchange rate in NDF transactions poses some market pressure on renminbi's official exchange rate. To control risk, the State Administration of Foreign Exchange issued a directive in October 2006, prohibiting Chinese banks from quoting renminbi-NDF rate overseas. This shows the influence of renminbi-NDF trading on the official exchange rate.

20.2.2 *Renminbi Exchange Market*

The renminbi exchange markets include exchange trading and over-the-counter trading. Such trading is analyzed in terms of trading volume and structure of trading.

First, in terms of trading volume, despite rapid rise in renminbi-related foreign exchange trading in recent years, its share in the global foreign exchange market is still small. The share of renminbi-related foreign exchange trading in the global market rose from 0.01% in 2001 to 0.10% in 2004 and 0.47% in 2007, while the share of dollar related trading in the corresponding year was 76.16%, 85.2%, and 86.35%.[4] The renminbi's share of total trading was even lower than that of other non-major international currencies such as the Mexican peso, the South Korean won, the Danish krone, the Russian ruble, the Indian rupee, and the Polish zloty.

Second, in terms of structure of trading, renminbi-related foreign exchange trading takes place mainly in spot market. In 2007, in all the five categories of foreign exchange trading for the renminbi, spot trading made up 60% and forward exchange took up 30%, while the other categories (swaps, options, and currency swaps) accounted for only 10% of the

---

[4] BIS (2007).

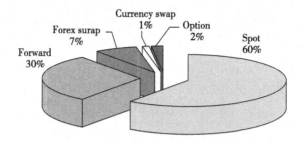

Figure 20-2   Renminbi's Transactions in Foreign Exchange Market
Note: This data reflects both exchange trading and over-the-counter trading.
Source: BIS (2007).

total (Figure 20-2). During the same period, however, dollar spot trading made up less than 30% of the total and forward exchange made up about 10%, while the remaining 60% were conducted in swaps and options. This major difference in the structure of foreign exchange trading shows that the renminbi-related foreign exchange market is still in its infant stage. The number of financial instruments for renminbi-related trading needs to be increased and the potential demand for such trading needs to be tapped.

Chapter 21

Cost-benefit Analysis*
of the Internationalization
of the Renminbi

In recent years, there has been an ongoing debate on the internationalization of the renminbi — should the renminbi be internationalized, and, if so, how? This is because while China stands to gain from the renminbi's internationalization, it also needs to pay a cost.

21.1 Benefits of Internationalizing the Renminbi

Internationalizing the renminbi will increase China's international influence and elevate China's international position. It will reduce exchange rate risk of the renminbi, create a favorable environment for China's economic development and bring in more revenue from seigniorage.

21.1.1 *Enhancing China's international position and influence*

The degree of internationalization of a country's currency reflects its international status and position. History shows that the internationalization of

---

* Data is from Miqieer (2002a, 2002b).

a country's currency goes hand in hand with a steady increase in its international influence, as was the case with Britain, the United States, Germany, and Japan. Promoting the internationalization of the renminbi will increase China's global competitiveness, give China more say in global economy, and strengthen its role as a global economic power.

The internationalization of the renminbi will increase China's economic power. It will help accelerate the growth of China's domestic financial market. The huge amount of capital thus made available and massive financial transactions will tremendously benefit China's finance sector and make corporate financing much easier. China's domestic economic development will be supported by ample supply of capital. Additionally, an internationalized renminbi will create another benchmark, along with GDP and foreign trade, for China's economic power.

Second, the internationalization of the renminbi will increase China's ability to participate in global economic and financial policy coordination as well as in regional and international political affairs. With the internationalization of the renminbi, its exchange rate would become an important issue in international coordination. From both the medium and long-term perspective, the renminbi's rising international status will help reduce the volatility of major reserve currencies and the resulting financial market turmoil. Furthermore, with the power to issue and regulate an internationalized currency, China would be in a better position when it comes to resources allocation and influencing the market, which would be a major means to counter attempts by some Western countries to block China's economic development. As the renminbi's internationalization advances, China's current state of being a "big trading country but small monetary country" will change.

The renminbi's internationalization will promote a more diversified international monetary system. As a new choice of reserve currency, the internationalized renminbi will enable countries to improve the mix of their international reserve assets.

21.1.2 Reducing Exchange Rate Risks While Promoting the Development of Trade and Investment

A country's foreign trade, introduction of foreign investment and outbound investment can all make its government and private sector hold large amount of international currencies or assets and bonds priced in such currencies. Countries whose currencies are not internationalized hold reserve currencies but face risks associated with fluctuation in the economy and consumer prices of the reserve currency issuing countries. Fluctuation in the exchange rate of internationalized reserve currencies will have a large impact on the foreign exchange reserves of other countries and their foreign trade and overseas investment. This is the drawback of currency mismatch.

At present, China is a victim of the Dollar Standard (Li Ruogu, 2008). As a large net exporter of "inclusive energy",[1] China has depleted its own natural resources and suffered from environmental pollution and degradation to sustain high consumption of other countries, chiefly Western countries. With the world's largest foreign exchange reserves, China suffered losses of RMB 435 billion in 2007 due to depreciation of the dollar.[2] The excessive dollar liquidity in the global economy has led to rise of global inflation. As a major importer of natural resources, China paid 18.4 billion more dollars to import oil in 2007 than it did 2 years before.[3] In recent years, China's foreign exchange reserves has grown rapidly. Despite a clear long-term trend towards dollar depreciation (Figure 21-1), the dollar still makes up the majority of China's foreign exchange reserves. As the global financial crisis spreads, the security and profitability of these reserve holdings is threatened. The value of China's huge foreign exchange reserves hinges closely on changes in the dollar's exchange rate. Internationalizing the renminbi will help address this problem, reduce risks associated with exchange rate fluctuation and promote the reform of the international monetary system. The internationalization of the renminbi will benefit both China and the world.

Chinese companies are rapidly expanding overseas presence, and China's dependence on foreign trade has increased. In 2008, the rate of China's dependence on foreign trade was close to 70%. Therefore, the impact of exchange rate fluctuation on China's economy is greater, particularly regarding manufacturing costs for import and export, price quotations, profit accounting and overseas investment. China's numerous

---

[1] *Ibid.*
[2] *Ibid.*
[3] *Ibid.*

(Billions of U.S. dollars)

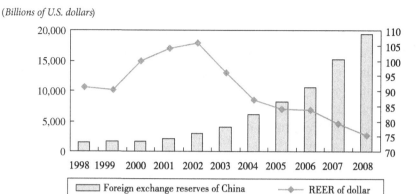

Figure 21-1   The Exchange Rate Risks Faced by China's Foreign Reserves (1998–2008)

Note: Data shown in the figure above is for the end of each year.
Source: Data and Statistics IMF, IFS (2009).

export oriented companies are mostly at the bottom of the value chain, which produce little domestic added value and have low profit margins. This makes them ill-prepared to deal with exchange rate, risks, and even mild fluctuation in foreign exchange market can deal a major blow to them and can even cause some of them to go bankrupt. As the renminbi is not internationalized, international transactions and investment by Chinese companies are mostly made in dollars. When exchange rate fluctuation occurs, Chinese companies making such transactions in dollars react by either advancing or postponing account settlements, which in turn will exacerbate exchange rate fluctuation. In a dollar-based international settlement system, all exchange rate risks associated with such transactions are borne by Chinese companies. The internationalization of the renminbi means that many of these transactions can be priced in the renminbi instead of the dollar, the euro, or the Japanese yen, thus reducing some of the exchange rate risks associated with such transactions. With less exchange rate risks and prospect of greater profitability in international trade, Chinese companies will have greater incentive to expand foreign trade and make more overseas investment. So the internationalization of the renminbi will benefit Chinese companies.

The internationalization of the renminbi will also benefit China's financial industry by cutting transaction costs and increasing revenues. For one thing, China's financial institutions are more familiar with the domestic market than their foreign counterparts. Using the renminbi to make transactions will reduce information costs, transaction costs, and exchange rate risks for them. Also, internationalizing the renminbi will increase China's trade with other regions and overseas lending and investment by China's financial sector. This will not only increase revenues to Chinese companies, but also benefit banking and financial services in other countries and regions. By widening the range of the renminbi's circulation, more international trade transactions can be conducted through China's banking channels and transaction costs will be reduced. This will improve the renminbi's international reputation and increase competition in banking sectors of other regions.

21.1.3 *Deepening regional economic cooperation and promoting Asian economic stability*

Based on close regional economic partnership, the internationalization of the renminbi will strengthen regional economic ties and promote regional economic stability. The economic shocks created by the global financial crisis have undermined the economic development and foreign trade of all countries, and exchange rate fluctuations have exacerbated the impact of the crisis. Against this backdrop, many countries are engaged in competitive currency devaluation, and the currencies of many of China's neighboring countries have depreciated significantly against the dollar. The renminbi, however, has remained fairly stable. It has become a major factor contributing to stability in the Asian economy.

Accelerated renminbi internationalization along with deepening of economic and trade ties between China and its neighboring countries and other countries in East Asia will help all these countries make more efficient use of their foreign exchange reserves and reduce lessen potential market shocks associated with acquiring foreign exchange reserves. Also, the convenience of using the renminbi as a clearing currency in international transactions will promote the development of regional trade. The development of a bilateral and even multi-lateral clearing system based on the renminbi will further the goal of achieving regional economic integration in East Asia.

21.1.4 *Increasing seigniorage and fiscal revenues*

Seigniorage refers to the difference between the face value of a currency and the cost of its issuance kept by the issuer of a currency. Under the current system of legal tender, the marginal cost for issuing bank notes is near zero.[4] Given this negligible marginal cost, seigniorage becomes a source of revenue for the issuing country. Statistics show that, between 1971 and 1990, the seigniorage fee levied by 90 countries (excluding China) averaged 10.5% of a given country's gross revenue,[5] which is a substantial amount. The United States has reaped huge profits from the dollar's status as a key international reserve currency.

21.2 Analysis of the Costs of Internationalizing the Renminbi

The Bretton Woods system established the Dollar's status as a global currency, but the "Triffin Dilemma" has remained unresolved. The current financial crisis is in a way a penalty against the United States for abusing the dollar's dominance. The financial crisis has also fully shown the risks and responsibilities the issuer of an international reserve currency faces. The internationalization of the renminbi will impose the same responsibilities and obligations on China.

21.2.1 *Increasing pressure for opening China's capital accounts*

Theoretically, a country's currency is the liability of that country's monetary authorities. After its internationalization and overseas circulation, the renminbi's reputation as an international currency can be upheld only when overseas holders of the renminbi can exchange it freely and use it as

---

[4] *Ibid.*
[5] *Ibid.*

a means of payment and as a vehicle of investment. If overseas holders of the renminbi cannot do so, the renminbi will have no credibility and its internationalization will be out of the question. Meeting the expectation of overseas holders of the renminbi requires the early opening of China's capital accounts. Of course, this opening process should be a gradual one and under control. However, this process must be completed at some point. To make the renminbi freely convertible and open capital accounts, China needs to have a solid financial system, a fully developed legal system and a developed and flexible capital market, which should be put in place in China in the next one or two decades.

21.2.2 *Less ability for China to control its money supply and increased currency risks*

Movements of the renminbi in or out of China will correspondingly increase or reduce China's domestic money supply. Outflow of the renminbi would work against measures taken by the People's Bank of China to increase domestic money supply to achieve a certain policy goal, and vice versa. During the 1970s and 1980s, Japan and West Germany were not eager to promote the internationalization of their currencies and restricted capital flows out of such concern. However, such impact on monetary supply is controllable. The renminbi would not only be used overseas to purchase Chinese goods, it would also circulate among other countries. Provided that China's economy remains stable, confidence in the renminbi would not drop and there would not be a sudden flow of vast quantities of the renminbi back to China. Furthermore, overseas renminbi pricing, clearing, and circulation would be more easily monitored and managed.

21.2.3 *Decreased independence of domestic economic development*

Here, independence of economic development means a country's economic development is not affected by changes in external economic conditions and spillover effects of economic policies of other countries. With the deepening of globalization and increasing economic openness, all countries need to cope with risks associated with less economic independence. These risks are greater for issuers of reserve currencies. As their financial systems and economy are more open and they have closer economic ties with other countries, they are more subjected to both positive and negative effects of an ever changing global economy in terms of pursuing economic development and adopting economic policies.

As for China, in the course of internationalizing the renminbi, we should consider not only the needs of China's own economy, but also the external economic benefits thus derived as well as the impact this process will have on other countries. Take for example, China's stock and real estate markets. After the renminbi becomes internationalized, international demand for it would rise, and overseas renminbi could flow into China's stock and real estate markets. This could then lead to a sharp rise in renminbi-based asset prices or even bubbles in these markets. Even minor policy missteps taken in correcting price instability in the stock and real estate markets would not only create problems for China's domestic economy but also cause shocks in the global economy. Internationalizing the renminbi also means that changes in China's economic development could affect other economies. Even short-term economic problems in China could shake the confidence of other countries and regions in the renminbi as a stable international currency. If they decide to have other currency assets rather than the renminbi, this could trigger panic selling of the renminbi, which in turn would cause severe currency risks to China.

The above mentioned analysis shows that there are both benefits and costs for the internationalization of the renminbi. However, China would face more difficulties and risks in not internationalizing the renminbi. Currency mismatch has led to a situation where the money China earns is not really what it can spend, and China is forced to save the money of other countries. Instead of showing gratitude to China for saving their money, these countries have time and again called on China to appreciate its currency. Therefore, for a country as large as China, it must have an independent monetary policy and necessary flexibility in pursuing economic development. The internationalization of the renminbi must move forward. As long as China maintains a firm control over its currency, risks associated with the internationalization of the renminbi will remain under control.

Chapter 22

Pathway Towards Internationalizing the Renminbi

China is already the world's third biggest economy, third largest trading country, and the sixth largest overseas investor. But the internationalization of the renminbi is still at an early stage, and its international status is incompatible with China's power in the global community. It is therefore necessary to create an environment which promotes the internationalization of the renminbi.

22.1 The Internationalization of the Renminbi is a Gradual Process

The global political and economic systems are going through profound change. The renminbi's internationalization is drawing close attention from the international financial sector, especially amid the current turbulent international financial situation. Actually, the internationalization of the renminbi is not something new. It already started when China and its neighboring countries in the region signed currency swap agreements and when the mainland and Hong Kong concluded the Closer Economic Partnership Agreement (CEPA).

At present, although the renminbi is not yet completely convertible, many countries around China have accepted it and even held it as a reserve currency. As the renminbi has kept stable for more than a decade, even during the Asian Financial crisis, these countries have confidence in it. Such confidence is also rooted in China's sustained, rapid, and healthy development in the past three decades since it began the reform and opening up program. The international community is also optimistic about the future development of China. So, keeping the renminbi means keeping a profitable asset. All these are favorable conditions for accelerating the internationalization of the renminbi.

However, the path towards internationalizing the renminbi is still a long one. In terms of the level of development of the financial market, financial innovation, financial infrastructure, legal rules, and financial expertise, there is still a big gap between China and developed countries which cannot be bridged overnight. China needs to do more to internationalize the renminbi.

22.2 From Neighbors to the World

In view of the current stage of China's economic development and the progress of monetary cooperation in Asia, China should first target its neighboring countries in its efforts to internationalize the renminbi. When the renminbi can freely circulate and be used in Asia, it will set the stage for accelerating the internationalization of the renminbi. This approach conforms to China's strategy for promoting its economic development and international cooperation.

22.2.1 *Strengthening economic, trade, and financial cooperation with regions around China*

As economic and trade cooperation is the basis for financial cooperation, China should promote economic and trade cooperation with its neighbors in phases, leading to customs union, economic union to monetary union.

In phase one, China should continue to expand bilateral economic and trade relations with its neighboring countries, increase demand for the renminbi and improve the management of and supervision on its offshore circulation.[1]

In phase two, China should establish multilateral free trade zones with its neighboring economies, namely, customs unions, with the renminbi serving one of the major pricing and clearing currencies in such zones. Since 2003 when the China–ASEAN Free Trade Zone was established, China has concluded over 10 free trade zone agreements, including CEPA with Hong Kong and Macao Special Administrative Regions (SARs), the China–Pakistan Free Trade Zone Service and Trade Agreement, etc. China should establish additional multilateral free trade zones so that they will be connected with each other. At present, China's nominal import tariffs are being cut, and the level of its tariffs in real terms is far lower than most other developing countries. Therefore, the mutual reduction of import tariffs between China and its neighbors will not be a big burden to China.

In phase three, China should establish a substantive Asian monetary cooperation mechanism, make China's renminbi capital account convertible, expand the size of free trade zones, and make the renminbi a major international reserve currency. Since there are still obstacles to the renminbi becoming an Asian reserve currency before a mechanism for closer

---

[1] In 2000, while working at the People's Bank of China, the author was responsible for compiling a research report entitled, "On Ways to Promote Asian Financial Cooperation and the Strategy for Renminbi Regionalization". The report proposed the establishment and development of the economic trade cooperation zones in areas near the borders, specifically: the Suifenhe Economic Cooperation Zone, and cooperation zones in Altai, Xinjiang, Manzhouli and Chita; the Yunnan Jiegao Customs Bonded Zone and Dongxing–Mangjie, Pingxiang–Liangshan, and Heke–Laojie Cooperation Zones. At present, these border-region trade cooperation zones have generally already been established. They will promote China's trade and investment across borders and play an important role in expanding the circulation and use of the renminbi and increase its international influence.

economic and trade cooperation is created, it is still premature to put Pan-Asia monetary cooperation on the agenda at present.

22.2.2 *Short-term strategic options*[2]

It is necessary for China to adopt a well developed plan and take active steps to internationalize the renminbi in a phased way through boosting economic and trade cooperation with its neighbors.

In geographical terms, the internationalization of the renminbi should begin with China's neighbors in the region on a bilateral basis, and then proceed to cover more countries and the whole of Asia.

Expanding economic and trade partnership with the Association of Southeast Asian Nations (ASEAN) countries should receive high priority. China has many advantages in this respect, such as sharing a long border with its neighbors, economic and trade complementarities, right products and technologies for these countries, excellent political relations, and a free trade zone between them. In addition, China should continue to strengthen its economic and trade cooperation with Russia and particularly with Mongolia. Mongolia is a close neighbor of China, and both countries have strong mutually reinforcing economic and trade ties and have maintained good political relations over the years. China should further promote cooperation with Mongolia. Mongolia also needs to strengthen cooperation with China in pursuing economic development.

Conditions should be created for the renminbi to be used as a pricing and clearing currency in countries around China and to increase the circulation and use of the renminbi in these countries.

Circulation of the renminbi based on border trade and tourist consumption in China's neighboring countries should be the initial stage of the renminbi internationalization. With China's growing economic and trade ties with other Asian countries, the renminbi will become a pricing unit and medium of exchange in trade between China and the rest of Asia.

---

[2] The main viewpoints are those detailed in the research report entitled, "On Ways to Promote Asian Financial Cooperation and the Strategy for Renminbi Regionalization" which was compiled under the sponsorship of the author in 2000. In the opinion of the author, some of the opinions expressed in this report are still relevant today.

In order to internationalize the renminbi through China's economic and trade cooperation with its neighbors, three specific steps should be taken: (1) Encourage China's neighbors to use the renminbi for making trade payments and for tourist consumption where it is convenient and on a voluntary basis. (2) Substantially increase renminbi priced investment in and assistance to these countries to expand the influence of the renminbi. (3) Further relax restrictions on the inflow and outflow of the renminbi and give incentives to governments and residents of China's neighboring countries to increase their use of the renminbi.

The currency swap agreements signed by China with its neighboring countries in 2008–2009 can be regarded as a major step in the internationalization of the renminbi. By the end of March 2009, China had signed currency swap agreements involving RMB 650 billion Yuan with the Republic of Korea, China's Hong Kong region, Malaysia, Belarus, Indonesia, and Argentina. These agreements will increase international acceptance of the renminbi.

The Chinese government is also promoting the use of the renminbi for cross-border trade settlement. In early April 2009, the Chinese Government decided to launch a trial program of using the renminbi to settle cross-border trade with onshore centers located in Shanghai and four cities in Guangdong Province (Guangzhou, Shenzhen, Zhuhai, and Dongguan). Hong Kong was chosen as the first offshore center, and testing of its clearing system has been completed. Using the renminbi for cross-border trade settlement will enhance its function as a unit of pricing and medium of exchange in foreign trade, improve China's trade environment and promote economic cooperation between China and its neighbors.

China should speed up regional cooperation and turn the renminbi into an Asian currency.

Since China is a major political and economic country in Asia enjoying good cooperative relations with other countries in the region, the renminbi should first be used as a major currency in the region and then be used as an international currency. Regarding the use of the renminbi in Asia, this author has the following proposals:

First, China should actively participate in and promote Asian economic, trade, and financial cooperation. Economic and trade cooperation is the foundation of financial cooperation, and the two are mutually reinforcing. For instance, the success of the euro is attributable to economic and trade integration in the euro zone. As Asian countries differ in economic development, political system, culture, and religion, China should call for putting in place a consultation mechanisms based on free and equal participation in carrying out economic and trade cooperation in Asia. Through broader, regular high level and working meetings, regional bilateral and multilateral economic partnerships can be developed to promote intra-regional economic ties. This will enhance Asia's monetary cooperation, and China can open its capital account in a phased way so that the renminbi can become a regional reserve currency.

The current financial crisis exposes Asia's excessive dependence on European and American markets and the dollar. Only by strengthening regional economic, trade, and financial cooperation can Asia better resist possible global economic and financial crisis. And it is now the ideal time to broaden economic trade cooperation in Asia. In particular, increased financial cooperation is of critical importance for Asian countries to guard against external risks and strengthen the stability of their financial systems. Such cooperation also creates the opportunity for the renminbi to speed up its internationalization.

Second, China should establish a renminbi-based domestic and foreign inter-bank clearing system. Since clearing is a key function of an international currency, the frequency and scope of use of a currency in international trade settlement reflects the degree of its internationalization. The above-proposed system would strengthen supervision and regulation of offshore renminbi trading, reduce renminbi clearing costs, facilitate economic and trade activities, and create profit making opportunities for businesses, financial institutions, and individuals.

Currently, border trade between China and ASEAN countries are flourishing. A plan to make Yunnan Province a trial renminbi clearing center for cross-border trade is under consideration. When this plan is implemented, renminbi clearing will be extended from border trade to general trade, from the current eight border counties and cities to the whole Yunnan Province, and from the current four neighboring countries of Burma, Laos, Vietnam, and Thailand to all 10 ASEAN countries. To establish a renminbi inter-bank clearing system between domestic and oversea banks, we need to make greater progress in adopting necessary policies and regulations to build an institutional framework and in upgrading related infrastructure.

Third, China should increase renminbi lending to its neighbors. In providing trade credit, investment and aid, the renminbi should be used wherever possible. This will defuse exchange rate risks, promote China's trade and investment in its neighboring countries and the economic growth of those countries.

Fourth, China should reform the renminbi exchange rate regime in a phased way under the regional currency cooperation framework and advance the regionalization of the renminbi. First, the short term goal should be maintaining the stable exchange rate of the renminbi. Then, China can strengthen the coordination of regional exchange rate policies so that the renminbi becomes a "nominal anchor" in a sub-region such as in the Chinese economic circle. Second, exchange rate regimes should be reformed under the framework of East Asian currency cooperation. Through institutional reforms, renminbi exchange rate elasticity would be enhanced to meet the goal of maintaining stable but flexible exchange rates.

China should improve the policy environment to support the internationalization of the renminbi in the following ways:

A regular meeting mechanism between China and its neighboring countries at both senior official and working level should be put in place to develop a plan for internationalizing the renminbi. As China's neighbors may have concern about the internationalization of the renminbi, it is necessary to ease such concern through effective dialogue. The internationalization of the renminbi provides China and its neighbors with an alternative currency, which can help stabilize international trade and financial market and benefit the export driven economy of China's neighbors.

Supervision and control over the cross-border use of the renminbi should be strengthened. Posts should be set up in all major border ports to monitor the outflow of the renminbi, and overall monitoring should cover all areas including trade, tourism, technical cooperation, labor services, anti-counterfeiting, and anti-money laundering. Swift steps should be taken to crack down hard on counterfeiting of money and money laundering. The relevant Chinese laws should be improved. Recently, China has released the Implementing Rules on Pilot Program of Using the Renminbi for Settling Cross-border Trade Transactions, which is an important move to speed up the reform of the renminbi clearing system. It is also necessary to review and update laws and regulations on offshore pricing, clearing and circulation of the renminbi and on the renminbi clearing, depositing, and lending services provided by the overseas offices of Chinese financial institutions in China's neighboring countries. This will create a favorable legal environment for increasing the circulation and use of the renminbi. It is also necessary to create a legal structure and adopt laws allowing foreign institutions and individuals to invest their renminbi holdings in China through domestic institutional investors.

While pursuing a strategy for regional cooperation, China should also work to improve the international environment. It should take an active part in the reform of the international monetary system and increase China's say. It should forge closer economic, trade and financial partnership with developed countries. China should be actively involved in regional economic, trade and financial cooperation and policy coordination and create a sound environment for regional cooperation.

In addition, the Chinese government authorities concerned need to develop an overarching strategy for the future development of the renminbi and a corresponding strategy for internationalizing the renminbi.

22.3 Internationalizing the Renminbi and Keeping Necessary Control over Capital Account are not Incompatible with Each Other[3]

The internationalization of the renminbi requires the support of supplementary policies. For instance, the government may consider allowing foreign institutions to purchase Chinese treasury bonds and corporate bonds. But this calls for opening the capital account. As China is still a

---

[3] Li Ruogu, "Reform of International Monetary System and Internationalization of the Renminbi", a presentation at Shanghai Lujiazui International Financial Forum on May 10, 2008.

developing country, its financial system has much room for improvement. The current control of the capital account is in keeping with the fundamental interests of China, and it is an example of China being responsible to other countries. However, capital control does not mean that the renminbi cannot be internationalized. Both theories and international practices suggest that currency internationalization and capital control are not fully incompatible with each other.

23.3.1 *Free currency exchange and currency internationalization*

In theory, while free currency exchange and currency internationalization are interrelated, they are two different concepts. First, a freely convertible currency means that the currency can be exchanged with no legal or quantitative restrictions, while an international currency means that the currency is widely accepted and used by non-residents and foreign governments for transactions, pricing, investment, reserve, etc. Second, a necessary degree of currency convertibility is a prerequisite for a currency to become an international currency. Without convertibility, there would be no wide acceptability. However, currency convertibility is generally determined by government policy and the development of the domestic economy in the country issuing the currency, while the internationalization of a currency is determined by foreign demand. Therefore, the basis of currency internationalization is foreign demand and preference for the currency of a country due to its economic strength. Thus, full currency convertibility is not a prerequisite for promoting currency internationalization. If there is enough foreign confidence in and preference for a currency, it could still become an international currency even if the currency issuing country imposes certain restrictions on its use in international trade and financial transactions.

23.3.2 *The dollar and the yen: Capital account restrictions and currency internationalization*

International practices have shown that complete convertibility is not always necessary for currency internationalization. In the 1960s, the

United States adopted a series of measures such as the Interest Equalization Tax Act of 1963 and Voluntary Foreign Credit Restraint Program of 1965 to restrict capital outflow. These measures, however, did not limit the internationalization of the dollar but actually stimulated the development of euro–dollar market and accelerated the internationalization of the dollar. It was not until 1980 when the Foreign Exchange Order was amended that Japan started to lift restrictions on yen convertibility and open the capital account. Yet, the internationalization of the yen had already begun in the 1970s. Japan made great progress in financial liberalization in the 1990s, but the process of the internationalization of the yen reversed during this period. From 1995 to 2008, the percentage of the yen in the global official foreign exchange reserves dropped from 6.8% to 3.27%.[4] Likewise, the percentage of the yen in international trade clearing and the percentage of the yen assets in foreign banks also dropped to varying degree. The major cause for reverse in internationalization of the yen was that the prolonged Japanese economic recession caused the international community to lose confidence in the value and stability of the yen.

Since the most important factor in promoting the renminbi's internationalization is China's overall national strength, although the renminbi is not yet fully convertible, this will not be a barrier to its internationalization. The renminbi has achieved convertibility under the current account. Over half of the transactions under the capital account are already convertible, and the percentage of sub-accounts still under strict control is not high. So, on the whole, backed by China's strong economy, the renminbi is already partially convertible. The renminbi will eventually become fully internationalized as a matter of natural development thanks to continued growth of China's economy and further development of its financial market.

22.4 Improve Domestic Financial Markets, Establish an International Financial Center, and Internationalize the Renminbi

A fully developed domestic financial market where a currency can perform its functions of trading, payment, and investment is the base for it to become an international currency. The major international currencies such as the pound sterling, the dollar, the Deutsch mark, and the Japanese yen are respectively represented by international financial centers in London, New York, Frankfurt, and Tokyo, where there are developed financial institutions, numerous financial products, rich financial expertise, and well-established laws and regulations. To internationalize the renminbi, China must fully develop a domestic financial market and build an international financial center.

Hong Kong is a window for promoting renminbi's internationalization since it is already a famous international financial center fully integrated into the global financial markets. With its developed financial markets and its special status as a special administrative region of China, Hong Kong can serve as an offshore market for the renminbi in which the process of its internationalization is controllable through policy coordination with the mainland. For instance, the current renminbi personal savings service in Hong Kong is provided with full reserve, so it will not lead to the creation of offshore renminbi liquidity. This provides a platform for testing water in conducting offshore renminbi services. On the basis of gaining more experience and at the proper time, other renminbi services can be introduced in Hong Kong so that more renminbi trading can be diverted from underground channel to the banking system. This will also create conditions for Hong Kong to become an offshore renminbi center.

With a good geographic location, a solid economic foundation, and a long history of financial market, Shanghai is well-poised to become an international financial center. In recent years, Shanghai's financial market has grown rapidly, with increasing financial transactions and financial products. So Shanghai is ready to become an international financial center. At the end of 2008, 864 companies were listed at the Shanghai Stock Exchange, with market capitalization amounting to RMB 10.7 trillion. This made the Shanghai Stock Exchange the sixth largest one in the world. Total sum raised through initial public offering (IPO) reached RMB 103.4 billion Yuan that year, the second highest in the world. Regarding the futures market, the Shanghai Futures Exchange (SHFE) had a total turnover of RMB 29 trillion in 2008, accounting for over one-fifth of China's total. Copper futures and steel futures trading at SHFE play an important role in international pricing. Because of Shanghai's financial strength, against the backdrop of the global financial crisis, the State Council officially announced in March 2009, the goal to turn Shanghai into an international financial center by 2020 in keeping with China's economic strength and the international position of the renminbi.

Of course, there is still a long way to go before Shanghai can become a developed international financial center. The main bottleneck is the lack of qualified and experienced professionals. For quite a long time, China's financial sector was not open enough to attract talents. There is a lack of experience in providing financial products, and Shanghai's integration with the international financial market is low. To become an international financial center, Shanghai needs to generate more self-driven demand. Second, Shanghai also needs to strengthen financial regulation and supervision. A well-established regulatory system is essential for building an advanced and developed financial market and ensure its orderly operation and growth. Lack of innovation is a major constraint on China's effort to build an international financial center, whereas only an adequate regulatory system can stimulate financial innovation. China should work harder to improve its regulatory system to address such weakness of its financial sector. Finally, there is a large gap between Shanghai's legal environment and competence of its legal professionals and those of other international financial centers. This gap should be speedily closed.

To internationalize the renminbi, the most important thing China needs to do is to grow itself. China should also deepen its financial market reform, raise financial regulatory standards, enhance capacity for financial innovation and actively participate in international financial cooperation so as to lay a solid foundation for the internationalization of the renminbi. Initial progress has been made in the internationalization of the renminbi. As China's economy grows and as it has more say in the world economy, the renminbi's internationalization will accelerate. In the foreseeable future, the renminbi will no doubt become a new international currency and an important force in stabilizing the international financial market. It will also help create conditions for establishing a new international monetary system (Li Ruogu, 2008).

Bibliography

English Editions

Aheame, Alan, "Global Imbalances: Time for Action", *Irish Times*, March 2007.

Artis, Michael and Zhang, Wenda, "International Business Cycles and the ERM: Is there a European Business Cycle?", *International Journal of Finance and Economics*, 2, 1997, pp. 1–16.

Bernanke, Ben, "The Global Saving Glut and the U.S. Current Account Deficit", remarks at the Homer Jones Lecture, St. Louis. April 14, 2005.

BIS, "FX Reserve Management: Elements of a Framework", Quarterly Report, 2003.

BIS, "Triennial Central Bank Survey: Foreign Exchange and Derivatives Market Activity in 2007", *BIS Quarterly Review*, 2007.

Bradford, Colin and Linn, Johannes, "Global Economic Governance at a Crossroads: Replacing the G7 with the G20", *Brookings Institution Policy Brief*, 131, April 2004.

Brooks, Stephen G and Wohlforth, William C, "Reshaping the World Order: How Washington Should Reform International Institutions", *Foreign Affairs*, March/April 2009, pp. 49–63.

Bryant, Ralph C, "Reform of IMF Quota Shares and Voting Shares: A Missed Opportunity", 2008. Available at http://www.brookings.edu/papers/2008/0408_imf_bryant.aspx.

Bryant, Ralph C, *Overhauling the Global Financial System*, Brookings, October 28, 2008.

Cecchetti, Stephen G, "Crisis and Response: The Federal Reserve and the Financial Crisis of 2007–2008", NBER Working Paper 14134, June 2008.

Cohen, Benjamin J, "The Seigniorage Gain of an International Currency: An Empirical Test", *The Quarterly Journal of Economics*, 85(3), 1971, pp. 494–507.

Cline, William R, *The United States as a Debtor Nation*, Washington, DC: Institute for International Economics, 2005.

Commission of the European Community, "One Market One Money — An Evaluation of the Potential Benefits and Costs of Forming an Economic and Monetary Union", *European Economy*, 44, October 1990.

Congressional Budget Office, Economic Projections for 2009–2019, March 2009.

Cooper, Andrew F, "The Logic of the B(R)ICSAM Model for G8 Reform", CIGI Policy Brief in International Governance 1 (May), pp. 1–11, 2007.

Corden, Max, "Monetary Integration", Princeton Essays in International Finance, p. 32, International Finance Section, Princeton University, April 1972.

De Rato, Rodrigo, "The IMF View on IMF Reform", 2005. Available at http://www.iie.com/prog_imf_reform.cfm.

Dhonte, Pierre, "Conditionality as an Instrument of Borrower Credibility", IMF Papers on Policy Analysis and Assessments 97/2, 1997.

Dooley, Michael P, Folkerts-Landau, David and Garber, Peter, "An Essay on the Revived Bretton Woods System", NBER Working Paper 9971, September 2003.

Dulder, H-J, "Monetary Policy and Exchange Market Management in Germany", in *Exchange Market Interventions and Monetary Policy*, Basel: Bank for International Settlements, 1984.

Eichengreen, Barry, "Global Imbalances and the Lessons of Bretton Woods", NBER Working Paper Series No. 10497, 2004.

Eichengreen, Barry and Razo-Garcia, Raul, "The International Monetary System in the Last and Next 20 Years", *Economic Policy*, 21(47), 2006.

Fischer, Stanley, "Seigniorage and the Case for National Money", *Journal of Political Economy*, 90(2), 1982, pp. 295–313.

Fischer, Stanley, "On the Need for a Lender of Last Resort", address to the American Economic Association, New York, January 1999.

Fleming, J Marcus, "On Exchange Rate Unification", *Economic Journal*, 81, 1971, pp. 467–488.

Frankel, Jeffrey A and Rose, Andrew K, "The Endogeneity of the Optimum Currency Area Criteria", NBER Working Paper 5700, August 1996.

Fukuda, Hiromasa, "The Theory of Optimum Currency Areas: An Introductory Survey", Keio University Mita Festival, 2002 paper. Available at http://www.clb.mita.keio.ac.jp/econ/kaji/mitafest/fBritainuda.pdf.

Galati, Gabriele, and Wooldridge, Philip, "The Euro as a Reserve Currency: A Challenge to the Pre-eminence of the US Dollar?", BIS Working Paper No. 218, October 2006.

Garnier, Julien, "Has the Similarity of Business Cycles in Europe Increased with the Monetary Integration Process?: A Use of the Classical Business Cycles", European University Institute: Badia Fiesolana, 2003.

Giavazzi, Francesco and Giovannini, Alberto, "Can the EMS Be Exported? Lessons from Ten Years of Monetary Policy Coordination in Europe", CEPR Discussion Papers No. 285, 1989.

Goldstein, Morris, "The Subprime Credit Crisis: Origins, Policy Responses, and Reforms", Peterson Institute for International Economics, 2008.

Hartmann, Phillip, *Currency Competition and Foreign Exchange Markets: The Dollar, the Yen and the Euro*, Cambridge: Cambridge University Press, 1998, pp. 35–39.

Hogan, Michael J, *The Marshall Plan: America, Britain, and the Reconstruction of Western Europe, 1947–1952*, Cambridge: Cambridge University Press, 1987.

IMF, "Classification of Exchange Rate Arrangements and Monetary Policy Frameworks", IMF Online.

IMF, "Reform of Quota and Voice in the International Monetary Fund — Report of the Executive Board to the Board of Governors", March 28, 2008. Available at http://www.imf.org/external/np/pp/eng/2008/032108.pdf.

IMF, *Financial Stability Report*, April 2008.

IMF, "The Recent Financial Turmoil — Initial Assessment, Policy Lessons, and Implications for Fund Surveillance", April 2008. Available at www.imf.org.

IMF, Currency Composition of Official Foreign Exchange Reserves (COFER), 2009.

IMF, *Global Financial Stability Report*, April 2009.

IMF, International Financial Statistics Database (IFS), 2009.

IMF, *World Economy Outlook*, August 30, 2005.

IMF, WEO Database, Available at http://www.imf.org/external/pubs/ft/weo/2009/01/weodata/index.aspx, 2009.

IMF, World Economic Outlook Update, July 2009.

Ingram, James, *Regional Payments Mechanisms: The Case of Puerto Rico*, Chapel Hill: University of North Carolina Press, 1962.

Ishiyama, Yoshihide, "The Theory of Optimum Currency Areas: A Survey", *IMF Staff Paper*, 22(2), 1975, pp. 344–383.

Ito, Takatoshi, "Global Financial Crisis of 2008: Crisis management and Competition Policy", 2009. Available at http://www.e.u-tokyo.ac.jp/~tito/.

Kamps, Annette, "The Euro as Invoicing Currency in International Trade", ECB Working Paper Series, No. 665, 2006, pp. 43–50.

Kenen, Peter, "The Theory of Optimum Currency Area: An Eclectic View", in P. Mundell (ed.), *Monetary Problems of the International Economy*, Chicago: Chicago Press, 1969.

Kirton, John, "From G7 to G20: Capacity, Leadership and Normative Diffusion in Global Financial Governance", paper prepared for a panel on "Expanding Capacity and Leadership in Global Financial Governance: From G7 to G20", International Studies Association Annual Convention, Hawaii, March 2005, pp. 1–5.

Krugman, Paul, "Policy Problems of a Monetary Union", in P. De Grauwe and L. Papademos (eds.), *The European Monetary System in the 1990s*, London and New York: Longman, CEPS and Bank of Greece, 1990, pp. 48–64.

Krugman, Paul, "Crisis Endgame", *New York Times*, September 18, 2008.

Little, JS and Olivei, GP, "Rethinking the International Monetary System", Federal Reserve Bank of Boston, Boston, 2002.

McKinnon, Ronald, "Optimum Currency Area", *American Economic Review*, 53, 1963, pp. 717–725.

McKinnon, Ronald, "The East Asian Dollar Standard, Life after Death?", World Bank Workshop on Rethinking the East Asian Miracle, July 1999.

McKinnon, Ronald, "The International Dollar Standard and Sustainability of the US Current Account Deficit", Instructions to Stanford Economics Working Paper, No. 01-013, 2001.

McKinnon, Ronald, "Can the World Economy Afford U.S. Tax Cut?: The International Dollar Standard Redux", *Finance & Development*, (6), 2001.

Ministry of Finance and Economy, "Korea's Crisis Resolution & Implications", MOFE, 1999.

Mortgage Finance, *Mortgage Market Statistical Annual 2006*, Vol. 2, Bethesda, MD: Mortgage Finance Publications, 2009.

Mundell, Robert, "The Theory of Optimum Currency Area", *American Economic Review*, 51, September 1961, pp. 657–665.

Mundell, Robert, "Exchange Rates, Currency Areas and the International Financial Architecture", November 2000, Delivered at an IMF panel, September 22, 2000.

Obstfeld, Maurice and Rogoff, Kenneth, *Foundations of International Economics*, Cambridge: MIT Press, 1996.

Pisani-Ferry, Jean and Santos, Indhira, "Reshaping the Global Economy", *Financial & Development*, IMF, March 2009.

Reinhart, Carmen M and Rogoff, Kenneth S, "This Time is Different: A Panoramic View of Eight Centuries of Financial Crises", 2008. Available at www.economics.harvard.edu/faculty/rogoff/files/This_Time_Abstract.pdf.

Roach, Stephen S, "Testimony Before the Subcommittee on Trade of the House Committee on Ways and Means", May 9, 2007.

Stephen Roach,"Adjustment for Global Economic Modes", 2008. Available at http://futures.hexun.com/2008-09-22/109042205.html.

Robin, Robert E, "Attention: Deficit Disorder", *New York Times*, May 13, 2005.

Rodgers, Jim, "Yijing Wufa Fusu de Meiguo JIngji" ("Unrecoverable US Economy"), *Appeal Monthly* (Japan), February 2009.

Roubini, Nouriel and Setser, Brad, "Will the Bretton Woods 2 Regime Unravel Soon? The Risk of a Hard Landing in 2005–2006", 2005. Available at http://ideas.repec.org/a/fip/fedfpr/y2005ifebx13.html.

Roubini, Nouriel, "No Hope for the Recession Ending in 2009". Available at http://www.reemonitor.com.

Roubini, Nouriel, "The Worst Financial Crisis Since the Great Depression", 2008. Available at http://www.rgemonitor.com.

Roubini, Nouriel, "The Transformation of the USA into the USSRA (United Socialist State Republic of America)", 2008. Available at http://www.rgemonitor.com/S&P/Case-Shiller Home Price Indices, http://www2.standardandpoors.com/spf/pdf/index/CSHomePrice_History_072943.xls.

Rueff, Jacques, *The Monetary Sin of the West*, New York: The Macmillan Company, 1972.

Schneider, Martin and Tornell, Aaron, "Balance Sheet Effects, Bailout Guarantees, and Financial Crises", NBER Working Paper 8060, 2000.

Stiglitz, Joseph and Greenwald, Bruce, "A Modest Proposal for International Monetary Reform", 2006. Available at http://web.gc.cuny.edu/economics/SeminarPapers/Fall,2006/international_monetary_reform-joe%20stglitz.pdf.

Tavlas, George S, "The 'New' Theory of Optimum Currency Areas", *The World Economy*, 16(6), 1993, pp. 663–685.

Thorbecke, Willem, "The Effect of Exchange Rate Changes on Trade in East Asia", RIETI Discussion Paper Series 05-E-009, 2006.

Tower, Edward and Willett, Thomas, "The Theory of Optimum Currency Areas and Exchange Rate Flexibility", special Papers in International Economics, No. 11, International Finance Section, Princeton University, May 1976.

Treasury of the United States, 2009. Available at http://www.ustreas.gov/tic/fpis.shtml.

Triffin, Robert, *Gold and Dollar Crisis: The Future of Convertibility*, Yale University Press, 1960.

Truman, Edwin M, "Budget and External Deficits: Not Twins but the Same Family", paper presented at the Annual Research Conference, held at the Federal Reserve Bank of Boston, June, 2005, pp. 14–16.

Truman, Edwin M, "A Strategy of for IMF Reform", 2005. Available at http:// bookstore.petersoninstitute.org/book-store/3985.html.

UNCTAD, Handbook of Statistics, 2008.

United States Government Printing Office, Economic Report of the President 2007, 2007.

United States Government Printing Office, Economic Report of the President 2008, 2008.

Van den Spiegel, Freddy, "The Euro's Challenge to the Dollar as An International Reserve Currency", Autumn 2005. Available at http:www.europesworld.org/ NewEnglish/Home/Article/tabid/191/ArticleType/articleview/AriticleID/ 20923/Default.aspx.

WEO Database, October 2008, April 2009.

Willett, Thomas and Tower, Edward, "Currency Areas and Exchange-rate Flexibility", *Review of World Economics* (*Weltwirtschaftliches Archive*), 105(1), September 1970, pp. 48–65.

Wolf, Martin, "The End of Lightly Regulated Finance has Come Far Closer", *Financial Times*, September 18, 2008.

World Bank, *World Economic Outlook*, January 2009.

WTO, *Global Financial Crisis and Global Trade*, March 2009.

Chinese Editions

Chen Baosen, "Meiguo de Zhaiwu Jingji he Quanqiu Jingji Shiheng", *Shijie Jingji yu Zhengzhi Luntan* ("US Debt Economy and Global Economic Imbalance", *Forum of World Economy and Politics*), 3 (2007).

Chen Biaoru, *Guoji Jinrong Gailun* (*Outline of International Finance*), Shanghai: East China Normal University Press, 1996.

Chen Xiaochen and Xu Yisheng, "G20 Fenghui Zhongdian Huofei Guoji Huobi Tixi, Gaige", *Diyi Caijing Ribao* ("Keynotes of G20 Summit may not be international Monetary System Reform", *CBN Daily*), November 11, 2008.

Chen Xiaolv, "Guanyu Hengliang Yingguo Shuailuo de Biaozhun Wenti — Ping Luobinsitan de Zibenzhuyi Wenhua yu Yingguo de Shuailuo", *Shijie Lishi* ("On Standards for Measurement of Decline in Britain: A Comment on Rubinstein's *Capitalism, Culture and Decline in Britain*", World History), 5, 2002.

Chen Yulu, *Guoji Jinrong* (*International Finance*), Beijing: China Renmin University Press, 2000.

Duan Yanfei, "Meiguo Zhaiwu Jingji de Guoji Xunhuan", *Meiguo Yanjiu* ("International Circulation of US Debt Economy", *American Studies*), 4 (2008).

Feng Zhaobo, "Xide Make 40nian: Jingyan Qishi Jiejian", *Jingjixuejia* ("Four Decades of DEM: Empirical Enlightenment and Reference", *Economists*), 1 (1989).

Guoji Jinrong yu Kaifang Jingji de Hongguan Jingjixue (Chinese translation of Giancarlo Gandolfo, *International Finance and Open-economy Macroeconomics*), Shanghai: Shanghai University of Finance and Economics Press, April 2006.

Gao Haihong, "Zuiyou Huobiqu: Dui Dongya Guojia de Jingyan Yanjiu he Fenxi", *Quanqiu Shijiaoxia de Renminbi Huilv: Zhengce yu Fengxian Fangfan* ("Optimum Currency Area: Empirical Study and Analysis of East Asian Countries", *A Global View of Renminbi Exchange Rates: Policy Selection and Risk Prevention*), Beijing: China Financial and Economic Publishing House, 2008.

Gao Haihong, "Zhongguo zai Yazhou Quyu Jinrong Hezuozhong de Zuoyong" ("Function of China in Asian Regional Financial Cooperation"), CASS 25th International Affairs Forum — "Global Financial Crisis: Challenges and Countermeasures for and of China", a thesis at the conference (1–7), April 29, 2009a.

Gao Haihong, "Qingmai Xiexi Xinjucuo: Yi Duobian Zhidu Hezuo Baozhang Yazhou Quyu Jinrong Wending", *Caijing Pinglun* ("New Move of CMI: Secure the Financial Stability of Asian Region through Multilateral Systematic Cooperation", *Finance and Business Review*), No. 09010, February 24, 2009b.

Ge Huayong, "Guanyu Guoji Huobi Jinrong Tixi Gaige de Sikao", *Zhongguo Jinrong* ("On Reform of International Monetary and Financial Systems", *China Finance*), 3, 2009.

Guan Zhixiong, *Riyuan Guojihua* (*Internationalization of Japanese Yen*), Beijing: China Financial and Economic Publishing House, 2006.

He Fan and Li Jing, "Meiyuan Guojihua de Lutu Jingyan he Jiaoxun" ("*Way, Experiences and Lessons of USD Internationalization*"), 2002. Available at http://www.doctor-cafe.com.

He Fan and Qin Donghai, "Dongya Jianli Huobi Lianmeng de Chengben yu Shouyi Fenxi", *Shijie Jingji* ("Cost-Benefit Analysis for East Asia to Establish the Currency Union, *World Economy*), 1, 2005.

He Fan, Zhang Bin and Zhang, Ming, "Dui Qingmai Xieyi de Pinggu ji Gaige Jianyi", *Guoji Jinrong Yanjiu* ("Evaluation on and Proposal for Reform of the Chiang Mai Initiative", *Studies of International Finance*), 7, 2005.

He Fan, "Meiyuan Guojihua de Lishi ji Qishi" ("History and Enlightenment of the Dollar's Internationalization"), 2004. Available at http://www.doctor-cafe.com.

Hu Guangyao and Yu Qianliang, "Suhatuo Yuanhe Xiatai", *Guangming Ribao* ("Why has Suharto stepped down?", *Guangming Daily*), May 22, 1998.

Huang Meibo and Lin Yang, Dongya Xinxing Zhaiquan Shichang Fazhan Yanjiu — Cong Benbi Zhaiquan Shichang dao Yazhou Zhaiquan Shichang (*A Study on Development of East Asian Emerging Bond Markets: From Local-currency Bond Market to Asian Bond Market*), Beijing: Economic Science Press, January 2008.

Huang Weiping and Zhu Wenhui, "Wentezhi: Meiguo Xinjingji yu Quanqiu Chanye Chongzu de Weiguan Jichu", *Meiguo Yanjiu* ("Wintelism: Micro Base for US New Economy and Global Industrial Restructuring", *American Studies*), 2, 2004.

Jiang Boke, "Guanyu Guoji Huobi Tixi de Yanbian yu Gaige", *Shijie Jingji* ("On Evolution and Reform of International Monetary System", *World Economy*), 1, 1985.

Jiang Boke, *Guoji Jinrong Xinbian* (*New International Finance*), 3rd Edition, Shanghai: Fudan University Press, 2008.

Kikkawa Mototada, *Jinrong, Zhanbai — Fazi Jingji Daguo Shoucuohou de Zhengyan* Chinese translation of *Financial Defeat: Advices from Economic Giant after Frustration*, Beijing: China Youth Press, 2000.

Li Ruogu, "Guoji Huobi Tizhi de Yanbian yu Qushi", *Guoji Jingji Hezuo* ("Evolution and Trends of International Monetary System", *International Economic Cooperation*), 4, 1986.

Li Ruogu, *Jingji Quanqiuhua yu Zhongguo Jinrong Gaige* (*Economic Globalization and Chinese Financial Reform*), Beijing: China Financial Publishing House, 2001.

Li Ruogu (chief editor), *Guoji Jingji Yitihua yu Zhongguo Jianguan* (*International Economy Integration and Financial Regulation and Supervision*), Beijing: China Financial Publishing House, 2002.

Li Ruogu (chief editor), *Guoji Jinrong Diaoyan Lunwenji* (*Collection of* Theses *on International Finance*), China Financial Publishing House, 2004.

Li Ruogu, *Zouxiang Shijie de Zhongguo Jinrong* (*Chinese Finance to the World*), Beijing: China Financial Publishing House, June 2006.

Li Ruogu, *Quanqiuhuazhong de Zhongguo Jinrong* (*Chinese Finance in Globalization*), Beijing: Social Sciences Academic Press, April 2008.

Li Ruogu, *Zhidu Shiyi yu Jingji Fazhan: Jiyu Zhongguo Shijian de Fazhan Jingjixue* (*Systematic Adaption and Economic Development: Development Economies based on Chinese Practices*), Beijing: People's Publishing House, 2008.

Li Ruogu, "Reform of International Monetary System and Internationalization of Renminbi", a presentation at Shanghai Lujiazui International Financial Forum on May 10, 2008.

Li Ruogu, "Views on Current International Economic and Financial Situations", *China Today*, May 19, 2008.

Li Ruogu, "Global Economic Imbalance not due to Renminbi Exchange Rate", September 2008.

Li Ruogu, "Global Financial Crisis: Impact on China and the World", a presentation at Beijing International Finance Forum, November 15, 2008.

Li Ruogu, "Quanqiu Jinrong Weiji yu Guoji Huobi Tixi Chonggou", *Shanghai Zhengquanbao* ("Global Financial Crisis and Rebuilding of International Monetary System"), *Shanghai Securities News*), November 24, 2008.

Li Ruogu, A speech on CCTV-2: *Outlook Today*, March 26, 2009.

Li Xiangyang, "Buleidun Senlin Tixi de Yanbian yu Meiyuan Baquan", *Shijie Jingji yu Zhengzhi* ("Evolution of Bretton Woods System and Dollar's Hegemony", *World Economy and Politics*), 10, 2005.

Li Yang, "Tuidong Guoji Huobi Tixi Duoyuanhua de Lengsikao", *Shanghai Jinrong* ("Calm Thinking on Promoting the Diversification of International Monetary System", *Shanghai Finance*), 4, 2009.

Liu Junmin, "Lijie Liudongxing Pengzhang: Meiyuan yu Guoji Huobi Tixi de Weiyuji", *Diyi Caijing Ribao* ("Understand Liquidity Expansion: USD and Crisis and Opportunity of the International Monetary System", *CBN Daily*), August 15, 2007.

Liu Zongxu, *Shijie Jindaishi* (*The Modern World History*), Beijing: Beijing Normal University Press, 2005.

Lu Shiwei, *Meiyuan Baquan yu Guoji Huobi Geju* (*Dollar Hegemony and International Currency Arrangements*), Beijing: China Economy Publishing House, 2006.

Luobote Telifen, *Huangjin yu Meiyuan Weiji* (Chinese translation of Robert Triffin, *Gold and Dollar Crisis*), Hongkong: The Commercial Press, 1997.

Ma Yaobang (Ben Mah), "Bei G20 Hulue de Wenti" ("Subjects Ignored by G20"), http://www.chdjx.com/, May 20, 2009.

Makesi, *Zibenlun*, Diyijuan (Chinese translation of Karl Marx, Capital, Vol. I), translated by Guo Dali and Wang Yanan, Beijing: People's Publishing House, 1963, pp. 72–132.

Maijinnong, *Meiyuan Benweixia de Huilv*: *Dongya Gaochuxu Liangnan* (Chinese translation of McKinnon, *Exchange Rates under the East Asian Dollar Standard: Living with Conflicted Virtue*), Beijing: China Financial Publishing House, 2005.

Mengdaier, *Mengdaier Jingjixue Wenji, Diliu Juan — Guoji Huobi: Guoqu Xianzai he Weilai* (Mundell, Robert, *Collective Works of Mundell on Economics* (*Vol. IV*) — *International Currency: Past, Present and Future*), Beijing: China Financial Publishing House, 2003.

Meng Xianyang, "Qianxi Buleidun Senlin Tixi", *Nankai Jingji Yanjiu* ("An Analysis of Bretton Woods System", *Nankai Economic Studies*), 4, 1989.

Miqieer, *Paergeleifu Shiji Lishi Tongji* (*Meizhoujuan*): *1750–1993* (Chinese translation of Brian R. Mitchell, *Palgrave International Historical Statistics 1750–1993: The Americas*), Beijing: Economic Science Press, 2002a.

Miqieer, *Paergeleifu Shiji Lishi Tongji* (*Ouzhoujuan*): *1750–1993* (Chinese translation of Brian R. Mitchell, *Palgrave International Historical Statistics 1750–1993: Europe*), Beijing: Economic Science Press, 2002b.

Mu Liangping, *Zhuyao Gongye Guojia Jinxiandai Jingjishi* (*Modern Economic History of Major Industrial Countries*), Chengdu Southwest University of Finance and Economics Press, 2005.

Qian Rongkun, "Jianxi Guoji Huobi Tixi de Yanbian (Shang)", *Nankai Jingji Yanjiu* ("Brief Analysis of Evolution of International Monetary System: Part One", *Nankai Economic Studies*), 2, 1988.

Qian Rongkun, "Jianxi Guoji Huobi Tixi de Yanbian (Xia)", *Nankai Jingji Yanjiu* ("Brief Analysis of Evolution of International Monetary System (I)", *Nankai Economic Studies*), 3, 1988.

Qiaozhi Suoluosi, Quanqiu Jinrongjie de Huaihaizi (*George Soros, the Bad Boy of Global Finance*), www.webtrade-USA.com, March 30, 2003.

Renminbi Xianjin Kuajing Liudong Diaocha Ketizu, "2004nian Renminbi Xianjin Kuajing Liudong Diaocha", *Zhongguo Jinrong* (Renminbi Cross-border Cashflow Survey Project Team, "Survey on Cross-border Cashflow of RMB in 2004", *China Finance*), 6, 2005.

Sun Lijian and Peng Shutao, "Cong Cijizhai Fengbo Kan Xiandai Jinrong Fengxian de Benzhi", *Jinrong yu Baoxian* ("Essence of Modern Financial Risks in View of 'Subprime Lending Market Chaos'", *Finance and Insurance*), 1, 2008.

Shijie Jingji Qiannianshi (Chinese translation of Angus Maddison, *The World Economy — A Millennial Perspective*), Peking: Peking University Press, 2003.

Tan Yaling and Wang Zhonghai, *Guoji Jinrong yu Guojia Liyi* (*International Finance and National Interests*), Beijing: Shishi Publishing House, 2002.

Tang Min, *Cidaixia Guoji Jinrong Tixi Chongxin Xipai Shi Zhongguo Zhanlue Jiyu* (Restructuring of International Financial System under Subprime Lending is a "Strategic Opportunity" for China), http://tangminblog. blog.163.com/blog/static/49568684200810410351 8578/.

The PBC, 2004 Statistics: Overview of Currencies. Available at www.pbc. gov. cn.

Wang Jianye, "Erlun Meiguo Changfu Nengli de Weiji — Meiguo Fuzhai de Jixian ji Kaiensi Zhuyi Zhengce", *Jingji yu Jinrong* ("Second Discussion Crisis of US Solvency: Extreme of U.S. Liabilities and Keynesianism Policy", *Economy and Finance* — Internal publication of Export–Import Bank of China), 14.

Wang Jianye, "Guoji Jinrong Zaipingheng yu Jinqi Shijie Jingji Zoushi", *Jingji yu Jinrong* ("Re-equilibrium of International Finance and Short-term Trends of World Economy, *Economy and Finance* — Internal publication of Export–Import Bank of China), 17.

Wang Yongzhong, "Meiguo Jinrong Weiji yu Guoji Jinrong Xintixi — Riben Xuezhe Guandian Zongshu" ("U.S. Financial Crisis and New International Financial System: Viewpoints of Japanese Scholar), Institute of World Economics and Politics of Chinese Academy of Social Sciences Working Paper, March 11, 2009.

Weilian Tabu, "Meiguo Zhaiwu Pengzhang Jingji Paomo yu Xindiguozhuyi", *Guowai Lilun Dongtai* (Chinese translation of William Tabb, *"Trouble, Trouble, Debt, and Bubble"*, *Monthly Review*, abstracted and translated by Wu Wei and Fu Qiang, published in Chinese Journal of *Foreign Theoretical Trends*), 11, 2006.

Wu Hanhong and Cuiyong, "Zhongguo de Zhubishui yu Tonghuo Pengzhang: 1952–2004", *Jingji Yanjiu* ("Seigniorage and Inflation of China: 1952–2004", *Economic Research*), 9, 2006.

Xia Bin and Chen Daofu, "Guoji Huobi Tixi Shihengxia de Zhongguo Huilv Zhengce", *Zhongguo Jinrong* ("China Exchange Rate Policy under Imbalance of the International Monetary System", *China Finance*), 1, 2006.

xinhuanet.com, "Faguo Zongtong Sakeqi Jianyi Chongjian Guoji Jinrong Huobi Tixi" ("French President Sarkozy Proposes to Rebuild the International Financial and Monetary System"), September 26, 2008.

Xinpaergeleifu Jingjixue Dacidian (Disan Juan)(Peter Newman, *New Palgrave Dictionary of Economics, Volume III*), Science Press, 2005.

Xu Qiyan and Li Jing, "Guoji Fengong Tixi Shijiao de Huobi Guojihua: Meiyuan he Riyuan", *Shijie Jingji* ("Currency Internationalization in View of International Division System: USD and JPY", *World Economy*), 2, 2008.

Xu Wei, "Luelun Meiguo Dierci Gongye Gemin", *Shijie Lishi* ("Brief Discussion on U.S. Second Industrial Revolution", *World History*), 6, 1989.

Yang Changjiang, *Renminbi Shiji Huilv Changqi Tiaozheng Qushi Yanjiu* (A Study on Long-term Adjustment Trends for Real Exchange Rates of Renminbi), Shanghai: Shanghai University of Finance and Economics Press, 2002.

Yuntong Wang, "The Asian Financial Crisis and the Need for Regional Financial Cooperation", KIEP, 1999.

Zhang Ming, "Cidai Weiji de Chuandao Jizhi" ("Transmitting Mechanism for Subprime Crisis"), Institute of World Economics and Politics of Chinese Academy of Social Sciences Working Paper, No. 0809.

Zhang Ming, "Quanqiu Jinrong Weijixia de Zhongguo Guoji Jinrong Xinzhanlue" ("New International Financial Strategy of China under Global Financial Crisis), International Financial Research Center, Institute of World Economics and Politics of Chinese Academy of Social Sciences, Finance and Business Review No. 09028, April 16, 2009.

Zhang Ming and Zheng Liansheng, *Huaerjie de Moluo* (*Downfall of Wall Street*), China Financial and Economic Publishing House, January 2009.

Zhang Yuyan, "Juezhu Huobi Baquan", Shangwu Zhoukan ("Compete for Monetary Hegemony"), *Business Watch Magazine*, January 16, 2009.

Zhao Xijun, "Guoji Huobi Tixi Gaige: Cong Keshou Danyi dao Zouxiang Duoyuan", *Jinrong Shibao* ("Reform of International Monetary System: from Sticking to Singularity to Diversification", *Financial News*, February 23, 2009.

Zhong Hong, "Guoji Huobi Tixi Gaige Fangxiang he Zhongguo de Duice Yanjiu", *Shijie Jingji Daokan* ("A Study on Orientation for Reform of International Monetary System and Countermeasures of China", *Journal of World Economics*, 1, 2007.

Zhong Wei, "Guoji Huobi Tixi de Bainian Bianqian he Yuanzhan", *Guoji Jinrong Yanjiu* ("Century Evolution and Prospects of International Monetary System", *Studies of International Finance*), 4, 2001.

Zhong Wei, "Guoji Huobi Tixi Gaige: Fazhanzhong Guojia de Shijiao", *Zhongguo Waihui Guanli* ("Reform of International Monetary System: A View from Developing Countries", *China Forex*), 3, 2001.

Zhou Xiaochuan, "Guanyu Gaige Guoji Huobi Tixi de Sikao" ("Thinking about Reform of International Monetary System") March 23, 2009. Available at www.pbc.gov.cn.

Zhu Dantao, "Zuiyou Huobiqu Pipanxing Pingxi", *Shijie Jingji* ("A Criticizing Analysis on Optimum Currency Area"), *World Economy*, 1, 2005.

Zuo Xiaolei, "Jianli Guoji Chubei Huobi de Tiyi Shifen Zhongyao", *Jinrong Shibao* ("Proposal to Establish the International Reserve Currency is Extremely Important"), *Financial News*, April 2, 2009.

Index

Printed in the United States
By Bookmasters